ORGANIC GARDENING

ORGANIC GARDENING

Natural Ways of Growing Fruit, Vegetables and Herbs

Peter Blackburne-Maze

WINDWARD

Editor: Maggie Daykin
Designer: Johnny Pau

Published by Windward,
an imprint owned by W. H. Smith & Son Limited
Registered No. 237811 England
Trading as WHS Distributors,
St John's House, East Street, Leicester LE1 6NE

ISBN 0 7112 0431 4

Phototypeset by Tradespools Limited, Frome, Somerset, England
Printed and bound in Italy
by L.E.G.O., Vincenza

CONTENTS

INTRODUCTION

The principles of growing vegetables, herbs and fruit 'organically' – or growing anything else in this way come to that – are as old as gardening itself. Only our approach to the subject has changed to any extent.

Perhaps we ought to look at just what is meant by 'organic', before we pull the concept to pieces. Where the word comes from in relation to growing plants is anyone's guess because it does not really mean anything. It does, though, convey an idea – that the plants are grown completely without the aid of modern chemicals.

However, a line has to be drawn somewhere between what is sensible and in line with good plant husbandry, and what is pig-headed dogma. There are distinct similarities between organic gardening and vegetarianism, and that is not meant unkindly. Both have rather blurred lines of demarcation between what is 'allowed' and what is not.

In essence, we are talking about a form of gardening that, for various reasons, rejects the use of modern and sophisticated pest, disease and weed control chemicals – along with their opposite numbers in the fertilizer world. This is carried to various lengths, some bordering on lunacy, but an ever-growing number of people are becoming worried by the amount of man-made chemicals that are finding their way into our food, and ultimately into our stomachs.

Along with this, is a genuine concern over the effect that these chemicals are having on the world we live in. We have seen what can happen if safeguards are inadequate or knowledge is insufficient; DDT is the obvious example. But the DDT case should also be taken as a gleam of light, because action was taken to put the matter right.

However, what we are talking about here is organic gardening – not United Nations policy on pesticide control. It all boils down to the fact that 'organic gardening' is a far from exact term and can mean whatever the speaker or writer wants it to mean.

With that established, the object of this book is to show you that gardening is not all dependent on the contents of a sprayer or fertilizer packet. There is a great deal of gardening that can be done without chemicals, though it is not a good idea to carry the doctrine to ridiculous extremes. Certainly we do not always need to use chemicals to discourage or destroy this weed, that pest or the other fungus but it is folly to suppose that we can garden efficiently and effectively by turning our backs on the problems and pretending that either they do not exist or that they will go away if we ignore them. That is certainly not the sort of gardening that we are advocating here. We leave all that to the 'muck and magic' brigade and their maggoty apples!

Peter Blackburn-Maze

THE SOIL

There are very few things that all gardens could be said to have in common but they all contain soil of some sort. It has to be expressed like that because soil is extremely variable. It is at this point that people tend to divide into those that take gardening seriously and those that do not; the latter refer to soil as 'dirt'. Let us have a closer look at soil and its composition and see why they are so wrong.

Soil is a living thing, teeming with life in an almost unimaginable variety. Indeed, it is this life that makes it possible for us to grow plants in soil as opposed to a desert, mud flats or a rocky ledge on a mountain. The life forms present in soil are a wonder in themselves and, in gardens, they range in size from being as large as moles right down to microscopic bacteria. All have a part to play and to ignore them is folly, since to so would begin a downward spiral that, were it allowed to continue, would eventually will bring us back to the desert or mud flat.

Apart from these living organisms, all soils exist in what are called three 'phases'. That is, everything that goes to make up a soil is either a solid, a liquid or a gas. That may sound rather obvious to some people and academic to others but it is the simplest way of catagorizing things when we have, as it were, put soil under the microscope.

By far the largest fraction of a soil is the mineral matter from which it is made and the nature of this is entirely dependant on the parent material – the clay, rock, sand, chalk and so on that underlies it. It is also the type and nature of this parent material that determines a soil's texture and type.

Most of us have heard of soils referred to as 'light' or 'heavy' and this is a reflection on what the soil is made from. For instance, a heavy soil has very small particles, such as clay or silt. A medium soil, the kind that we all wish we could garden on, is one with medium-sized particles. You might expect to find this kind overlying rock. A light soil is one that consists mainly of large mineral particles; typically, a sandy soil.

The texture of a soil is more or less in the lap of the gods, in that you have to put up with what you are sitting upon. However, there are certain things that we can do to alter the texture slightly. For example, we can add soil of the opposite texture. However, this has a limited effect and should be considered only in an emergency.

Something that we *can* do to improve the texture of a heavy soil, by employing the same principle, is to add horticultural sand or grit. This will open up the soil and make it better draining but this only forms part of the remedial action, as we shall see later.

Organic matter in soil

Still with the 'solid' phase, we come to the most important constituent of any soil; the organic matter. Without organic matter, a soil could be termed 'dead', because it is in organic matter that all the microbes and other minute forms of life exist.

The organic matter in a soil also helps to provide the plant foods that are so necessary for strong and healthy growth. Organic matter in the soil can be both living and dead. We have already established that the micro-organisms and other creatures, of various sizes, are one important group. The other is the vegetation: all the soil fungi and plant roots. All these living things are vital in carrying out chemical and physical changes in the soil, and they are just as important once they have died. It is from the *dead* remains that the plant nutrients are derived in nature. The present generations of these once living things decompose the remains of their predecessors and release the nutrients they contain, so helping to perpetuate the biological cycle that keeps the soil in good heart.

Water in soil

Moving on to the liquid content of the soil – hardly surprisingly, this is in the form of water.

Clearly, water is vital for the health and well-being of all growing plants, but it also has two other very important functions. One is that all soil organisms and micro-organisms are completely dependent on it for their existence. Without it, at the worst they die and at the very best they cease to carry out effectively their vital work of breaking down dead organic matter in the ground. The other, and possibly even more important, job that water does in the soil is dissolve and transport the various plant nutrients. Indeed, until these have been dissolved in water, they are quite useless to the plants.

Water, therefore, is not only important in keeping all forms of life within the soil alive and active, it is also responsible for getting nutrients to the plant roots, in a form that is acceptable to them.

Gases in soil

In the final soil phase, gases, we are most concerned with oxygen and carbon dioxide. Just as oxygen is the one gas that all living animals need, so it is just as necessary to plants. And it is not only needed by the above-ground parts of the plant, it is just as vital to the roots. This

TESTING THE SOIL

1. To find out if your soil needs draining, dig a hole in the garden 60 cm (2ft) deep, and fill it with water.

2. Cover the hole with something to keep out rain: a dustbin lid will do.

3. If no water remains after 24 hours drainage is good. If there is water after 48 hours, drainage is necessary.

is clearly shown when we consider a waterlogged soil.

It is not the fact that it is waterlogged that does the damage, but the lack of oxygen around the roots of the plants. Water plants such as rushes and water-lilies have adapted to this sort of existence but the vast majority of those that we grow in gardens have not.

Water is not the only factor to influence the presence or absence of oxygen in the soil. Compaction of the soil can have the same effect; simply because there are not enough – or not large enough – air spaces within the soil to provide the necessary oxygen.

Carbon dioxide may seem a little odd in the context of soil, because it is the gas that the leaves absorb and turn into carbohydrates. However, it is also given off in the process of respiration – and the roots respire as well as the leaves.

If there is a build-up of carbon dioxide in the soil because it cannot escape, due mainly to compaction, there is a corresponding shortage of oxygen. Also, it must be remembered that it is via the spaces in soil that water escapes downwards, or drains. If it cannot, the ground becomes waterlogged and we go back to square one.

Types of soil

Having looked at what soil is made of, let us next examine the different soils that we are likely to come across and how they are influenced by their ingredients, and structure.

Clay and silt soils Let us start by looking at heavy soils as it is these that most of us garden on and which are likely to present the most problems. Heavy soils (clay and silt) are characterized by their small particle size, or fine texture. This results in them frequently being poorly drained, so that the ground becomes waterlogged more easily.

Along with this is the likelihood that the soil will get compacted more often. While this obviously effects the drainage, an even worse result is the difficulty which roots have in penetrating it. If a plant has to struggle to push out sufficient roots to sustain it, growth is unlikely to be good.

Heavy soils are also slow to warm up in the summer – mainly because of their normally high water content. This is not always important but it is worth remembering if early crops are wanted.

In a dry summer they have the tiresome habit of becoming bone hard the moment there is a shortage of water. Either that or, if they have been recently dug, they turn into a mass of indestructible lumps.

From this, you could be forgiven for imagining that heavy soils have a formidable list of vices and few, if any, virtues. This is not so; in fact, far from it.

Probably the least obvious benefit of heavy land is that, being firm and comparatively unyielding, plants can get a very firm foothold in it. That is, once they get established. Most plants will also grow much better in heavy soils because they have a far greater reserve of plant nutrients in them.

Taking these two considerations alone, once a plant – particularly a tree or shrub – establishes itself in clay, it is likely to grow far better than its companion growing in sandy soil.

The water retention properties of heavy land can also be an advantage. Just as they hold a lot more water in the winter, so do they hold a good supply in the summer. They are, therefore, the last to dry out when there is a water shortage.

Sandy soils At the opposite end of the soil scale are the sandy soils. These are far less common than clay and, apart from little local pockets, they are found mainly in areas such as Surrey, Bedfordshire and Cheshire/Lancashire – the market gardening regions of the country.

This gives us an excellent clue as to their suitability for gardening: by and large, they are first rate. These soils are coarse textured and, as such, are very quick to dry out because any rain that falls on them soon drains away. Also, the water carries a lot of plant nutrients with it so sandy soils are often starved, from the plant's point of view.

Plants grown on well-drained soil (left) and waterlogged soil (right). The plant on well-drained soil shows healthy leaf growth and root system; poor growth results from waterlogged ground.

However, the quick-drying characteristic does have advantages. Sandy soils warm up early in the year and are excellent for the production of early crops. Such soils are also very easy to cultivate. Any plants that resent too much water are likely to thrive on sand, because of its drip-dry nature.

The big advantage, though, is the readiness with which roots are formed and with which plants grow in it. Hence its popularity with market gardeners. Putting it in a nutshell: once a plant is put into a sandy soil, it is up to the gardener how well it does, not Nature.

One very important thing to remember about sandy soils is that, whereas clay soils can be either acidic or alkaline, sand is always acidic.

Medium-textured soils Not surprisingly, soils with a medium texture tend to have diluted versions of the advantages and disadvantages of clay and sand. In other words, they are as near perfect as one could wish. They can be cultivated quite easily, plants grow well in them, they have a reasonable reserve of nutrients, and they hold water well but also have good drainage.

If we are not blessed with this Utopian soil, however, we need never despair. With time and effort, even the most uninspiring soil can be turned into a first rate one that will do everything that is asked of it.

Although the three groups so far mentioned cover the majority of soils in this country, there are several others that are found in certain areas.

Chalky soils The most widely spread is probably the thin soil that overlies chalk. This can be found in Wiltshire around Salisbury Plain, through to the Chilterns and Hertfordshire and just into Cambridgeshire. There, the band of chalk disappears underground to reappear in a small area around Hunstanton in Norfolk. Other well known chalky areas are the North and South Downs.

Soils on chalk are often thin and may be acidic, though only in new gardens where the soil has not been disturbed. Once cultivation starts, the chalk imparts its alkalinity throughout. The texture of chalky soils can vary greatly but is normally on the heavy side.

These soils have a couple of advantages, both of which are derived from the porous nature of chalk. The first is that they tend to be well endowed with reserves of water – the chalk acts as a sponge and really can hold a remarkable amount. Secondly, this porosity means that chalky soils are usually well drained. They may be wet clay on top but, underneath, there is very little chance of waterlogging.

Where solid chalk is near the surface, difficulties can be experienced in getting trees and shrubs established. The problem stems from the impenetrability of the chalk until fissures have been created for the roots to travel along. When a garden is overlying chalk and you want to plant trees and shrubs, it is usually necessary to break up the chalk to a depth of at least 60 cm (2 ft), with a pick or crowbar, to give the roots a reasonable start in life. Once they have acquired a bit of strength, they can usually manage for themselves.

This problem is highlighted in beech woods on downland, where nearly every gale has its victims. You can quite easily see the enormous platforms of roots, with hardly any penetration into the chalk.

Limestone soils Chemically close to chalk, are the limestone soils of Derbyshire, the eastern half of Yorkshire and parts of Somerset. These have the same characteristics as chalky soils except that they are usually much lighter in texture because limestone breaks down into an almost sandy material.

Both chalk and limestone soils are really quite common and are nothing to be frightened about.

Peaty and fenland soils These are much rarer and are normally found in flat, low-lying districts such as south-east Yorkshire, Somerset and the Fens of Lincolnshire. However, they can also occur in almost mountainous areas along the Pennines, in Derbyshire, Cumbria and many places in Scotland.

These highly organic soils are often very fertile and physically perfect for growing plants in. But they require careful handling if you are not used to them, because there is very little reserve of nutrients and the high organic matter content is soon broken down once cultivations start.

Those in the north are very acidic but the Somerset ones are less so because of the proximity of limestone (for example, Cheddar). These soils can often be improved by importing a heavier grade from outside the district.

Acid, alkaline or neutral? The question of acidity and alkalinity has already cropped up while looking at the different types of soil, so let us now look at it in a little more depth, particularly regarding the effect that it has on both the nature of the soil and the types of plant that are best suited to it.

Acidity, neutrality and alkalinity are expressed as the pH value of a soil. For gardening purposes, the scale runs from about pH5 to around pH8, with neutral being anything from pH6.5 to 7. The lower the figure, the stronger the acidity. Most of the soils that we garden on are probably in the range pH5 to 8.

Although the optimum pH for different plants varies, 6 to 6.5 is generally the balance to aim for as this suits the greatest number of plants. It is slightly acid but not sufficiently so to cause any problems.

The pH of a soil is really quite easy to alter. All that has to be done is to add material with the opposite reading. Therefore, if you garden on a strongly acid soil, the answer is to apply chalk or lime. Gardening on chalk or limestone may necessitate dressings of peat or, in extreme cases, even powdered sulphur.

If a soil is strongly acidic or alkaline,

USING A SOIL-TESTING KIT

1. Pour solution into the tube with the soil in it, then cork and shake.

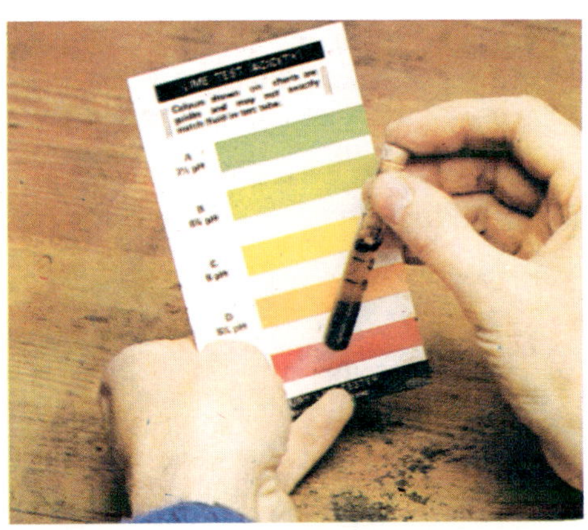

2. Allow soil to settle, then compare colour in tube with colours on chart.

the number of different kinds of plants that can be grown in it will be reduced. For instance, most gardeners know that ericaceous plants (rhododendrons, azaleas, heathers and so on) will not tolerate a high pH. This is a clear example of the reaction of a plant to the chemical nature of the soil. In this particular case, the problem is that the plant's internal mechanism for absorbing essential nutrients can only operate successfully in neutral or acidic soils.

In alkaline soils, certain essential elements are converted into a chemical form that is unavailable to the plants; the roots just cannot absorb them.

There are several ways round the problem, the most convenient being to apply the elements in what is called a chelated form, or as a sequestrene. These are unaffected by the alkaline conditions and can be absorbed by the roots. Another way is to build an acid border for the plants to grow in, by constructing a raised bed, using bricks or peat blocks to retain a quantity of acid soil. This is more effective than digging out a depression and filling it with the special soil because, over the years, alkalinity will creep in from the sides. In a raised border, this cannot happen.

Nearly all plants dislike strong alkalinity to a greater or lesser extent and this is often shown by pale and sometimes mottled yellowish leaves.

The best answer to this is to increase the organic matter content of the ground, which will effectively 'dilute' the chalk or limestone. The addition of moss peat is especially beneficial because of its strongly acid nature.

In extreme cases, the ground should also be treated with powdered sulphur or iron sulphate. Both are completely harmless and the only effect they have is in lowering the pH (acidifying) the soil. They are applied at the rate of 120 gm per sq. m (4 oz per sq. yd).

These situations are rare with the vast majority of gardens. Plants – and most gardeners – will never have experienced them.

Acid soils can also have their problems. Just as a chalky soil will 'lock up' certain elements, so will an acidic soil, though not usually the same elements. Acidic soil conditions also reduce the population and, therefore, the beneficial effects of many of the soil micro-organisms. In this case, the plants are not able to make full use of the naturally occurring plant nutrients, normally because they are taking longer to break down into an available form.

The simplest way to reduce the acidity (and raise the pH) of a soil is to treat it with ground chalk or limestone, or agricultural lime. In most cases the first two choices are better than agricultural lime, because they are far 'gentler' to any plants with which they come in contact. For this reason, lime is best applied only after winter digging, when it will be washed in during the winter and be integrated well before anything is planted. However, lime does have about double the corrective value of chalk or limestone.

Fortunately, there are fairly accurate guidelines as to how much chalk/limestone should be applied to a soil to have a given effect. As a rule, to raise the pH of a soil by 1.0 you need to apply 500 gm per sq. m (1 lb per sq. yd).

Soil's structure

Now it is time to look at the meaning of another word – structure. This is often confused with texture and one word is frequently used when the other is meant.

Whereas the texture of a soil refers to its actual character and the size of the individual soil particles, its structure is exactly what the word implies – the way in which it is put together. Imagine that the individual soil particles are represented by ball-bearings. These are of different sizes but heavy soils are predominantly small ones while light soils are large. That is how we can think of the 'texture' of a soil. Now put those 'ball-bearings' into polythene bags and pack them into a huge crate.

If the bags are very large and the ball-bearings are mainly small (as in the case of clay soils), there will be very little room for air in the crate. There will also be hardly any spaces for water to drain through if it rains, so it will tend to lie on top of the bags, and the crate becomes saturated and heavy.

This is very similar to the situation that we would find with a soil having what is called a 'massive' structure. Each of the individual blocks of soil particles are large and present very little pore space for water to drain away or roots to travel through. This is the situation with clay and silt.

At the opposite end of the scale, we would find a sample of predominantly large ball-bearings, representing a sandy soil. These would be packed in small bags. When placed in the crate, there would be a large amount of air between the bags, as well as between the individual 'ball-bearings'. Air can flow through the crate quite easily, as can water. Roots can grow more or less unhindered. This is called a 'loose' structure and it has its problems just as much as a massive structure does. When we come to medium textured soil we find that not only are the ball-bearings just about an equal mixture of large, medium and small, but so also are the bags in which they are packed. This gives us a soil that is truly between the two extremes with, one hopes, the best of both types.

The *texture* of a soil is very difficult to alter as it would mean adding ball-bearings of different sizes and hoping that they would get into the bags and alter their size and shape. However, it is perfectly possible to improve the *structure* of the soil.

Nature's way of achieving this improvement is to return dead vegetation to the ground and encourage it to be incorporated not only into the polythene bags but also around and between them.

Dead vegetation has the remarkable ability to bind together loose-structured sandy soil and break up clay and silt. In the former case it enables the soil to hold more water and plant foods. In the latter, it allows water to drain away easier and so improve a soil that hitherto lay wet. Thus, the structure of all soils can be improved, whether they be heavy, medium or light.

However, the dead vegetation (or organic matter), does not last for ever in a soil. The more there is, the greater the population of micro-organisms and, hence, the faster the organic matter is decomposed. The end result of this decomposition is a substance that is known to all gardeners – humus.

Humus is the end product of the decomposition of organic matter; it is not simply another word for organic matter. It is also a very mysterious substance that has a mainly chemical role in the soil rather than the largely physical effect that organic matter has before it fully decomposes.

All soils contain organic matter and humus, and the level of both must be maintained if plants are to grow properly. From the gardener's point of view, there is little we can do to add pure humus to the soil but there is a great deal that can be done to increase the organic matter content, which will ultimately break down into humus.

The effect that organic matter has on the soil has already been discussed, that is, it opens up heavy soils, binds together sandy soils and generally improves the structure of all of them. So, let us now move on and look at the various sources and forms of this marvellous stuff that we call organic matter.

ORGANIC MATTER

Because organic matter is the very essence of the types of gardening that we are concerned with here, we must clearly understand the different sorts that we are likely to find and use.

Broadly speaking, they fall into two groups. Those that are bulky and which are used mainly for improving the structure of the soil. And those that are applied in small quantitites as a source of plant nutrients. The latter we will cover when we discuss feeding plants.

There are also other types that we shall look at as we go along.

Farmyard manure

In years gone by, the most common form of bulky organic matter was farmyard manure (FYM) and most gardening went on in the country where the supply of this commodity was virtually limitless.

There is still no shortage of FYM but the number of gardens has increased so dramatically that there is just not enough to go round. Added to that, there are now many more town gardens than there used to be so the problem of supply crops up.

Fortunately, although FYM is still thought by many to be the elixir of plant life, science has taught us that this is far from the case; there are alternatives. Also, the quality of FYM can vary greatly, due to a number of factors. The percentage of straw or other litter will have an effect, as will the type of animal that produced the manure. The degree of decomposition will also influence its value. By and large though, a good sample of FYM should contain approximately 76 percent water, 0.64 percent nitrogen, 0.23 percent phosphates and 0.6 percent potash. This may not sound very much as against 21 percent nitrogen in sulphate of ammonia. Indeed, it is not, but it does represent a useful amount. Also, as we have seen, it is not the nutrient value of bulky organic manures but their physical effect on the soil that is important.

One thing that can be said for *all* these bulky forms of organic matter is that they contain the trace elements, but more about these later.

Straw

While FYM or stable manure is not always easy to come by, straw is. And not only is there a lot of it about but it is also far easier to transport and a much less anti-social material.

Straw is of little value to gardeners until it is composted, but then it provides a perfectly good alternative to FYM. It also has 0.5 percent nitrogen, 0.2 percent phosphates and 1 percent potash.

Sewage sludge

This used to be a common material for spreading on the garden but we tend to take rather a dim view of it in the 1980s. Yet we are quite happy to use animal manures. Odd. Raw, but dried, sewage sludge on its own is of low value as a soil improver but it is a valuable manure when mixed and composted with straw.

A typical sample would contain as much as 60 percent more nitrogen than FYM, about the same amount of phosphates but rather less potash. It is mainly a source of nitrogen and organic matter.

Domestic waste

An increasing number of town councils are now turning their domestic rubbish into a 'material', for want of a better word, that can be worked into the soil. This is mainly organic in nature, the glass and metal having been removed, and it certainly is quite useful. However, unless it is composted and used in conjunction with something like straw or normal garden waste, its value is really rather limited. The combination, though, is well worth using, if you can get it at a reasonable price and a supply is close at hand. A typical analysis would be something like 0.8 percent nitrogen, 0.54 percent phosphates and 0.43 percent potash. Wastes will also contain some valuable trace elements.

Wool shoddy

This used to be a splendid form of bulky organic matter. It is the waste from the wool mills of the north. Unfortunately, man-made fibres have reduced the amount of pure shoddy considerably, but it can still be found.

The mixed grade of shoddy now being produced is by no means useless. The nitrogen content is reduced but its physical effect on the soil is just as good, if not better, as the man-made fibres take much longer to rot down than wool.

The highest grade of pure wool shoddy would have a nitrogen content of 12–15 percent. Lower grades would be 5–10 percent and contain 75–80 percent organic matter.

Peat

When one thinks of peat, it is normally as a constituent of seed and potting composts, or as a material to use for improving the soil when planting trees and shrubs. This is mainly because of the rather high price of proprietary brands. Where it is available in large quantities at relatively little cost though, it is a useful soil conditioner. It is not in the same class as FYM, straw or garden compost, but nevertheless, it is still worth while.

The trouble with peat is that the particles are very small so the physical effect on the soil is less than that of coarser materials.

The nitrogen content varies from 1.5 to 2 percent, phosphate about 0.03 percent and potash 0.1 percent so you can see that its nutritional value is almost nothing. However, peat's real worth lies in its acidifying action when applied to alkaline soils. The pH of peat may vary from 3.0 to 6.0, depending on its type (moss peat is the lowest, sedge the highest). The most valuable would be in the range pH 4–5.

Pulverized pine bark

This material is increasing in popularity. It has much the same uses as peat but is far longer lasting in the soil because of its hardness. This hardness also means that its physical effect on the soil structure is much greater. And when used as a mulch there is not nearly the same tendency for it to blow away.

The plant food value is virtually nil but, with a natural pH of 4–5, it is a valuable acidifying agent. Beware of some brands though if you want the completely unadulterated product as they have additives that are designed to increase the nutrient value and reduce the acidity.

Spent mushroom compost

This is readily available in some areas and makes a useful soil improver. It consists mainly of straw composted with horse manure and with ground chalk added to raise the pH. Once again, the plant food value is low but the soil improving qualities are good.

One thing to remember about spent mushroom compost is that the chalk content makes it unsuitable for use among ericaceous plants.

Sawdust, wood shavings and chippings

These are all quite easily found in some areas, as waste products from timber and furniture works. The worst thing about any wood material is that it will rob the ground of nitrogen if applied 'raw' and uncomposted. They should either be composted with other waste vegetation before use or they should be applied in conjunction with a source of nitrogen. This is simply because, during decomposition by micro-organisms, a lot of nitrogen is used up.

Leafmould

One of the most valuable sources of bulky organic matter is leafmould. In rural areas this is often quite easy to find but, before collecting it yourself out of woods, do make sure that this is allowed. In most woods, the best leafmould will be found a few inches below the surface as it will have lain there for several years and therefore will be well rotted. But its removal will upset the ecology of the area, so it is advisable to look for another source.

Freshly fallen leaves are perfectly all right but they should be composted for upwards of a year before they are fit for use. Raw leaves will not only need nitrogen to rot down, like sawdust, but they will also blow about all over the garden, if used as a mulch. Once again, the nutrient content is low but their value to the soil is high.

Seaweed

Near the coast, there has always been a strong leaning towards seaweed as a bulky manure and it certainly does do a lot to improve the soil. Fresh seaweed has a similar nitrogen content to FYM, but much less phosphate and about twice as much potash. It has the same organic matter value but rots down a lot quicker because of its physical nature and nitrogen content. In fact, it is excellent for adding to straw to rot it down quicker.

It also has a useful amount of trace elements, principally iron, manganese and zinc. However, the real benefit of seaweed lies in its alginate content. These extraordinary chemicals even have a number of uses in industry, but their particular interest to gardeners lies in their ability to open up clay soils and bind together sandy ones. What seaweed therefore lacks in fibre, it more than makes up for in alginates.

Garden compost

The last source of bulky organic matter that we need to look at is the cheapest and most readily available of all. If you have a garden, then the raw material is sitting there in front of you – garden compost. We shall see next how easy it is to make and how to go about it but, here, we are concerned with its value as a soil improver and supplier of plant foods.

Contrary to what most people believe, garden compost normally has a higher plant food value than FYM: 2–2.5 percent nitrogen, 0.5–1 percent phosphates and 0.5–2 percent potash. This makes it a very valuable manure. The figures are extremely variable because it depends entirely on what constitutes the compost.

Because the amount of fibrous material also varies greatly, the soil-improving value of garden compost is rather unpredictable but the average sized garden will have enough raw material to make composting worthwhile. After all, it costs virtually nothing.

MAKING LIQUID MANURE

1. One method of making liquid manure is to hang a hessian bag of well-rotted animal manure in a bucket of water.

2. After several days, the liquid in the bucket should be brown. Dilute it to a straw colour before using it.

Another method of making liquid manure is to dilute urine with water until it is the colour of straw.

MAKING COMPOST

The type of compost we are talking about here is the properly rotted waste vegetation from the garden and home and should not be confused with seed and potting composts. These are special materials in which to sow seeds and grow plants and they are always used in containers such as seed trays, pots, tubs, window boxes and hanging baskets, not for treating the ground.

Garden compost is usually applied to the soil and can consist of any or all of the following: lawn mowings, weeds, hedge clippings, spent vegetable plants, dead flowers, leaves of all sorts, soft prunings, sawdust and wood ashes, straw and hay, pet droppings and animal manures.

Along with these, we can add household waste such as cabbage leaves, vegetable peelings, tea leaves, egg shells and more or less anything else of organic origin from the kitchen. When we talk about garden compost, we are referring to the decayed or decaying remains of these materials.

'Well rotted' compost is a dark brown, rich material that is dry and easily breaks up in the hand. Woody materials such as thick hedge clippings and prunings, take a long time to decompose but will, eventually, provide the most humus as this is mainly derived from the lining in woody material.

As long as twigs and the like are chopped up into small pieces with a shredder, or something similar, they can be a valuable raw material but are still best mixed with softer tissues. If large prunings and bits of wood are available, they should first be burnt and the ashes added to the compost heap.

Carpet sweepings used to be a first rate material but, as with shoddy, they now contain a lot of man-made fibre. Newspaper in small amounts, such as from the bottom of pets' cages, is fine but large quantities should be avoided. Not only does it take a long time to rot down, it also adds very little of value to the soil.

There are extremely few things of organic origin that cannot be turned into compost but some materials are only suitable in small amounts. We have already mentioned newspaper, but too many evergreen leaves or pine needles have the same problem. They take a long time to break down. The roots of perennial weeds – such as docks, thistles and ground elder – must be dried and killed before composting them or they should be burnt. Rhubarb leaves are often said to be bad in a compost heap but they are perfectly safe in what might be called domestic quantities. It is when large amounts are put on for weeks on end that trouble might arise, by making the heap too acidic.

Plants infested or infected by pests and diseases are also frowned upon by many gardeners but the majority are destroyed either by the heat generated in the heap or the very fact that they are in a hostile environment for a considerable time. Some are best avoided though. These are the ones that live and move and have their being in the soil. They would include the victims of such things as club root disease, cabbage root fly and carrot fly. Because they are used to life below ground, being buried in a compost heap seldom worries them.

Lawn mowings are perfectly all right to add to the heap, in fact they frequently form the backbone in summer, but they are much better if mixed with other things first. In a thick layer, they are apt to lie cold and soggy after the initial heat generation. Another point to bear in mind about mowings concerns those that come from a lawn that has been treated with a selective weedkiller. If the treatment took place from April to the end of July, the mowings can be added to the compost heap and it will be quite safe to use the compost in the autumn. If the treatment was *after* July, then it is better to leave the compost until the spring. This is worth mentioning because many gardeners beg or borrow raw material for their compost heaps with little knowledge of its history.

While on the subject of selective weedkillers, it used to be quite common practice to grow tomatoes in partially decomposed straw bales. This is still fine in principle but it must only be done if you can be sure that the corn crop from which the straw came was not treated with a hormone type weedkiller shortly before it was harvested. Tomatoes are particularly sensitive to these weedkillers and are easily damaged by them.

To return to composting and to summarize the raw material aspect; the greater variety there is in a heap, the better will the resulting compost be. A mixture of firm and soft materials can only give good results.

How compost is formed

Having looked at the sort of things that can and cannot be put in the compost heap, it is helpful to know how compost is formed so that we can use the knowledge to our advantage.

The decomposition of waste vegetation is carried out by beneficial micro-organisms that need air (oxygen) and moisture to survive and operate efficiently. The amount of air and moisture required, while not critical, does have limits. Too much air will lead to the raw materials drying out and too little will encourage the wrong type of microbe. Too much moisture will force out a lot of the air and thereby reduce the microbe population. At the same time, it will discourage the build-up of heat within the heap. Too little moisture will cause the whole process to grind to a halt.

A good supply of nitrogen is essential to the micro-organisms, as this forms an important part of their diet. While a certain amount is provided by the plants' remains, the whole composting process is greatly speeded up if extra is added. This is referred to as an 'activator' or 'accelerator', and there is one particular proprietary product which dominates the market. However, if a more natural material is preferred, any bird or animal manure can be used instead.

In fact, given a correctly built heap made with the right material, decomposition will occur by itself but the use of an accelerator will certainly hasten the process. This speeding up may not seem particularly important but it means that more heat is generated during decomposition and this is vital if weed seeds and other undesirables in the heap are to be destroyed.

The word 'heap' keeps cropping up in relation to composting and this is certainly the traditional way of making compost. However, there are heaps and there are heaps and an untidy one is an abomination, whether it be large or small. Anything that looks like a heap of garden rubbish thrown into a corner is likely to produce correspondingly awful compost, as well as creating a general air of slovenliness.

Before we start making compost, therefore, there are several questions that have to be answered concerning the type of heap, or container, that is going to be most convenient for us.

- How much raw material is likely to be available?
- How much compost is going to be needed?
- Is the compost going to be required all at once or as a steady supply right through the year?

If there is only a small amount of raw material or the need for compost is strictly limited, then a small heap or, better still, a readymade composting bin, is probably the answer. On the other hand, if waste vegetation is plentiful and all the compost that can be produced is used, then one or more large heaps would be more sensible. This would also be the best system where compost is only needed once a year for, say, digging in during the autumn. If it is going to be wanted for various jobs throughout the year, it would be wiser to have a number of small heaps or bins with compost maturing on a sort of production line.

Where it has been decided that bins are inappropriate, the question arises as to what is the best way of containing a heap so that it looks tidy and operates to full effectiveness. The heap should be as near round or square as is convenient to encourage the quickest and most even decomposition. The width should be not much more than 1.2–1.5 m (4–5 ft) but the length can be up to about 1.8 m (6 ft). The width is the important measurement because, with a wider heap, air will have difficulty in penetrating to the centre. For the same reason, 0.9–1.2 m (3–4 ft) would be about the maximum desirable height.

The importance of having sufficient air within the heap cannot be overstressed; it really is the crux of making good compost. Satisfactory decomposition can only take place in the presence of sufficient oxygen, so every effort must be made to achieve this.

There are two different types of decomposition: aerobic and anaerobic. Aerobic decomposition needs free oxygen to take place whereas anaerobic decomposition occurs when there is no free oxygen available. Under the latter conditions completely different micro-organisms do the decomposing and the results are seldom satisfactory, but always smelly.

The absence of air in a heap is usually the result of compaction of the raw material – either by firming it down too much or by the nature of the raw material itself. For example, grass mowings pack down tightly without any firming and this may well exclude air. Hence the need for a good mixture of raw materials.

This slatted wooden bin can be bought or made. Simply add slats as you build the heap.

Where this is difficult, or where the heap is large, occasionally push a hoe handle (or something similar) into the heap in several places to provide ventilation holes.

Some proprietary composting bins are equipped with air holes and some are not. With bins of a normal size, plenty of air will get in via the top and bottom to make special holes quite unnecessary.

Siting a compost heap

The ideal site for such a heap would be in the angle of a fence or wall where two sides are already provided.

In most cases it is better to put a sheet of tin or something similar against the wall to prevent its deterioration or the bridging of any damp-course. The other two walls can be similarly made of corrugated iron with holes driven through it or planks nailed 1.3 cm (½ in) apart to upright supports. However, wood is generally considered superior to corrugated iron because it looks nicer and provides better insulation against heat and cold. If possible, choose a level site for the heap or bin.

Choosing a compost bin

If the choice is to have a bin, as opposed to a heap, there are several models to choose from or you can even make your own. Bins which incorporate perforated polythene sheeting or which are made of more substantial plastic, wood or even bricks all have the ability to retain heat and moisture quite well, in spite of the small inside volume.

The important factor is that the bin should have a top, as this will not only keep the heat and moisture in but will also prevent the contents getting wet by being rained on. Incidentally, the necessity for a top is not confined to bins, traditional heaps also operate far better when covered.

Compost bins are about the shape of a large dustbin but their shape, material or manufacture and effectiveness are about as variable as their price. Unfortunately, the high price of some models has deterred many newcomers to gardening from even setting foot on the composting ladder. They assume that all other aspects of the art are equally expensive. This is absolutely wrong and the makers of highly priced but rubbishy bins are doing neither themselves nor the gardeners any good at all.

A VARIETY OF COMPOST CONTAINERS

This proprietary compost container consists of a strong black polythene bag, with air holes in it, suspended from a circular frame. Spare bags are provided.

If possible, make a double bin, so that one heap can be left to mature as another is started. This bin has walls of corrugated iron, supported by stout stakes. The aeration layer at the base is made from parallel rows of land drain pipes.

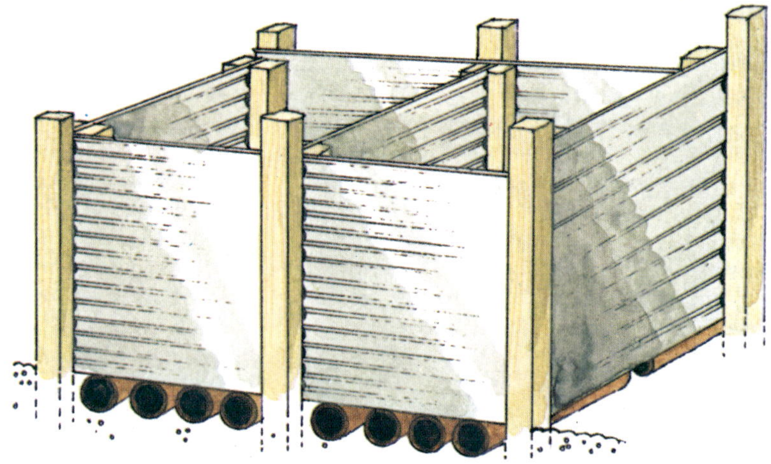

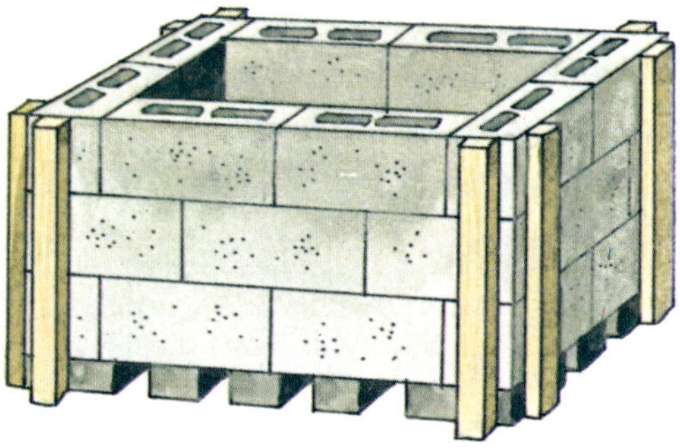

An effective compost bin may be made from concrete breeze blocks, anchored at the corners by wooden stakes (treated with a horticultural wood preservative). In this case the aeration layer is at the base; it consists of rows of bricks with gaps between.

A slatted wooden bin is easy to make. The gaps between the slats allow good aeration, and the slats are removable for ease of access to the heap. Make a sloping roof from corrugated iron.

A simple circular container can be made of wire netting. Improve its heat insulation by lining with waste timber and cover with a roof.

If you fancy having a go at making your own bin, very good results can be had from old dustbins with the bottoms knocked out and some holes punched in the side.

Or you can make a wire netting cylinder 0.9–1.2 m (3–4 ft) high and not less than about 75 cm (30 in) across. Support this by canes woven through the netting and place a bottomless dustbin bag inside it to enclose the 'heap'.

Compost materials

Having set the scene, the time has come to start composting. Most gardens produce a range of useful materials and, for best results, these should be mixed together as the heap is built up in layers. If an accelerator is being used, this should be added every 15–25 cm (6–10 in).

Mix dry and wet materials together so that the moisture content is reasonably even. If anything is dry, it should be thoroughly soaked *before* it is added to the heap. When fairly woody materials are used a careful firming down of the material is needed, to exclude large air pockets. If the heap appears to be drying out in the summer, it is perfectly safe to wet it so that activity is maintained. Do not overdo this though or excessive cooling can take place.

Before the days of effective accelerators, it was common practice to build up a compost heap in the course of one year, turn it inside-out and upside-down and leave it for another year. This ensured that it was completely and evenly rotted and in a fit state to use. If an accelerator and a good heap or bin are used, this is not usually necessary.

When a heap or bin is complete and has been properly made, cover it and leave it to decompose. This process will start very quickly and should be complete before you use it. The time it takes for compost to become sufficiently decomposed to be usable will vary enormously because there are so many variables. Not least amongst these are the nature of the raw materials used and the time of year.

If soft material is being composted in the summer, it can be fully decomposed in a matter of two to three months. On the other hand, chopped up prunings added in the late autumn are unlikely to be fit for at least six months. Among the slowest materials to decompose are autumn leaves. These normally take in excess of a year and large quantities are really better composted on their own.

That takes care of the main points involved in making your own garden compost, but there are a number of others that are worth noting.

Sometimes, one sees recommendations for adding layers of soil to a heap to provide additional micro-organisms. Although the introduction of soil in the natural course of events – such as on plant roots – is quite in order, the deliberate formation of layers of soil can seriously interfere with the composting process by creating cold layers in which no breaking down occurs at all.

If you anticipate that a particular batch of material will be reluctant to break down, the addition of activator immediately on top of it normally evens things up.

Lawn rakings We discussed the situation as regards lawn mowings and those treated with weedkiller but lawn rakings are also a valuable source of material for composting. These are perfectly safe as they are, even if they contain a fair percentage of moss. Although this may not rot down completely, there is no risk whatsoever of spreading moss to other parts of the garden when the compost is finally used.

Leafmould There are occasions when a lot of the same material turns up all at once; autumn leaves are a good example. In reasonable amounts, these can be mixed in with the other vegetation to be composted but if there are a lot, it is usually best to deal with them on their own and the addition of an activator is a great help.

The formation of good leafmould usually takes at least a year but this will vary with the type of leaves. Beech and oak are of the quickest types to rot down. Plane, sycamore and horse chestnut take a lot longer because of their thick veins and stalks. Evergreen leaves and pine needles are best added to the normal mixed compost heap because, on their own, they can take literally years to rot down. No leaves need be rejected, they all make good compost if treated correctly. It's just that some take longer to decompose than others. All leaves should have plenty of water when being composted.

Sawdust is tricky material but also very valuable if dealt with properly. Its woody nature makes it an excellent raw material for humus, but it does take a long time to break down. In small amounts it can safely be added to the general heap. If a lot is available, it is best composted separately, as advised for leaves. The answer is to build the heap with thoroughly wet sawdust and mix in an activator as the heap is being made.

Straw Small amounts can be mixed with grass mowings and added to the heap. The grass will make much better compost than on its own and the straw will break down quicker. Again, large amounts are best composted separately. There are several ways of doing it. You can just water the straw. You can water the straw and layer it with green and sodden material. Or, you can layer the straw with sodden, green material but not water it and allow the rain to provide the moisture. This last method takes the longest of all.

When composting straw, make sure that it is thoroughly loose and always stack it high rather than wide so that it decomposes much quicker. One of the best ways is to build a sort of stockade of bales and fill the middle with loose straw. This keeps the heap tidy and allows it to decompose right up to the edges. When completed, tread the whole thing down and give it a soaking.

The retaining wall need not be bales; planks or boards are just as effective if held in place with stakes. But there is an advantage in using bales. When the composting of one batch is finished those used for the wall will be half rotted also and can be shaken out for the next batch of compost while fresh bales are used for new walls. As a rough guide, two tons of dry straw will need a heap about 2.7 m (9 ft) square while 6–10 tons will need it to be about 5.4 m (18 ft) square.

If materials other than straw are included in the heap, spread them out evenly. Then tread the heap down as before and give it enough water to soak it thoroughly. Decomposition will be quickest if an activator is used.

A heap can perfectly well be built without walls but it will not be as efficient and, of course, the straw does not rot down right to the edges. Should you wish to build without walls, first make the outside of the heap with longish material to about 15 cm (6 in) high. Then fill the centre with shaken out straw until it reaches the top of the edges, when the process is repeated. Once you get high enough, tread it all down and soak it thoroughly. In this case, 'high enough' is about 1.8 m (6 ft) and this will sink to about 1.2 m (4 ft) during decomposition.

Bracken and seaweed In some parts of the country, plants like bracken and seaweed are in plentiful supply and these two make particularly good compost. Bracken contains a lot of potash and is best treated like straw. We have discussed the virtues of seaweed already but, for composting, it should first be allowed to drain so that most of the salt goes. The best system is then to mix it with straw before composting it. Normally, no activator is needed because of the readily available nitrogen seaweed contains.

Annual weeds If a lot are going to be put on a compost heap there is always a danger that any seeds they are carrying will be distributed when the finished compost is spread. The best way to avoid this is to 'harvest' the weeds before they come into flower. If you don't have an opportunity to do this, they should be put in the centre of the heap and covered with other material. The greatest heat is produced in the middle and it should kill the seeds.

The weeds are covered so that they will not continue growing. This is particularly important in the winter when weeds are apt to stay alive, even when uprooted, in the cool and damp conditions that are found on top of the heap.

Turf Something that falls quite neatly into the category of composting is the use of turf to form the basis of the other kind of compost: seed and potting mixtures for growing plants in. If you are making your own John Innes type of compost, you will need a good supply of fibrous loam. One of the best sources of this is old grassland. Start by stripping the turves off so that there is about 5 cm (2 in) of soil below the grass. Lay the turves on the ground, grass side up, and put the next layer on them, grass side down, to form a sort of grass sandwich. Carry on building, like this until all the turves have gone. If you want to hasten the death of the grass and its decomposition, sprinkle an activator such as poultry manure into the middle of each 'sandwich'.

Using the compost

Well rotted garden compost certainly does work wonders. All plants derive enormous benefit from the improving effect that it has on the soil. Having looked at its manufacture therefore, what are we to do with it once it is ready for the garden? There are four main ways in which it can be used.

The most common way, and probably the one that springs immediately to mind, is digging it into the soil to a depth of about 30 cm (1 ft) to improve the structure and to add to the plant foods already there. The usual – but quite wrong – method of doing this is to dig out the first trench on the plot, spread the compost in the bottom of it and then turn the next lot over on to it. This is wrong because the compost is buried out of sight and completely out of reach of the plant roots. A plant has to be well established and growing strongly before the roots come in contact with the

STAGES IN BUILDING A COMPOST HEAP

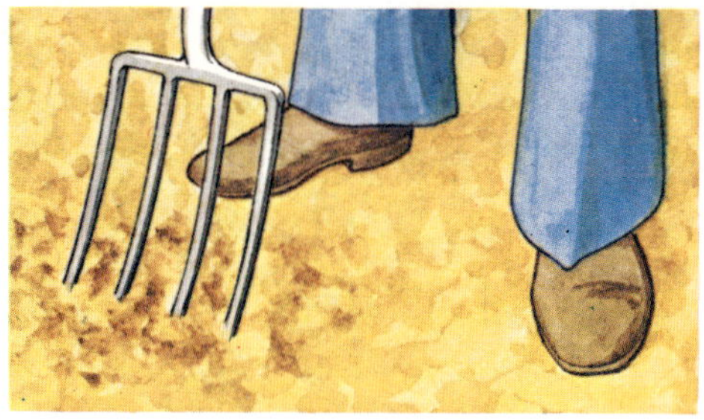

1. Before starting the heap, lightly fork over the soil to make it easier for earthworms to tunnel into the heap.

2. Build the aeration layer first, at the base of the heap – in this case, it is a layer of thick, woody prunings.

3. If possible, thoroughly mix the garden and kitchen wastes with a fork and moisten them with water.

4. Fork a 15–22 cm (6–9 in) deep layer of pre-mixed waste into the bin (here it is a slatted box) and level.

5. Put a thin layer of an activator, such as poultry manure, onto the first layer of pre-mixed waste.

6. Scatter enough lime on the next layer of waste to colour it white. Cover this with soil if necessary.

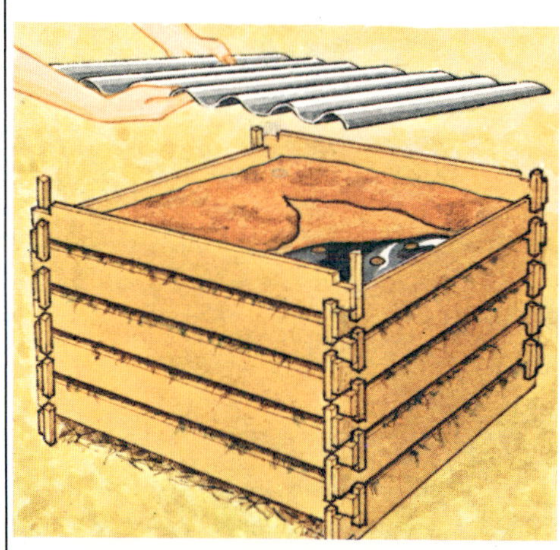

7. Cover the heap with a sheet of black polythene with holes in it, followed by sacking and the roof.

8. The compost is mature when it is dark brown and crumbly. It can then be used on your crops safely.

A mulch of straw around growing plants will discourage weeds.

compost. Burying it at the bottom of a trench destroys the whole object of the exercise, which is to help plants to grow from the moment they are put in the ground.

Clearly, therefore, the compost has to be spread through as great a depth of soil as possible. And the way to achieve this is *not* to throw it into the bottom of the trench but to spread it in front of you over the face of the trench so that the full depth of soil benefits. In that way the plants are helped immediately they germinate or are planted. There is also a right and a wrong way of doing the actual digging, and we will be looking at that on pages 30–31.

Another common use for garden compost is as a mulch instead of peat or bark. For anyone new to gardening, mulching is the practice of covering the ground between plants with a layer of organic material 10–15 cm (4–6 in) deep. This has a number of benefits:

- It helps to prevent the soil from drying out and capping in the summer – the compost forms a blanket on the soil surface so that much less water is lost by evaporation. For this reason, the mulch must be put down at a time when the ground is thoroughly moist. If it goes on when the ground is dry, it simply acts as a Macintosh and stops any rain from soaking in. April is a good time to mulch.
- Mulching will help to keep the weeds down. Weed seeds operate in the same way as any other seeds. They have to be near the surface to germinate and grow properly. If they are buried deeper than Nature intended by being covered with several inches of compost, they are either not going to germinate at all, in which case many will rot, or, if they do germinate, they perish before they reach the surface. Unfortunately, this does not apply to established perennial weeds; they have to be killed by other means.
- Mulching adds organic matter to the soil. In fact, this is about the only way in which it can be added once a fruit area has been laid out and planted. No deep cultivations are possible so we have to rely on Nature to incorporate it with the help of earthworms and other similar creatures.

Garden compost can also be used in the making of seed and potting composts, but here we come to a big snag – weeds. Unless the compost is particularly well rotted or great care has been taken to exclude weed seeds, the most awful mess can result. Weeds will spring up everywhere and the seeds we *want* to grow will be smothered in the resulting forest.

One way round this is to heat sterilize the seed or potting compost after it has been made, rather than just the loam beforehand. On the whole, though, it is infinitely wiser not to rely on homemade seed and potting composts but to buy properly made ones. When you are spending quite a lot of money on seeds, the saving in the cost of compost is too high a price to pay on the off-chance that things will be satisfactory. They seldom are. However, for preparing your own liquid plant food, there is little better than well rotted garden compost. FYM has been used for this purpose for years, so why not compost, since the nutrient values are similar?

The process is exactly the same as for manure-water, in that a bag of garden compost is hung in a water tub so that the 'goodness' seaps into the water. This is then used to feed plants. There are no weeds, no pests, no diseases and, unlike manure-water, no smell; well, hardly any. Here's how to set about it. Fill some sacking with well-rotted compost and tie it at the top. Then submerge the whole thing in a container of water, preferably rainwater. Make sure that the sacking is tied to something outside the container because, if a 40 gallon drum is used, it can present difficulties when the bag is just dropped in and you want to retrieve it. In about a week, the liquid should be ready to use.

The way to work out how much compost to use is to allow about 1 lb for every gallon of water. No dilution is required when the infusion is drawn off. Whenever any is taken out, top up the container with more water. A bag of compost should last for 5–6 weeks, after which time most of the nutrients will have gone and a fresh start will have to be made. The spent compost can be used on the garden.

Other soil improvers

Before leaving the subject of garden compost and composting, it would be worth while having a quick look at one or two other materials that are available for improving the soil. Some of these purport to do away with the need for bulky organic matter.

Ground calcified seaweed Probably the most readily available, this perfectly natural material is derived from a seaweed that is more like a coral than a plant. It has a very high calcium carbonate content and, as such, a high pH as well. In all honesty, it is an expensive way of buying chalk or limestone but it does have the advantage of containing trace elements. It is used in the same way as lime is, in that it is applied to the ground after digging and it then helps to create a good tilth for sowing or, planting.

Ground seaweed Another form of seaweed that is of more value in improving the soil is also a completely natural material, that is seaweed that has been harvested, dried and ground up. This also has trace elements but by far its greatest virtue is that it is rich in alginates, the material mentioned earlier as being first rate at improving the structure of all soils, whether they be heavy, medium or light.

Both these products are natural, genuine, and they work – within limits. Neither profess to do away with the need for bulky organic matter but, certainly, the composted seaweed is a great help in creating a good tilth.

PLANNING

It is one thing to own a garden and to grow plants in it. It is quite another to use it to the limit of its potential. Most gardens have the capacity to produce a lot more than they actually do. It is not normally the standard of gardening that is responsible for any shortage of efficiency but, purely and simply, a lack of forethought, or planning.

What goes where – and when

Just sowing vegetable seeds and planting plants, be they vegetables or fruit trees and bushes, is all very well but there must be some overall plan. In fact, there should be two. One is a properly drawn plan of the garden, so that the position of every row or tree and bush can be worked out and plotted in relation to all the others. Only in this way will the ground be used to the full. Along with this, you need to form a time plan, or cropping programme, so that you can properly work out when such-and-such a crop is sown, when it is harvested and when it is cleared to make room for the next. If these two plans are drawn up together, the best use is going to be made of the land.

There is no need to go into all the different possibilities with fruit and vegetables as regards planning. In the sections of this book dealing with them, you will find all the information needed when considering time and space (in the horticultural rather than philosophical sense). This, after all, is the essence of planning: what goes where and when. You may still make a few mistakes – but they won't be difficult to rectify.

Vegetables

When working out a vegetable plot, it is often convenient to include any greenhouse in it. But this is by no means essential and it is normally a case of where it will fit rather than where it is wanted.

Naturally, one should try not to have the vegetables in the most eye-catching part of the garden but it is equally silly to have the plot at the back of beyond, if this can be avoided. The reason for this may not be obvious in the summer but, if you have to trudge through the snow to gather a few sprouts, it will quickly become clear.

Other features which are normally best placed in the vegetable section are the composting area and any tool sheds. The compost, because it is from the vegetables that most of the raw material will be coming, and the tool shed simply for the sake of appearances.

If you wish to have a physical barrier between the decorative and productive sections, an evergreen hedge, such as a Leylandii conifer, is one of the best choices. This will provide a visual barrier all the year round as well as a windbreak for whenever the need arises. However, do not have this kind of hedge if it has to be less than about 2.4 m (8 ft) high as Leylandii is very vigorous and will need clipping almost as often as the lawn needs mowing.

For immediate effect, woven sectional fences are good as plants can soon be grown up them to give the impression of maturity. In the actual vegetable area, the first consideration should be the direction in which the rows will run. North to south ensures that everything gets the maximum amount of light. But it is more important that the length and direction of the rows are right rather than them having the best aspect.

Perennial plants, such as rhubarb and artichokes, should be grouped together as they will be there for some years. Also, many gardeners like to include strawberries among the vegetables. These fruits should be treated as perennials.

Before sowing or planting anything, make sure that there is going to be room for it; hence the need for a plan drawn more or less to scale.

Where the whole garden – or maybe just the vegetable section – is limited for space, concentrate on growing those vegetables which are unusual and difficult to buy or those which, for one reason or another, are expensive. For example, it is pointless to waste valuable land on something as low in value as maincrop potatoes. But it is a very good idea to have a row or two of earlies, to mature when shop prices are high.

Crops like peas and beans, especially runner beans, are always worth growing. Not only do they crop for weeks on end but, if there are more than you can cope with at any time, the surplus can be frozen. Remember also that some varieties of peas and broad beans are suitable for sowing in the autumn, for maturing early in the following summer.

Intercropping is an important part of any cropping programme. This is the practice of growing two or more completely different crops together. The normal system is to have a long-standing vegetable, like Brussels sprouts, with a quick-maturing crop, such as lettuces, set between the rows when the sprouts have just been planted. In this way, the ground between the sprout plants is not wasted and is producing a crop that, otherwise, you might not have had. The lettuces are out of the way long before they interfere with the sprouts.

A similar example is to plant alternate rows of later winter cabbages and seedling wallflowers. The cabbages go in at the recommended spacing with the wallflowers between the rows. By the time that the two crops are touching (October/November), the wallflowers will be ready to be planted in their final positions.

Fruit

With the exception of strawberries, planning for fruit is possibly the hardest. Not only are the individual plants much bigger, and therefore in need of more room, but they are also likely to be there for a considerable time. To give an idea of the life spans involved, bush and cane fruits should have an active life of 12–15 years and fruit trees from 20–40.

Along with this, it must be remembered that fruit trees are probably going to be the 'bones' of a garden with many of the other features being planned around them. If, therefore, they are planted in the wrong places, the result can be chaotic from a planning point of view.

Fruit of any kind should always be in a sheltered position that receives plenty of sun. If there is a choice, the north end of the garden is best as it can be in the sun and yet create no shade for other plants.

Trees that you want to train to a wall or fence should face south or west to take full advantage of the warmer conditions. This is particularly so with the choicer varieties of pear and gage but is also important for peaches, nectarines and apricots, all of which need every bit of help we can give them to ripen.

Later flowering varieties of apple and pear are quite happy on an east facing wall because the likelihood of sharp frosts is probably over by the time they come into flower. This may seem completely unconnected but it is the early morning sun striking the frozen blossoms that kills them. You get just the same effect when you turn a blow-lamp onto frozen water pipes – they burst.

The only fruit that can tolerate a north facing wall is the Morello cherry, a very sour variety that is only used for cooking and making jam.

If trees are to be grown as cordons trained to wires in the open garden (not against anything), the rows should run north-south to give equal sun to both sides. Incidentally, they make an excellent boundary between the ornamental and vegetable sections; a useful one as well.

If space permits, it is well worth setting aside a special area for fruit. This can combine free-standing as well as trained trees along with all the other types of fruit. Management of the trees and bushes is much easier if they are all together and anyone wishing to use sprays can do so without the risk of them drifting on to vegetables that are, perhaps, ready for harvesting.

Where it *is* possible to have a fruit area, there is no reason at all why, in its early years, it should not also be used for growing other things between the trees and bushes. In fact, a sensible system is to have the bushes between the trees. By the time the trees are getting large, it will probably be necessary to pull out grub the bush fruit anyway because of old age.

In gardens where space is at a premium, a greater use should be made of intensive tree forms such as cordons, espaliers, fans, dwarf pyramids and even spindles. These take up much less room and some forms can be grown against walls and fences, where they occupy hardly any ground at all.

In these smaller gardens, trees should be planted around the sides rather than in rows across the plot, where they would largely prevent the cultivation of other crops close by. Oddly enough, large trees – such as half-standards – are far more convenient and valuable if they are treated as decorative, and planted as specimens in the lawn or flower borders.

In really small gardens, and those where there is no soil at all but merely concrete or flag-stones, fruit trees and bushes can still be grown but they have to be in very large pots or other decorative containers.

Herbs

Planning for herbs is a much easier job because there are fewer to think about. However, as with vegetables, it is more convenient to have the shrubby ones and perennials together and the annuals, like parsley, in another group.

The only thing that really is important is that the herb area is as close as is reasonably possible to the kitchen door. There are few things worse than having to go to the other end of the garden in a thunder storm simply for a few bits of mint. It is also worthwhile spending some time getting to know the characteristics of particular herbs. Mint, for instance, is rampant, and will invade your garden rapidly, but it can be restrained by being planted in a container which when sunk beneath the soil will be concealed from view.

TOOLS

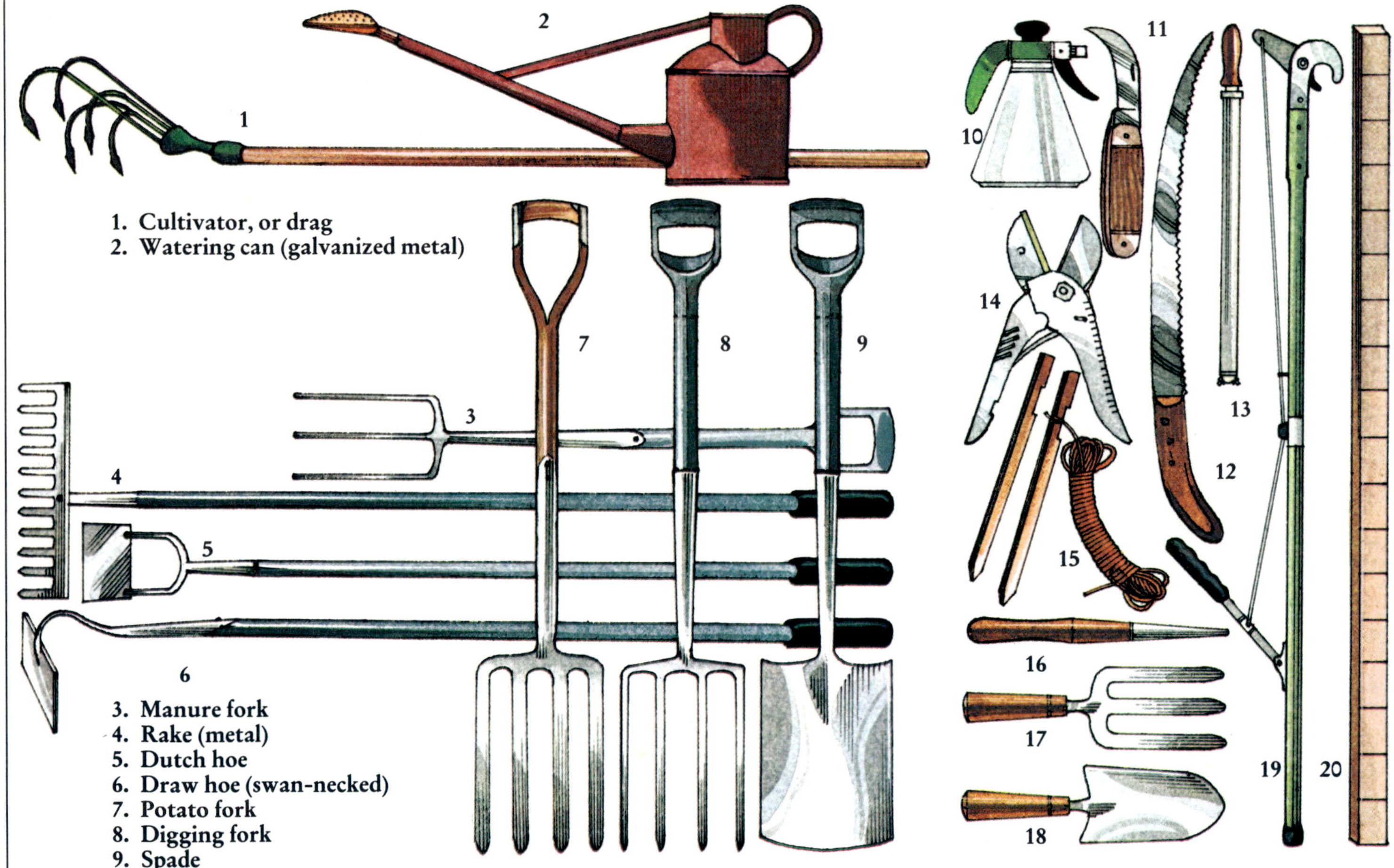

1. Cultivator, or drag
2. Watering can (galvanized metal)

3. Manure fork
4. Rake (metal)
5. Dutch hoe
6. Draw hoe (swan-necked)
7. Potato fork
8. Digging fork
9. Spade

10. Sprayer
11. Gardener's knife
12. Pruning saw (curved, one-sided)
13. Syringe (two nozzles)
14. Secateurs (single-cut)
15. Garden line and sticks
16. Dibber (steel-tipped)
17. Hand fork
18. Hand trowel
19. Long-handled pruner
20. Measuring stick

Gardeners who have been engaged in gardening for some years will already have their favourite tools and, apart from buying the occasional replacement or improvement, will be very conservative in the way they go about choosing and using them. What the newcomer to gardening has to learn first is that some tools are essential whereas others are expensive gimmicks that can well be done without. The hardest job is learning to distinguish between the two.

One thing that should always be borne in mind is that there is no such thing as a bargain where tools are concerned. Good tools cost a lot of money and any that appear to be cheap will be so for a very good reason. That reason becomes apparent soon after the tool has been put to use. The general rule is that you should always buy the most expensive tools you can afford. They will be the best. A good spade, for example, will last a lifetime; very probably two.

Stainless steel is certainly the best material for spades, forks and hoes but it should be avoided for things like knives and secateurs because it never seems to hold its edge as well as ordinary steel. Some tools, especially shears and cutters of that sort, can be made of ordinary steel coated with a special hardened plastic that makes them virtually rustproof. They will retain the keenness of edge that is not attainable with stainless steel.

The most important thing to remember about all tools is that, once they have been bought, they must always be kept clean and in good working order. Not only will rusty tools wear out sooner, but they will also be far less efficient at doing their job and may well damage the plants you have otherwise tended so well. Can you imagine a pair of rusty secateurs being any good for cutting anything?

Nor should anyone run away with the idea that stainless tools need not be cleaned. They should be kept just as clean as any other. Their main advantages are that they are easier to clean and the shinier surface tends, in the case of tools used for cultivating, to make them slip through the ground easier.

Basic tools

For general gardening, the following are the basic tools that everyone will need.

Spade This is the main digging tool that is used for all primary cultivations. It is suitable for use on all soil types, although a digging fork is sometimes used in its place on very heavy land simply because a fork is easier to work with in such conditions.

Spades can be made of ordinary steel or stainless. It is well worth buying a stainless one if you can afford it but it is certainly not essential.

A good spade will always have a narrow step welded on to the top of the blade where the foot rests when digging. This is to prevent boots and shoes being ruined by continuous pressure on the otherwise sharp edge. It is the sort of refinement that I look for and which turns a good spade into a first rate one.

It is also better to have the rivets that join the handle to the business end running from front to back and not side to side. Whenever a handle breaks, it always seems to be along the line of the top rivet of a 'side-to-side' model. A small point but one worth remembering.

Fork This is used for shallower digging or, as mentioned, for heavy clay. A common use is as a follow-up in the spring after deep digging with a spade in the winter. This is the first step towards creating a tilth suitable for sowing or planting. A fork is also useful for shallow digging among standing plants. It does far less damage to the roots.

Stainless and ordinary steel is available, as for spades.

Incidentally, most tools, and certainly spades and forks, can be had in a variety of sizes to suit all uses and physiques.

Rake This is used almost exclusively for breaking the soil down into a fine tilth suitable for sowing in. Lawn rakes with springy tines are a completely different tool and are not intended for tilling the soil but for raking out moss and other debris from the surface of lawns.

Dutch hoe (push hoe) This is the standard weeding tool. It can also be used for moving the soil shallowly either to prevent or destroy a surface crust. Move backwards when using it so that you work out your footmarks as you go.

Draw hoe (swan-neck hoe) Also used for weeding but useful as well for drawing up the soil over potatoes, for making seed drills, for working the soil shallowly and for thinning out rows of seedlings.

Dibber Essential when planting out brassica seedlings, a dibber is used to make the hole in which the roots are put and for firming the soil back around the roots. The result is much firmer planting than is achieved with a trowel or fork.

Garden line No good gardener will ever try to draw out a straight seed drill or plant in a row without a line, no matter how short a distance is involved. Plastic lines are quite commonly available now and are virtually indestructible; unless you happen to chop them with a spade.

Trowel and hand fork These are very useful for planting young plants and seedlings and for working among standing plants in a confined space.

Those are the basic tools that are required for general gardening but a few more will be needed for tending fruit trees and bushes.

Secateurs These are the standard pruning tool for removing shoots and small branches up to about 2.5 cm (1 in) thick. Two basic types are available. One has a curved cutting blade which works with a scissor action against another blade. The other type has a sharp blade that cuts through the wood on to a soft metal or plastic anvil. The latter tend to be cheaper but are believed by some gardeners to bruise the bark that is in contact with the anvil.

Loppers While not essential, loppers are useful for pruning established trees and bushes where branches up to about 4 cm (1.5 in) thick often have to be cut.

Their main use is for cutting out complete black currant branches at ground level where it is impossible to use even a special pruning saw.

Pruning saw An indispensible tool when pruning larger trees where complete branches have to be removed. The blades of pruning saws are of a specially designed, narrow shape to make it easy to get them into awkward places.

While extra large branches can sometimes justify the use of a bow saw, a carpentry saw is utterly useless and should never be used. There is at least one excellent pruning saw that shuts up like a pocket knife.

Knife This had better be mentioned if only to warn against the use of a blunt knife for any gardening purpose at all. A blunt knife is an abomination. Not only does it not perform the task for which it is intended but, oddly enough, it is far more likely to cut the user than is a sharp one.

Long-arm pruner This is only needed when trees reach a height that prevents them being pruned with conventional tools from the ground. In these circumstances it is one of the most useful tools ever devised.

One make dominates the market. The cutting blade is operated by a thin metal rod attached to a lever handle. Those which have a blade that is worked by pulling a cord are vastly inferior.

So, those are the tools that will be needed and will serve you well. Now we can get on with the actual gardening.

Machinery

Presumably there is no one reading this who believes that chemicals are indispensible to gardening. There may, though, be some who have a deep-rooted belief that they have to have machines for doing more or less every job in the garden. Without them, they seem to feel helpless and, apparently, in some way inadequate. Just as there are gardeners who firmly believe that chemicals are essential to gardening, rather than an aid, so there are also those who feel the same way about engines, be they petrol or electric.

Just stop and think for a moment what machines can do in the garden. There are grass cutters for fine lawns, for domestic lawns, for rough grass amongst trees, for grassy banks, even for tidying up round the base of trees or close to anything else where a mower will not go. If you want to cut something, there is a machine to do it. You can cut hedges, or chop up raw materials for composting and as for cultivating the ground, well, there are more machines than most of us would know what to do with.

But how many of these are really necessary and how many are just an expensive and often rather useless luxury that is used a few times and then put in the corner of a shed? The answer to that is really dependent on such circumstances as the size of the garden, what you are growing, the depth of your pocket and your approach to machinery and gardening.

All too often you see someone dashing hither and thither over a modest area of lawn with a powerful mowing machine, almost big enough for a playing field. It is puzzling trying to understand what induces the purchase of such a thing, especially when these vast machines are frequently the cause of much unwanted noise.

What all this boils down to is that people who buy machines tend to fall into one or more of three groups. There are those who wish to impress others. Those who think, or who have been convinced, that a machine makes life easier or a particular one is something that they cannot do without. And there are those gardeners who genuinely benefit from them.

There may, of course, be a number of very good reasons for needing a machine but there are two that dominate the rest. One is that there is genuinely too much work for one pair of hands to do without mechanical help as, for example, when mowing large lawns or cutting long or tall hedges. The other is that, for some perfectly good reason, you do not have the physical ability to do the job in question. This becomes increasingly relevant the older we get.

In all honesty these are the only reasons that justify buying a particular piece of machinery. However, if you fancy a gadget and can afford it, disregard all this so-called common sense and go ahead and buy it. You will probably feel much better for it.

It is safe to say that most machines do the job for which they are intended. Obviously there are exceptions but they are fairly rare these days as word soon gets round and they die a natural death.

This is neither the time nor the place to go into the pros and cons of every type of machine on the market but it is worth taking a closer look at just a few.

Powered rotavators Having covered soil cultivations, the question is bound to arise: how valuable is a powered rotavator?

The short and not very helpful answer is that they are a blessing and a curse. Let us deal with the good points first. The main one is that they make an excellent job of breaking down roughly dug ground and in a fraction of the time that it takes by hand. This is not particularly important in a small garden but it can be a boon in a large one in the spring when everything seems to need doing at once and a big black cloud hovers.

There is also no finer way of clearing the ground after one crop in preparation for setting the next. Everything is chopped up nice and small so that it can easily be dug in or just left as it is with the next crop being sown or planted without further cultivations.

A rotavator is also an excellent, if rather grand, tool for weeding between rows of vegetables or fruit. It should, however, only be used very shallowly for this purpose and when the soil is dry. And this task should not be left until the weeds are in flower and seeding.

Unfortunately, the design of some of the cheaper and less professional machines is so poor that they are good for very little. This has led to them being used for completely the wrong purposes, particularly digging. There is not a single garden rotavator that can take the place of a spade and never let anyone try to convince you otherwise. For a start, almost none will go deep enough; 15–23 cm (6–9 in) is about as much as you can expect from the best of them. You need to dig at least 30 cm (12 in) deep to do any good.

Also, if used in place of a spade, they break up the ground much too finely and create a puffy tilth. This is not what is wanted from deep digging and, if ground in this state has to stand the winter, it will be mud in no time.

Another failing of rotavators – or rather the users – is that, because all plant debris is smashed to pieces, it is assumed that this rough treatment will kill it. While this is so in many cases, it does not apply with things like bindweed or ground elder roots. If these are present in the land, a rotavator is the finest way of *propagating* them by spreading them about.

Lastly, the continual use of a rotavator can create a solid pan just a few inches below the surface. This is caused by the blades smearing the soil at their lowest penetration point. But, of course, these are not faults created by the rotavator but by gardeners using them for tasks for which they were not intended.

One of the worst things you can do with a rotavator is use it to blast a soil in poor condition into a good tilth. We are back to that business of battling with the soil. A machine may have the power to chew up the ground when it cannot be done by hand but it will also destroy the structure.

To summarize, a rotavator used sensibly at the right time and to do the correct job is a terrific help and can save a lot of work. In the wrong hands it can ruin the soil, and your garden.

Nor does it pay to buy the cheapest you can find. As with other tools, you get what you pay for. Always buy a robust make that is not going to fall to pieces once it has hard work to do. A salesman is unlikely to tell you the whole story.

Compost shredder Another type of machine that can be very useful to gardeners who are on what might be unkindly called 'the organic kick' is a compost shredder.

These are infernally noisy and not really suitable for Sunday afternoons in the summer but they make a grand job of smashing up bits of vegetation that are too large and hard to go straight into a compost heap or bin without it first being chopped up smaller.

Where a compost bin is being used, shredders really are terribly useful as they chop up everything to a size that will rapidly decompose.

Obviously, there is no point in putting soft vegetation through a shredder but, for chopping up prunings, brassica stalks, thick hedge clippings, tougher flower stems and even newspaper, it is well worth using as virtually nothing of vegetative origin need be wasted. A good shredder will make short work even of branches up to 2–3 cm (¾ in–1¼ in) across. But do get a powered model. Hand-cranked ones are hard work and not very effective. Remember, however, that the more woody material you put into a heap or bin, the more need there is going to be for an activator to provide the additional nitrogen needed.

A chain saw, powered by an electric or petrol motor, is ideal for felling small trees.

MAKING A START

CLEARING A NEGLECTED SITE

1. Before attempting to double-dig, remove all obvious surface rubble, large stones and refuse.

2. Sort rubble into piles; useful pieces of timber and bricks should be kept, other rubbish carted away.

If you are starting from scratch with land that looks as though it has never been cultivated before, even if it has been, the first problem could well be the removal of turf or a mass of weeds, and possibly builders' rubble as well.

Surface problems

Obviously the priority is to get rid of any rubble and, if the ground is heavy, it could be gainfully used for making a soakaway. To do this, all that is needed is for a pit to be dug at the lowest point of the garden and for the rubble to be thrown into it. This is then covered over with turf or sticks (to stop it getting blocked), and finally the topsoil that you previously dug out. Any left over at the end can be spread over the garden. Very often this simple job will make a whole area of wet ground perfectly fit for gardening.

Having got rid of the junk, attention can then turn to the soil. If the plot is brand new and was previously a field, the surface is likely to be turf. This can be skimmed off in strips about 5 cm (2 in) thick and stacked in a corner of the garden. The purpose of this is to save the basic ingredient for your own seed and potting composts, good fibrous loam.

Almost inevitably the turf will contain seemingly immortal weeds such as docks, thistles, dandelions, ground elder, bindweed etc. These should be dug out, preferably before skimming off the turf. If, for one reason or another, this is not done, the roots will be clearly seen after skimming and can be removed then instead.

On land that was previously a jungle, the main problem is going to be removal of the weeds and unwanted brushwood, such as brambles and elders. As much of this as possible should be dug out and left on the surface to dry and die before making a bonfire of it. Even the most ardent garden composter should shrink from putting the roots of perennial weeds on the compost heap but the ash from a bonfire is splendid.

There is no easy answer to the bramble and elder problem. Both will have to be dug out and burned. Just cutting them down to the ground will simply make them grow even stronger once they recover.

If there is little in the way of brushwood, it will probably be safe to cut the weeds down and turn them into garden compost. However, one has to be slightly guarded about this because, towards autumn, an enormous number of seeds are being produced. If the compost fails to heat up sufficiently during decomposition, these will simply germinate and grow when the compost is used. In this instance, it is normally safer to burn the top growth rather than run the risk of propagating weeds.

Improving the soil

Once the ground has been reasonably well cleared, it can be dug. Although one's free time may not be sufficiently abundant to be able to choose exactly when a particular operation is carried out, the best time to dig is during the autumn or winter when other activities such as propagating plants, are less intensive than in the growing season.

Where possible, heavy land should always be dug in the autumn or early winter to give it plenty of time to weather. Heavy land should never be dug, or cultivated in any way, if it is wet. It simply ends up worse than ever. Light land can be dug at any time because the weathering is not important.

Adding organic matter The structure of a soil, be it open and sandy or compact and mainly clay, can be altered to a great extent by the addition of organic matter which will eventually break down in the ground to form humus. This material enables a soil to absorb air and moisture and ensures that all plants form a strong and healthy root system.

There are several ways of supplying the soil with organic matter, a subject we have already dealt with but, to summarize, the time-honoured method is to dig in farmyard manure. This, though, is far from easy to obtain if you live in a town and, even if it is easily come by, the cost is very often far higher than the material is worth.

A much cheaper and better idea is to make your own garden compost from the waste vegetation that every garden produces (see page 20). All soils are improved by adding bulky organic matter and, at this stage in the procedings, the best way of incorporating it is to dig it in.

Single digging When you have to dig a plot of land, in particular a brand new one, it is best to divide it into two, or even more sections if it is large.

We have already seen that just heaping compost or FYM into the bottom of the trench and burying it out of sight as you dig the ground is no way to go about it. Instead, you should start by digging out trench A and stacking the soil at B. Then spread the compost or FYM over the face and floor of the trench. The next strip of soil, C, is then turned over and forward on to it, thus leaving another trench.

Repeat the process until you are left with trench D at the end of the first half-plot. Fill this trench in with soil from E and carry on digging until the final trench, F, is filled with soil B. This is the simplest form of digging and is called 'single' digging.

Double digging More often than not, however, a new plot of land will have been undug for many years or will be so compacted by building machinery as to be more like a road. In this situation, 'double' digging is what is needed. With this technique, instead of going down to the depth of just one spade, the ground below that is also dug.

The system is perfectly simple, if rather wearying, and is started in just the same way as for single digging. However, instead of turning the second strip of soil straight into the first trench, the bottom of that trench is itself dug. The best way of doing this is with a digging fork so that at least another 30 cm (1 ft) of depth is thoroughly worked. There is no need to turn over the bottom 'spit', as it is often called. All that is required is for it to be loosened and moved so that roots can penetrate easily into it in search of the abundant plant foods and moisture that this subsoil often holds. If the soil is particularly bad, put extra compost into the bottom of the trench so that it can be incorporated during the forking.

One thing to be careful of is that the top spit and the bottom spit do not become inverted so that you end up with the poorer quality subsoil on the surface and the good topsoil underneath it. There is no harm, in fact there is benefit, in mixing the two together to a certain extent but not to the point where the better topsoil suffers.

The importance of keeping the two layers separate not only applies to double digging. It should be done at all times and on all soils. Chalk is a prime example – it is thoroughly bad practice to dig up large lumps of chalk so that they lie near or on the surface.

As mentioned, a certain amount of mixing is good, because it increases the depth of good soil, but never overdo it.

Leave it to 'weather' Once any plot of land has been dug for the first time, it should be left undisturbed for as long as possible. In fact, until shortly before it is wanted for sowing or planting. If the digging is done during the autumn or winter, as is best, leaving it rough until the spring will ensure that it has as long as possible for the frost, wind, rain and snow to work on it to create a 'weather tilth'. If this is possible, it is better than all the chemical soil conditioners ever invented.

The most important part of all soil cultivations is the ability to judge when a soil is in the right condition for working. For those gardeners on light and sandy soils, the problem seldom arises but, for most of us, working the ground at the right time can mean the difference between success and failure. The golden rule is that the land must only be worked when it is in such a condition that it can be broken up easily and does not turn either to mud, because of wetness, or simply into somewhat smaller bricks, because of drought.

No matter how new or raw a heavy soil is, there is always a stage at which it can be cultivated to give the right tilth. This normally follows winter weathering but, at other times of the year, it occurs when a soil is drying out after rain. If you pick the right moment, it falls to pieces like sugar. It is not only freezing and thawing that breaks up the soil; it is also alternate wetting and drying. If a soil is wet enough to stick to your boots, leave it alone until it has dried out a bit. Even walking on it can ruin its structure. On the other hand, if all you can do is smash it into smaller lumps, wait until a drop of rain has softened it.

Above all, never have a battle with the soil; it will always win, leaving you bloody and bruised but, we hope, wiser.

Breaking the ground down after digging is often done with a fork. This is used to knock the clods to pieces and to level the land so that all the hills and holes disappear. A fork is not the only tool for the job but it certainly is the most economical as it can be used for a great many other jobs as well.

Hand cultivators are probably the best implements for breaking down dug land but never be tricked into buying some complicated and expensive gadget that has no other uses and does not even perform this one well. The most effective hand cultivators can best be described as 'turned down forks'. They are rather like ordinary digging forks but with long handles – like a hoe – and the tines are curved over so that they are at ninety degrees to the handle.

Several variations on this theme are available, some having 'arrowheads' welded to the ends of the tines. At least one of this type has the tines in pairs with the facility to remove any pair to alter the effective width of the tool. You can even take out the centre one so that the cultivator can be used to move the soil on either side of a row of seedlings.

Planting and sowing considerations

After breaking down the surface of the plot, the next move depends on the use to which the ground is then going to be put. If it is for planting or for sowing large seeds, like peas and beans, there is

DIVIDING A PLOT

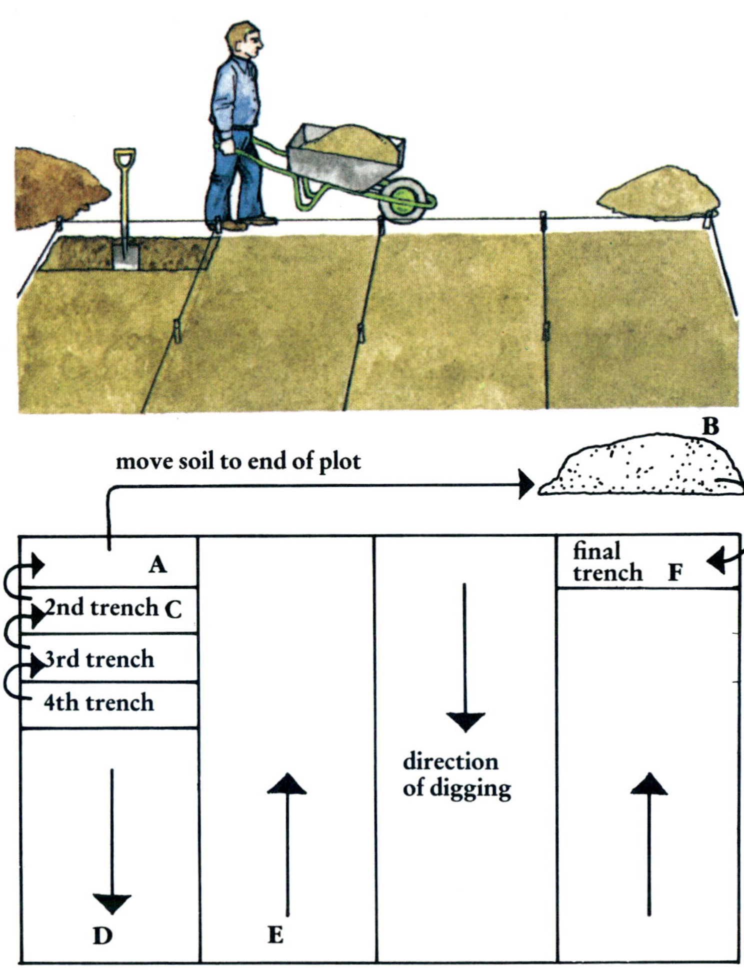

Divide a large plot into more manageable strips, using pegs and string. Start by taking out a trench across one end of the first strip. Move this soil to the other end of the plot. Then dig out the next trench, turning over each spit into the first trench, and so on, as shown by the small arrows. Depth of digging depends on the method. If needed, fork manure into trenches as you dig. When you reach the end of the plot, fill in the final trench with soil taken from the first one. Large arrows indicate the direction of the digging.

SINGLE DIGGING

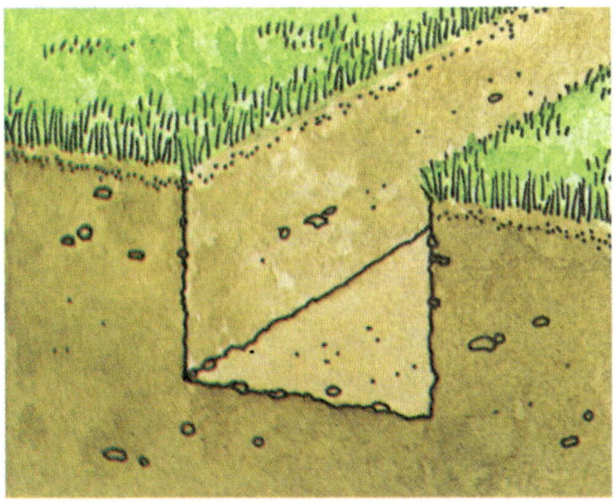

1. Take out a trench about 25 cm (10in) deep and 30 cm (12 in) wide. Remove soil to end of plot.

2. If you wish to add manure or other organic matter, scatter it over the bottom of the trench, using a fork.

3. Take out 25 cm (10in) deep blocks of soil and throw them well forward into trench, turning them over.

DOUBLE DIGGING

1. Take out a trench about 25 cm (10in) deep and 60 cm (24in) wide. Take soil to end of plot.

2. Break up bottom of trench to depth of 25 cm (10in) and fork manure well into this broken-up subsoil.

3. Take out blocks and turn over into trench – in stages, as 60 cm (24in) widths are too heavy. Dig base of next trench.

probably no need to do anything more. In neither case is a fine tilth necessary or desirable.

Many beginners make the mistake of breaking the soil down into as fine a tilth as they possibly can, no matter what they are going to use the land for. But a fine tilth has two big drawbacks. It encourages the germination of all weed seeds, especially the multitude of small ones, and it is easily capped following rain (a surface crust forms). Never, therefore, break down the soil any finer than is needed for the job in hand.

A coarse tilth, on the other hand, will discourage the germination of small seeds and will resist capping to a much greater extent.

In a nutshell, most soils that are in good condition and which are being worked at the correct stage can usually be broken down into as fine a tilth as is necessary with a hand cultivator or fork.

This is also the time at which any fertilizers that might be needed should be incorporated. Work them in a few centimetres/inches deep so that they are evenly distributed through the soil and are available when the roots need them.

On heavier types of land when sowing seeds smaller than peas and beans, and one or two others, you will usually need to rake the surface to produce a sufficiently fine tilth for good germination. If it is not fine enough, the seeds may be surrounded by comparatively large pieces of soil that will dry out quite quickly. It is also virtually impossible to bury the seeds evenly and to the correct depth. Both these faults lead to uneven germination and patchy crops.

If, for one reason or another, the land just will not break down finely enough, the problem can usually be overcome by applying sifted garden compost, peat or bark to the area and working it in with the cultivator at the same time as any fertilizer.

How to sow or plant

Once the ground is in the right condition for sowing or planting, use the garden line to mark out the row so that all is ship-shape and tidy.

When sowing, make the drill to the depth recommended on the seed packet and never sow thicker than you need. Not only is it a waste of seed if crops later have to be thinned out but it also creates tall and spindly seedlings that are far more likely to be attacked by fungus diseases because of the overcrowding.

Cover the seeds evenly and to the correct depth with a rake and then use the flat of the rake to pat down the soil along the row. If the ground is dry, it should be watered to give the seeds the moisture they require for germination.

Some gardeners water the drill *before* sowing the seed, the reason being that it prevents puddling the soil (turning it to mud) around the seeds as can happen when watering after sowing. However, it is by no means easy to rake what might be very wet soil over the seeds so, on balance, it is better to water after sowing and covering. Water lightly and with a fine rose, to avoid flooding.

FEEDING PLANTS

This is the point at which the organic or 'no chemical' gardener would start to break away from what might be called 'mainstream' gardening. This is because anyone who does not intend to use chemicals will almost certainly frown on the use of what are referred to as artificial fertilizers.

Artifical fertilizers are manmade plant foods as opposed to those which occur naturally but, once again, there is no clear dividing line between the two. It is left largely to one's conscience and likes and dislikes as to which ones are considered ethical and which are not.

For example, there can be very few fertilizers more natural in origin than hoof and horn but where does basic slag fit into the picture? This material is a by-product of the steel industry and was widely used as a phosphatic fertilizer. The phosphorus comes from iron ore during the smelting process – it is necessary to remove it to prevent the iron being brittle. It certainly is not an organic material but is it a natural one?

Fortunately, not all fertilizers are as hard to classify. Those like sulphate of ammonia, superphosphate and sulphate of potash can definitely be considered out-of-bounds, along with ammonium nitrate and magnesium sulphate. Though one would not shrink from using the latter, medicinally, as Epsom Salts. As we discussed when talking about organic matter, all the various forms do contain plant nutrients to a greater or lesser extent but none have sufficient to make it unnecessary to add specific nutrients to the soil.

The problem is that, in nature, there is a complete cycle in which everything returns to the ground and is then used by the next generation of plants. These, in turn, die and are returned to the soil and so on. But in gardens this does not happen. The moment we start to grow crops for eating, we break the cycle if we do not replace what we are taking out. So, we have to replace it in some other form and the conventional way is with fertilizers. It would be quite impracticable for most of us to rely solely on returning it as compost or FYM.

Fortunately, the choice of naturally occurring materials that contain sufficient plant foods to be termed fertilizers is very large, so we have plenty to choose from. However, we immediately come across what to some people could prove to be a nasty problem of conscience.

We have already seen the difficulty of distinguishing between natural and man-made materials. We now have to decide whether or not we wish to draw a further distinction between organic and inorganic and, once again, where is the dividing line? Here is a poser. Chalk and limestone are largely calcium carbonate and, being formed from the dead bodies of minute sea creatures, are organic in origin. But that was millions of years ago, so are they *still* organic in the same way that hoof and horn is?

If one is not to use inorganic, although perfectly natural materials, then the situation is rather complicated. Let us say that both organic and inorganic are allowed; there can be few objections to that.

Twelve essential elements

We have looked at some of the problems of conscience that might crop up, but so far, nothing has been said about the actual plant food value of the different 'natural' (for want of a better word) fertilizers.

There are twelve elements that are absolutely essential to a plant's diet if it is to be strong and healthy. These are divided into six major elements and six trace elements. The major elements are nitrogen (N), phosphorus (P), potassium/potash (K), magnesium (Mg), calcium (Ca) and sulphur (S). The trace elements are manganese (Mn), iron (Fe), copper (Cu), zinc (Zn), boron (B) and molybdenum (Mo).

The word 'minor' is sometimes used instead of 'trace' to describe the latter but this should not be interpreted as meaning that they are of minor importance. Far from it, all twelve elements are vital. Where the distinction comes is in the quantities required.

Major elements are needed by the plants in relatively large amounts whereas trace elements are only required in minute quantities – a few parts per million.

On the whole, fertilizers that are derived from recently living plants or animals, such as hoof and horn, fish meal, seaweed meal and treated town refuse, contain trace elements as well as major elements. However, despite the fact that most truely organic materials contain all the essential elements in varying proportions, there is nothing consistent about them as a group or even as individuals. For example, hoof and horn contains 12–14 percent nitrogen and 1–3 percent phosphates. Bone meal, on the other hand, contains only about 4 percent nitrogen but 22–25 percent phosphates.

This illustrates very clearly that not all natural fertilizers contain sufficient quantities of all the elements required by the plants. It is often necessary, therefore, to use two or more of them to supply a plant with its needs. This has to be considered alongside the fact that FYM or garden compost are also being given and these also contain plant foods.

Natural fertilizers

Let us look at the different natural fertilizers (as opposed to the bulky manures) and see just what they contain and roughly how much. The conventional classification is in terms of the N, P and K content, these being the elements needed in the greatest amounts. The figures given in the charts that follow represent percentages.

Nitrogen fertilizers There is a simple explanation for the large number of materials containing nitrogen. It is part of the protein molecule and, as such, is found in virtually all living things. Many of these natural materials are extremely variable however, and this has to be taken into account when applying them. Branded products carry the element percentages on the pack but these are frequently as loose as those above. Luckily, these fertilizers are seldom damaging to plants, even if over-applied. If you want to find out the element percentages of unbranded, or loose, materials, the retailer should be able to tell you or failing that, you could contact the supplier.

Nitrogen fertilizers

	%N	%P	%K
Dried blood	7–14	1–2	1
Feathers	8–9	–	–
Fish guano	6–10	4–7	0.5–0.8
Fish meal	8–9	9–10	1
Hair waste	8–10	–	–
Hoof and horn	12–14	1–3	–
Leather waste	5–7	–	–
Meat and bone meal	6–12	1–20	–
Poultry manure	4–6	3–5	2–3
Rapeseed meal	5–6	1.5–3	1–1.8
Soot	2–11	–	–

Two terms that often crop up in relation to fertilizers, especially those containing nitrogen, are 'slow release' and 'quick release'. These refer to the speed with which the nitrogen, or other element, is released from the fertilizer and becomes available to plants.

Which is the more suitable one to use will depend largely on the time of year and the crop in question. For example, fruit trees and bushes prefer a slow release form, such as hoof and horn, because the nitrogen is released over a longish period rather than all at once in a rush. Lettuces and other fast growing vegetables are better with a quick release fertilizer, for example dried blood, that gives them a boost when needed.

Phosphatic fertilizers Moving on to this type, it will be immediately apparent from the list that there are not nearly so many to choose from. However, phosphates are not used by plants in large amounts and, being comparatively insoluble in water, they tend to remain in the soil longer than nitrogen and potash, so less needs to be applied. Often, in fact, applying it every other year is perfectly adequate.

Bones are one of the main sources of phosphates. Here are some of the more commonly used:

Phosphatic fertilizers

	%N	%P	%K
Bone ash	–	35	–
Wood ash	–	2–4	5–15
Basic slag	–	6–22	–
Raw bone meal	4	22–25	–
Steamed b.m.	2–4	27–30	–
Fish guano	6–10	4–7	0.5–0.8
Fish meal	8–9	9–10	1
Gull guano	2–12	10–20	2–3
Meat and bone meal	6–12	1–20	–
Mineral phosphates	–	25–35	–
Steamed bone lour	0.75–1	27–30	–

Potash fertilizers are also less plentiful than those rich in nitrogen but there are still several to choose from and it must not be forgotten that some of those already mentioned contain useful amounts of potassium.

Potash fertilizers

	%N	%P	%K
Wood ash	–	2–4	5–15
Cement kiln dust	–	–	5–6
Flue dust	–	–	trace–6
Kainit	–	–	14
Dried kelp	2.5	1.5	15
Manure salts	–	–	20–30

One thing should be apparent from all the above examples: they are all in solid form. That is, they are applied dry and rely upon the moisture in the soil to dissolve them and make them available to the plants. This is not always convenient. Sometimes, a faster acting liquid feed is more appropriate – as with plants in containers.

We know that garden compost can be soaked in water to produce a very acceptable plant food and this can also be done with FYM to produce manure-water. But you should bear in mind that the smell is not always socially acceptable when used indoors.

Dried blood is fairly soluble in water and makes a good nitrogen feed when dissolved at the rate of 30 gm to 9 litres (1 oz to 2 gal) of water. This is first rate as a pick-me-up for the plants. Various other concoctions and infusions have been dreamed up over the years but none seem to have any particular advantage over the more orthodox ones.

However, there is one material that really surpasses all others – concentrated seaweed extract, sold as Maxicrop. This is available in several formulations, some of which have manmade soluble fertilizers added to increase its strength and suitability for different crops. The one described as 'natural' is the pure seaweed extract with no additives.

This type of feed has a number of advantages. First, it is a complete feed in itself, trace elements included. Secondly, it is excellent as a foliar feed (one applied to the leaves) as well as a root fertilizer. Thirdly, it is mild enough to be used on newly-emerged seedlings and is equally suitable for mature plants.

Plus and minus factors

Having mentioned the three main ways of feeding plants – dry and liquid root fertilizers, and foliar feeds – what are the advantages and disadvantages of each?

Dry fertilizers There is no doubt that these are convenient to use. All that has to be done is to sprinkle them on the ground, if appropriate hoe them in, then sit back and wait for things to happen.

With regards to use for vegetable crops, they are applied on two principal occasions; before sowing or planting and, later, during the growth of the crop. The first is called a base dressing and the second, a top dressing.

The normal system with vegetables is to apply only a base dressing to quick growing crops, like lettuces, other salads and summer cabbage, but follow this with a top dressing for those vegetables that crop for a long time, such as French and runner beans and peas.

Dried poultry manure, though a bit smelly, is a good general fertilizer for these crops. It is applied at 120 gm per sq. m (4 oz per sq. yd). In fact, it can form the basis for a great many feeds as it has an N.P.K. ratio of about 2:2:1. To make it richer in nitrogen, dried blood or hoof and horn could be added. To raise the potash level, mix in bonfire ash or one of the other potash fertilizers.

Feeding fruit crops is carried out on a rather different basis because we normally give them fertilizers just once a year, in the spring. This means that the slow release types are more appropriate so we should be using things like hoof and horn, bone meal and kainit or dried kelp (a seaweed especially rich in potash).

Observant and/or experienced gardeners will realize that dry fertilizers have one important short-coming. They need water from one source or another to dissolve them so that they are in a fit state to be absorbed by roots. If they remain dry after application, they are completely useless. This is a fairly rare happening in the UK but it does sometimes occur in the summer.

Liquid feeds If plants need feeding during periods of drought therefore, and many will, the answer lies in the use of liquid feed. This serves the double purpose of supplying both water and nutrients. In addition, liquid feeds are quickly taken up by the plants. One can also make use of this virtue at other times when a rapid response is wanted; as well as when feeding plants in containers.

Unfortunately, liquid feeds also have a snag. As a direct result of being readily soluble and quickly available, they are soon used up or washed out of the soil and need to be replaced fairly frequently. The speed of their disappearance is dependent on such things as the type of soil (heavy soils retain them longer) and the rainfall.

A very general recommendation for using liquid feeds on vegetables growing in the open ground would be to apply them about every fortnight as a routine procedure.

Foliar Feeds If a really quick response is wanted, a foliar feed like seaweed extract should be used. The elements within this are readily absorbed by the leaves as well as by the roots and, because the material reaches the leaves instantly, the response is really fast. That means you should expect to see results in well under a week in the summer.

Incidentally, older gardeners may well remember the popularity of soot-water. This was made by hanging a bag of soot in a water butt in the same way that one does with FYM or garden compost. The resulting brew made a good foliar feed by supplying nitrogen. It also had some powers of dissuasion towards certain pests and diseases; but more of that in the next section.

LIQUID FEED

Liquid feed needs to be measured out very carefully, as surprisingly small quantities are required.

Apply liquid feed either by watering in around crops, or as a foliar feed using a fine spray.

One important point about foliar feeding is that it should never be regarded as the main way of feeding plants. Unless you use a complete feed, like seaweed extract, the diet is likely to be incomplete and, beside that, it would need to be applied so frequently as to become a chore. The roots are the organs that a plant uses for absorbing food; keep it that way.

Foliar feeding really comes into its own when a plant is either suffering or you want it to put in just that little bit more effort. Plants that have recently been moved will derive enormous benefit from a foliar feed because it will sustain them until the roots have become established and can take over. Also, by strengthening the leaves and making them operate better, foliar feeding will encourage the roots to grow and take over all the quicker.

Those then are the three main ways of feeding plants, and circumstances will dictate which is best for a particular type of plant at a given moment. Plant nutrition is an extremely complicated science but, fortunately, we do not have to know the why and wherefore of it all because nature has endowed plants with almost boundless tolerance.

However, a bad gardener and one who fails to feed the plants properly will soon find that there is a limit to their patience. It is worth bearing this in mind because, and here we come to the financial burden of 'going organic', 'natural' fertilizers are a great deal more costly than 'artificials'. As a result, there may come a time when it is felt that putting the plants on a diet will do no harm – but it will.

One final thought on the subject of feeding plants. It is quite often felt that plants grow better when fed with natural fertilizers. There is no scientific evidence to support this. A plant cannot tell whether a nitrate has come from sulphate of ammonia or from hoof and horn. To the plant, it is just another nitrate.

It is certainly true that natural fertilizers often contain *more* trace elements than artificials do but, in the small quantities that they are used, this is unlikely to make a noticeable difference. No, the more probable answer is that gardeners who use natural materials are also likely to be paying more attention to the general growing conditions and not just heaping on fertilizers. Anyway, natural materials are certainly less potent than manmade fertilizers and there is far less risk of newcomers to gardening damaging plants by overdosing.

A system of feeding plants that has been gaining in popularity in recent years is the use of fibre sticks that have been impregnated with fertilizer and which are pushed into the soil among the roots of plants. These are intended for vegetables, herbaceous plants and pot plants, but there is a large type available for shrubs and trees.

While neither could be described as organic, they do represent a convenient and extremely safe way of feeding plants. In another, similar system 'pills' of fertilizer are pushed into the ground near to the plants that are to be fed.

Damaged and distorted runner bean leaves: the effects of capsid bugs are seen above.

An infestation of black bean aphis, commonly known as black fly, on a runner bean shoot.

Even more than the use of artificial fertilizers, it is the chemicals used to control pests, diseases and weeds that incense people. This is not the place to become embroiled in the argument for and against these materials. Millions of words have been written and spoken on the subject and, no doubt, many more are yet to come.

What we are concerned with here is how to garden efficiently and effectively either without them or by using only those that may be considered 'safe'. In fact, a great deal of what is going to be said is equally applicable to what might be called 'normal' gardening, where chemicals are not necessarily frowned upon.

The control of pests and diseases is very different to that of weeds so we will look at them separately.

Pests and diseases

The first thing that every gardener must understand and learn to live with is that pests and diseases, like poverty, are always with us. That is to say, no matter how tight a rein we keep on things, there are always going to be 'nasties' about. Trying to get 100 percent control will worry you into an early grave. A good gardener learns to tolerate a certain amount of trouble but will know when and how to act.

There are two approaches to the problem of pests and diseases; prevention and cure. Cures will come later as they may involve the use of chemicals.

Prevention

Preventing pests and diseases from attacking our plants is clearly better than having to join them in battle once they are established. By that time they will have built up their strength and caused damage. They will be far harder to get rid of and, if chemicals are to be used, a greater quantity will be needed to overcome them.

Prevention should be the watchword and top of the list of priorities is that we must all grow our plants as well as we possibly can. A strong plant is better able to withstand, and even in some cases repulse, attacks from its enemies.

Adequate nutrients Growing better plants will involve several things but, the number one essential must be to maintain an open and fertile soil with an adequate nutrient content. If the roots can flourish, so usually will the top.

Adequate watering Keeping plants well watered and fed is an obvious way of helping them to grow better. However, it is not generally appreciated that, besides suffering in the obvious way, wilting plants give off a stronger scent than turgid plants (those fully charged with water). This is especially important with a vegetable like the carrot because its main pest, the carrot fly, is attracted by the smell of carrots. If wilting is allowed to take place during and straight after thinning, trouble is much more likely. Always, therefore, water plants thoroughly after thinning or moving so that they recover as quickly as possible.

Similarly, all root crops should be kept as evenly moist as possible throughout their growing season. Sudden soakings after long periods of drought encourage splitting. This will happen with gooseberries and currants as well. And besides the actual splitting, which is damaging enough in itself, the wounds will be breeding grounds for fungus diseases.

Good ventilation

Along with growing plants under conditions in which they will thrive, we must also do everything we can to avoid those that encourage the presence, development and spread of pests and diseases. Although this is usually more applicable to a greenhouse than to the open garden, in that adequate ventilation is the best disease preventer, it can also apply outside.

Avoid overcrowding Never allow seedlings to become overcrowded. It leads to them getting drawn and weak and can frequently create a micro-climate that allows pests and diseases to flourish. Overcrowding can easily be avoided by sowing thinly and transplanting or thinning out the seedlings as soon as is reasonably possible. Not only will overcrowded seedlings and young plants create an environment favouring the nasties but, by being close together and touching, trouble will spread like wild fire.

Fungus diseases, such as Botrytis (Grey Mould), thrive in the close, cool atmosphere created by overcrowding.

Hoe with care When hoeing among plants, be careful to avoid nicking them with the hoe. This not only scars root crops like turnips and beet but it also provides a perfect point of entry for fungus diseases and, frequently, slugs. This happens also with uneven watering.

The effects of brown rot on fruit – the brown fruit often remains 'mummified'.

Good hygiene Garden hygiene in general is extremely important.

In particular, badly diseased and dead plants must be removed as soon as possible. If they are left where they are, they simply act as a source of further infection. The good habit of not putting plants infested or infected with soil-borne pests and diseases such as Club Root and Carrot Fly on the compost heap comes in here as well. Such plants should be consigned to the dustbin or, better still, burnt.

Care for tools A rather more specialized form of preventing the spread of infection concerns virus diseases effecting fruit trees, bushes, canes and even strawberry plants. Viruses can be spread by contaminated tools as well as by greenfly, and other insect pests, passing on the organism by feeding on the sap. Never, therefore, knowingly use the same tool for dealing with healthy plants after handling virused ones. A good example of this is the common mosaic virus disease that infects raspberries. Avoid digging up infected canes and then using the same spade to plant up the gaps with new and healthy ones. Infected sap could easily be on the spade.

Pruning tools, such as saws and secateurs, can also carry viruses from infected to previously healthy stock.

'Alternative hosts' Something often ignored by gardeners, or perhaps they have just not stopped to think about it, is the fact that most pests and diseases attack more than one crop, that is, they have alternative hosts. Now clearly there is very little point in protecting a crop from this or that pest or disease if it is simply being attacked from elsewhere. These other hosts are normally other plants in the vicinity of the crop but they could equally well be over the fence in the nextdoor garden. This is a distinct possibility that should not be ignored.

However, normally it is just a question of, for example, club root disease of brassicas also being perfectly happy on the roots of ornamentals like wallflowers or weeds like Shepherd's Purse.

Certain pests are also guilty of maintaining more than one home. Most greenfly are just as happy eating weeds as they are lettuces, for instance. Never ignore or treat this aspect of pest and disease control lightly, it is just as important as any other.

Crop rotation This is a time-honoured way of reducing unwelcome invaders and simply means not growing the same crop, or even type of crop, on the same bit of land every year. In the past, this was done more from the point of view of making sure that a particular piece of land did not run out of specific nutrients by growing the same crop on it year after year. This has largely been overcome now by the greater understanding and choice we have of modern fertilizers but there still remains its other purpose – that of preventing a build-up of specific diseases.

These are not diseases like the mildews that attack the tops of plants but are essentially soil-borne ones, like white rot of onions and club rot which go for the underground parts. If susceptible crops are grown on the same land the year after an attack, there are no prizes for guessing that the disease will turn up again, only worse. Nor is it the least bit of good practising crop rotation if alternative hosts are allowed to survive, flourish and carry over an infection to the following year.

There is also a less obvious side to rotation. Some of the soil-borne diseases have only a limited life in the soil in the absence of a suitable host. Unfortunately, club root is not one of them.

It used to be thought that the number of soil pests was also reduced by crop rotation. While this might happen to a small extent with largely immobile creatures like wireworm, the vast majority are active enough to move on when the need arises.

Immune crops The last method of what we call 'cultural' pest and disease control concerns the varieties of vegetables that we grow. Despite what the cynics might think and say, modern plant breeders are putting all their resources into the creation of varieties that are either resistant or immune to attack from as many pests and diseases as is humanly possible. This is achieved to a large extent by delving back into the past and finding wild varieties of plants that exhibit a tendancy to throw off attacks by nasties.

One of the most exciting recent discoveries is a wild cabbage, with an unpronounceable name, from central Europe. This is far more resistant to club

BEATING THE CABBAGE ROOT FLY

1. Melt a hole about 2.5 cm (1in) in diameter in the base of each plastic yoghurt carton. Then cut the sides down to 2.5 cm (1in) high.

2. Carefully thread the roots of young brassicas through the hole in each cut-down carton at transplanting time.

3. Plant the brassicas, protected by their plastic collars, firmly in trowel holes, burying 1.3 cm (½in) of the collar.

An alternative is to use squares of roofing felt to prevent root-fly attack. Cut a hole in the centre for the stem.

PRUNING TO CONTROL DISEASE

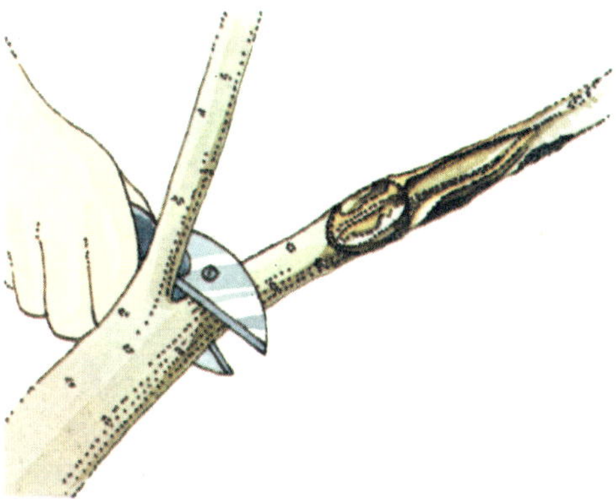

1. With a badly infected branch, it is best to remove the entire branch. Put the diseased wood on the bonfire.

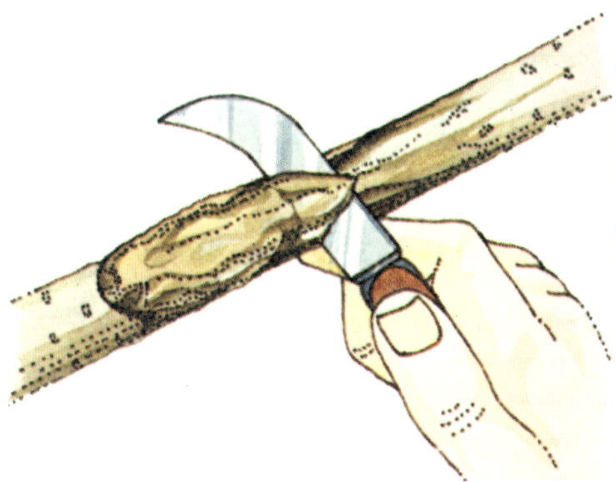

1a. If the branch is not so badly infected, pare off the diseased wood until healthy tissue is reached.

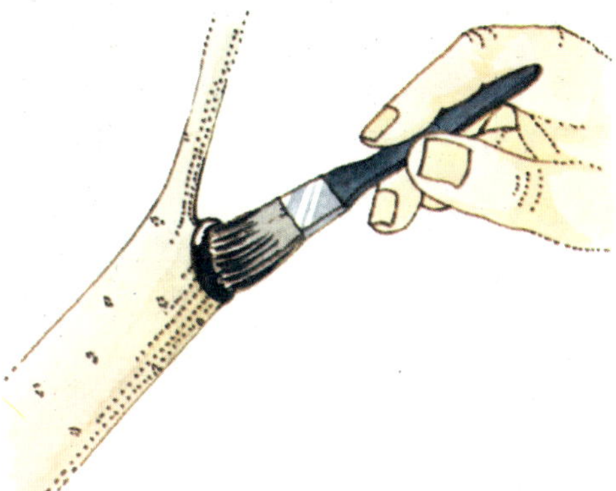

2. After pruning or paring away diseased wood, paint over the cut surface with an anti-canker paint immediately.

3. Immediately after using them on diseased wood, dip secateurs or knife into disinfectant solution.

root than anything else we have yet seen and is being used in breeding programmes to see if the resistance can be passed on.

This part of the operation is fairly simple; the difficult part comes when you try to create a usable vegetable with these characteristics. At the moment, the best that can be produced is a very third rate brassica, but the really important thing is that it does still have the resistance factor, so we live in hope.

Most gardeners also know about disease-resistant varieties of tomato. These have all but done away with many of the more serious soil-borne diseases, as well as disorders like Greenback.

Fruit crops are also coming into this picture a lot more now. The brand new gooseberry variety Invicta is practically immune to American gooseberry mildew; certainly the worst disease that the crop can get. The other good thing about Invicta is that it crops better than the standard variety Careless.

Anyone who has grown raspberries will probably know the virus disease that was mentioned earlier. This is transmitted from plant to plant by greenfly and, while it is virtually impossible to create immunity – or even resistance – to viruses, most of the new varieties of raspberry are resistant to many types of greenfly. This is because the plants have a smell that turns the greenfly off rather than attracting them. Clever stuff.

Wherever possible, therefore, always use varieties of vegetables and fruit that are resistant or even immune to the worst pests and diseases.

Cures

At the moment, and no matter how many of the above precautions you take or how seriously you take them, it is inevitable that every garden will get its fair share of pests and diseases. The problem then arises as to what should be done to combat them.

Even without using chemicals, there are several things that we can do but we must do them fast. The number one rule, therefore, is to keep a sharp eye open for any trouble and to act the moment it is seen. The idea that you can wait until you can be bothered or can find the time is useless; every hour that action is put off will allow whatever it is to get worse. In the case of a fungus disease, this means it spreading further on the original victim and even on to other plants. With pests, a delay in action will mean these, too, will quickly spread – and it is also possible that breeding or egg laying will take place.

Remove and burn diseased foliage Always remember that the more deep seated a problem becomes, the harder it is to control. The simple and obvious thing to do when a disease is seen is to pick off and burn the infected leaf, flower, fruit or whatever it is. This will prevent it spreading. If the disease has got really well established and has infected the stem of the plant, the only sensible course is to pull the plant up and destroy it. This may seem harsh but if the plant is left it is simply going to make matters worse.

Stamp out pests Much the same goes for the control of pests. But here we come to a method that is definitely not for the squeamish. If you can pick off the offender, do so and tread on it. If not, then you have to close your eyes and squash it where it is. There is no point in being faint-hearted about it. Use your fingers or, if you cannot stand that, wear gardening gloves. Whichever of these methods you adopt, the result is the same; a dead pest that will cause you no more bother.

Caterpillars, too, are very quickly disposed of by picking them off the plants individually and destroying them as you think best.

This physical approach to pest control is not to everyone's liking, although there is no denying that two half-bricks adminster a considerably quicker, more effective and less unpleasant end to slugs than does a sprinkling of salt. However, slug traps consisting of sunken jamjars half filled with beer are possibly the best of all.

'Old Wives' cures Among what might be termed 'alternative' methods of combating this, that and the other nasty, come the Old Wives Tales. While they should never be taken too seriously, nor must they ever be ignored as, if all else fails, they could well work and solve the problem.

Many books have been written about these sometimes rather bizarre methods of preventing or banishing problems and they are certainly worth reading. It does not always do to take them too seriously though. Some are very definitely written with tongue in cheek.

On the other hand, they must all be based on fact or they would not have survived so long and held such wide acceptance. Here are a few to get you thinking:

- To keep club root disease away from brassicas, bury a stick of rhubarb near the crop.

I cannot follow this one at all. Club root is a disease that is encouraged by acidic soil conditions and anything more acidic than rhubarb is hard to imagine. The best control of club root is certainly to keep acid soils alkaline by regular applications of chalk or lime.

- To get rid of peach leaf curl, pick off the infected leaves and hang mothballs or those naphthalene anti-moth rings in the trees.

I've never tried this myself but it seems odd that an insecticide should also be so effective against a fungus disease. Still, this is not unheard of and a coal-tar derivative (naphthalene) would certainly have the properties of a sterilant.

Of course, even the use of mothballs might be rather too chemical for some people. For them, and everyone else, the most effective control of all against peach leaf curl, where the trees are being grown against a wall, is to erect a small roof or canopy above the tree. This need only jut out 30–60 cm (1–2 ft) from the wall. It has the effect of sheltering the foliage from the rain, thereby keeping it dry and, in consequence, disease-free.

There are many more reputed remedies for pests than there are for diseases:

- One of the best known is using garlic to ward off greenfly. The normal recommendation is to plant a garlic clove beneath each bush because something within the garlic is exuded into the soil and then absorbed by the roots in much the same way as is a systemic insecticide. Apparently, garlic only smells when in flower so, provided that you take the precaution of removing the flower heads as soon as they appear, there should be no bother.

Personally, I cannot stand garlic at any price and, given the choice, would probably settle for the greenfly.

Other members of the onion family are said to be effective, but not to the same extent. Chives, though, would probably look the least out of place of any.

- French marigolds (or any other Tagetes) are quite a well-known remedy in the greenhouse to keep white fly away from tomatoes and fuchsias. A lot of people still swear by this so it is well worth a try.

Another possible cure for the same problem is Nasturtium plants. These though are allegedly a good cure against woolly aphis in apple trees. I find this particularly hard to swallow as Nasturtiums frequently get plastered with greenfly themselves and woolly aphid is simply another variety of the same pest.

If you believe the next 'cure', you will believe anything.

- Caterpillars originate in Tartary to the east of the Caspian Sea and are carried here on the east wind. Windbreaks erected to keep this wind at bay will protect a garden from caterpillars.

There's no answer to that.

Possibly the most widely followed remedies are the plant associations, like garlic amongst the roses. There are several of these and their devotees have almost maniacal faith in them. It would be quite wrong to write them off as useless but I have never heard of a single one that has worked for everybody and they must certainly be brought into operation before there is a sign of the problem. In other words, they may help to ward off an attack of a particular pest or disease but they will not get rid of one after it has struck.

Attract blue tits by hanging up fat or a coconut.

Using natural predators This far more effective, and widely practised, method has been used commercially for some years now but the big snag is that it can only be carried out with any chance of success in a greenhouse. The reason for this is obvious; there would be no control over the 'goodies' in the open air and most would simply disappear.

Two that have been used widely, both of which are available to amateurs, are the natural predator of the glasshouse red spider mite (Phytoseiulus) and a parasite of the glasshouse whitefly (Encarsia). Both are very effective, but the system as a whole has certain drawbacks. The main one is that it is difficult to control other pests by any chemical means without upsetting the goodies.

Like many garden birds, the robin is invaluable as a destroyer of pests. Protect your birds and feed them.

In the open garden, the nearest we can really get to this Utopian arrangement in which Good always prevails is to encourage the naturally occurring predators and parasites. Unfortunately, this has to be done in a rather negative way because the only method of attracting, for example, ladybirds, is to keep a thriving aphis population. Rather self-defeating. Really, the only thing we can do to encourage natural pest control is to avoid using sprays that will kill the predators and parasites. This rules out more or less all of them.

The trouble is that natural pest control in a garden just does not work, and let no one try to tell you otherwise. The moment you create a garden, you are doing something unnatural. For a start, you are planting rows and rows of similar vegetables and flowers. No amount of juggling with nature will produce enough ladybirds to control all the aphids. For this reason, the idea of ever

A hoverfly settles on a flower. The adults feed on nectar and pollen, but their eggs hatch into slug-like larvae which are efficient predators of many types of aphid.

being able to sit back and leave things to look after themselves is just unrealistic. There could well come a time, therefore, when the desire to garden efficiently outweighs one's praiseworthy principles and the help of insecticides and fungicides is sought.

This is not the time to throw up your arms in despair because, out of the vast array of pesticides that can be found in every garden shop and centre, there are a certain number that are quite definitely of natural origin. In other words, if you are prepared to use hoof and horn fertilizers, there is really no logical reason for shunning these. Unless, of course, you are against them on principle.

Insecticides Probably the best known and most widely used insecticide of natural origin is derris. This is the powdered roots of the Derris and Lonchocarpus plants, two tropical legumes that contain the insect poison rotenone. Derris is available as a dust or a spray and is of very short persistence. Edible plants may be harvested one day after treatment. It is effective against aphids, caterpillars (the younger the better), red spider mite, thrips, gooseberry sawfly and raspberry beetle.

Another good natural insecticide is pyrethrum, also available as a spray and a dust. It is a material which, once diluted, is quickly rendered harmless by sunlight so that, as with derris, edible crops treated with it can be eaten a day later. Pyrethrum is effective against a wide range of pests including aphids, white fly, caterpillars, thrips and beetles.

Although nicotine is another natural material, logic could be said to leave the scene if this is included as a 'safe' insecticide because it is about four times as poisonous as pyrethrum and is far more dangerous to fish, birds, livestock and wild animals. It gives effective control against aphids (including woolly aphid), capsids, leaf miner, thrips and gooseberry sawfly. Edible crops should not be harvested until two days after treatment.

Where insecticidal chemicals end and insecticidal materials begin is anyone's guess but there are a number if near-chemical remedies that are also practiced. One that often has good results is dragging a paraffin soaked piece of cloth along rows of brassica seedlings to keep cabbage root fly away. The smell of the paraffin masks that of the plants. There are quite a few combative ploys like this and it is well worth asking older gardeners about them as most of them are from a pre-insecticide era.

These are adult seven-spot ladybirds. Both the adults and the larvae (black with four white spots) are aphid destroyers.

Fungicides Of the effective fungicides, only two could really be said to fall into the category of natural.

- Copper gives excellent control of a large number of fungus diseases including canker and scab on apples and pears, cane spot of raspberries etc., celery leaf spot, peach leaf curl, potato blight, damping off and tomato leaf mould. There are several formulations and brands with additives so read the labels thoroughly if you are at all worried about their suitability.
- Sulphur is also found under various guises, some of which give excellent control of apple and pear scab and the various downy mildews. Flowers of sulphur is much used for dusting things like dahlia tubers before storage to protect them from diseases. It is sold as ordinary yellow sulphur and dyed green.

As we saw with the old wives' tales, there are many other remedies of varying efficacy that can be tried. One of the best known is almost certainly soapy water.

Another favoured by many is an infusion of rhubarb leaves as an insecticide. It also makes the saucepan you brew it up in sparkling clean.

Mulches Regarding weed control, there are really very few unusual methods as most rely on hoes of one sort or another. However, a system that most certainly should not be ignored is the use of mulches. Garden compost is the most widely used mulching material and this has already been fully covered.

A complete departure from organic matter involves the use of black polythene. Clearly, this has no place in flower borders but there is no reason at all for banning it from vegetable and fruit plots. One of its best uses is for covering the ground between rows of strawberries in place of straw. Here, though, it should be thoroughly punctured so that rain is able to pass through it. If this is not done, the fruits are likely to sit in puddles of water, which rather defeats the object of the exercise. Indeed, this holing should be done in most cases or the underlying ground will soon dry out.

Potatoes are another crop that can be grown well through a black polythene mulch as it does away with the need to earth them up after their first covering.

Probably the most appropriate kind of polythene sheeting is a proprietary brand that already has thousands of small slits.

Hoeing The most important non-chemical method of controlling weeds, hoeing, may need some explaining as there is a right way and a wrong way of going about it. Hoeing should be done the moment weed seedlings are visible. In this way they are very easily killed and so are thousands more that you cannot even see. Always hoe before the weeds are in flower but if, for any reason, they are large and nearly flowering, they should be hoed and then raked off and composted before they do actually flower. Semi-mature weeds left lying on the ground can remain alive and flower if the weather is damp.

Never hoe deeply, the object of the operation is to sever the weed from its roots just below the surface. That is the surest way of killing them.

Only hoe when the soil is dry. Wet soil will simply clog up the hoe and the weeds will never be killed but they will simply be transplanted.

Always hoe carefully so that wanted plants are not damaged. Keep all hoes sharp as they are cutting tools and, as such, are useless when blunt.

-VEGETABLES-

Probably the crops that most home growers associate with the ideal of gardening organically, are vegetables – simply because when commercially grown they are usually subjected to a greater blast of chemicals than most other plants.

Of course, even as private individuals we are subject to economic pressures. The great majority of us grow vegetables for the purely practical purpose of eating cheaply and well, rather than for the undeniable satisfaction we can derive from seeing crops flourishing. But we do have an extra, personal incentive in choosing to grow organically: it is our own health and well-being that we're thinking about. The benefits very quickly speak for themselves.

Having said that, it must be added that – with the possible exception of apples – organically grown vegetables do have the tendency to suffer more than other plants/when pests or diseases strike – that is, if nothing has been done to protect them in advance.

The emphasis, therefore, is on paying attention to preventing troubles arising rather than waiting until they become established, then having to counteract them with chemicals. There are, of course, certain 'permitted' chemicals that can be used if, having already taken all due precautions, you are faced with a problem that does seem insurmountable. Before resorting even to these, do look again at the section on Problems (beginning on page 35) to check that you no longer have any other option.

Always bear in mind that it is vital to give vegetables sufficient nutrients. There are two main reasons for this. First, there is the obvious one that all living things need food – and without adequate nutrients the vegetables will inevitably be very small and poor. Second, there is the fact that strong and active plants are also likely to be healthy plants. They are thus far better able to withstand attacks from pests and diseases and come through without any real damage having been done.

Which vegetables to grow is, of course, a matter which only the individual grower can decide upon, since personal preferences must figure large in the choice. However, on the following pages you will find all of the most popular vegetables and a few which though less commonly grown, are worthwhile 'extras'.

You will notice that virtually no varieties have been named. This is deliberate; the different seed houses all have their own favourites and any list that I give you now will probably be out-of-date long before you cease to have need to refer to this book – indeed, I hope that it will continue to be a useful source of reference.

Opposite A well organised vegetable garden in a suburban setting. *Below* Fine specimens of cabbages, beans and leeks.

CABBAGE

Sowing to harvest time Summer and winter varieties: 10–17 weeks. Spring varieties: 20–25 weeks.

Soil No particular likes and dislikes. Ordinary, well-drained soil suits cabbages well. It should be firmed well and without air pockets at planting time.

Yield 1–2 kg (1.5–4 lb) per plant.

Cabbages may be round-headed or pointed. Because they tolerate a wide range of soil and weather conditions, they are easily grown and are likely to succeed almost anywhere in the U.K. However, choose the varieties carefully so that best use is made of the space available. There are varieties for winter, spring and summer cropping.

Sowing and planting
Garden compost should be incorporated with the digging and any lime required should be applied in early winter so that it is washed well in.

Seed should be sown thinly in nursery rows 1.3 cm (½ in) deep and 23 cm (9 in) apart. Sow winter varieties, and red cabbage, outdoors in late April/May and transplant in June to 45 cm (18 in) apart. Sow spring varieties outdoors in July/August and transplant in September/October to 15 cm (6 in) apart in rows 30 cm (12 in) apart. In early spring, as the plants grow and become crowded, take out and use alternate ones. Sow summer varieties under glass in February/March and transplant outside in April or May to 45 cm (18 in) apart. Alternatively, sow outdoors in April/May and transplant in June.

Because of their liking for firm soil, cabbages are often best planted in ground that has been dug for the previous crop; particularly if the soil is light. Lift and plant the seedlings firmly when they are about 15 cm (6 in) high. Water in thoroughly.

Cultivation
Hoe regularly to keep the weeds down. Water as required. This is especially important during hot summers as drought conditions give a rather strong flavour to cabbages and later varieties are apt to stop growing before they reach their maximum size.

Pests and diseases
Cabbage root fly, several species of aphid, caterpillars of Large White and Small White Butterfly and Cabbage Moth are all likely to be troublesome.

The soil borne fungus disease club root can be devastating on acidic land.

Harvesting
In the main, cabbages are far better if they are left standing until required for use. However, the Dutch White varieties can be cut and hung upside-down in a shed for use during the winter.

SAVOY

Sowing to harvest time 13–16 weeks.

Soil As for cabbages.

Yield 2–4 kg (4–9 lb) per plant.

Savoy cabbages are easy to grow and are particularly popular in the North and Scotland because of their excellent winter hardiness. They are crisp and tasty and their crinkly leaves and solid hearts make the best coleslaw.

Sowing and planting
Savoys should be raised in the same way as winter cabbages, that is, sow outdoors in late April/May and transplant in June, but they should be planted out 60 cm (2 ft) apart.

Cultivation
Pests and Diseases and Harvesting: as for cabbages.

HANDY HINT

Store cabbages on a rack of chicken wire in an airy, frost-free place. They should keep for several weeks.

SOWING CABBAGES OUTDOORS

1. Prior to sowing, prepare the ground with an application of a suitable compound fertilizer.

2. Prepare the seed-bed just before sowing by raking the soil to a fine consistency. The soil must be dry.

3. Using the side of a draw hoe blade, take out a narrow drill about 1.3 cm (½in) deep and a few centimetres wide.

4. Cabbage seeds are large enough to sow individually. Space them in the drill about 8 seeds per 30 cm (12in).

5. When the drill is filled, use a trowel to cover over the seeds with a thin layer of fine soil or peat.

6. When sowing is complete, use the back of a rake to smooth over and firm the surface of the seed-bed.

TRANSPLANTING

1. If your soil is acid, lime the permanent bed in early winter, so the soil reaction is slightly alkaline.

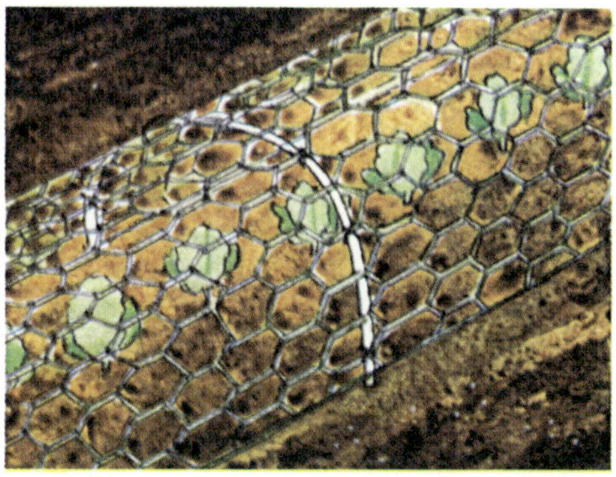

2. Birds, particularly wood pigeons, can be very destructive; netting seedlings is the best solution.

3. Thin the seedlings when the true cabbage leaves appear; thin to between 30 and 60 cm (1–2ft) apart.

4. If you are transplanting in dry weather, water the plants and the permanent bed thoroughly.

5. Lift the young plants with a trowel; transplant them into a hole larger than the root ball.

6. When transplanting the crop, plant a few extra in a cold frame to use as replacements if any die.

BRUSSELS SPROUTS

Sowing to harvest time 14–18 weeks.

Soil Should contain plenty of organic matter and must be very firm for planting into or the buttons are apt to develop loosely.

Yield About 1 kg (2 lb) of sprouts per plant.

Brussels sprouts are among the most popular winter vegetables and they are a rich source of vitamin C. By choosing the right varieties, it is possible to have a supply of fresh sprouts from October to March. In most households, it is better to grow 'pick over' varieties rather than 'single pick' ones. The former are picked from the base up as the sprouts mature, whereas the latter are intended to be picked all at once.

Sowing and planting

The soil for Brussels sprouts should contain plenty of organic matter and must be well limed to avoid over-acidity. As with cabbages, but even more importantly, the land should be cultivated well in advance of planting so that it has plenty of time to settle.

Seed should be sown thinly in nursery rows outdoors, 1.3 cm (½ in) deep and 23 cm (9 in) apart, from March to May, according to variety. Depending on the vigour of the variety, transplant to 60–75 cm (24–30 in) apart when the seedlings are about 15 cm (6 in) high. Plant them very firmly, preferably with a dibber, and water in if the soil is dry.

Cultivation

Hoe regularly to discourage weeds, and keep the sprouts growing steadily by watering when required.

Except in the most sheltered gardens, the plants will need to be tied to canes for support in the autumn.

Pests and diseases

As for cabbages, plus the possibility of pigeons in rural areas during hard winters.

Harvesting

Start to pick the sprouts from the bottom of the stem when they are about 2.5 cm (1 in) across and still hard. This will encourage sprouts further up the stem to develop. Sprouts may be deep frozen if desired but only if there are too many to eat at a time. Normally, they should be left on the plant until required.

HARVESTING

1. As the crop reaches maturity, the lower leaves will start to yellow; cut or pull them off when this happens.

2. Pick sprouts from the bottom of the stem upwards; split sprouts off the stem with a sharp, downward tug.

CAULIFLOWER

SELECTING AND TRANSPLANTING SEEDLINGS

Reject seedlings with bluish tint; they will produce small curds.

Avoid six or more leaves; they have grown old too quickly.

'Blind' seedlings with no growing point will not form curds.

A healthy seedling: short straight stem, good leaves and plenty of root.

1. When lifting seedlings, keep as much soil as possible around the roots.

2. In warm weather, fill hole with water before inserting the seedling.

3. After transplanting, firm the soil carefully around the young plant.

Sowing to harvest time 9–11 weeks for summer and autumn varieties; 15 weeks for winter varieties.

Soil Cauliflowers prefer soil that was dug in the autumn or winter and which has had plenty of organic matter incorporated into it. Rich loams are best but sandy soils are fine if they contain plenty of organic matter. For summer varieties, the ground should be friable and fertile, to encourage rapid growth.

Yield 1 kg (2 lb) per plant.

Summer cauliflowers mature from July to September, autumn varieties from October to December and winter ones from January to March.

Sowing and planting

Summer varieties should be sown under glass in February/March, for planting outside during April to mature from July onwards. Autumn varieties are sown outside in April/May and transplanted in late June. Winter cauliflowers (formerly known as heading broccoli) should be sown outdoors in May and transplanted in July.

Cauliflowers sown outdoors should be 1.3 cm (½ in) deep, and planted out 60 cm (2 ft) each way. Summer varieties need to be grown fast or they tend to bolt before the curd has reached full size. Make sure that the ground is fertile and well-watered.

Cultivation

Summer and early autumn varieties benefit from a base dressing of high nitrogen fertilizer, such as hoof and horn, before planting or of a more soluble kind (for example, dried blood) twice during growth.

Most modern varieties of winter cauliflower have incurving leaves which protect the curds from harsh weather. If this appears not to be the case, break off a lower leaf and place it over the curd.

Pests and diseases

As for cabbages.

Harvesting

Cut cauliflowers when they are still small and tender. Summer and autumn varieties are best when cut in the morning.

4. Form a long low earth ridge in autumn to keep the plants wind-firm.

5. Protect heads in very cold weather by covering them with dry straw.

BROCCOLI

Sowing to harvest time 8–12 weeks for calabrese; nearly a year for spring maturing purple and white sprouting broccoli.

Soil Much the same as for Brussels sprouts, that is, heavy, firm and well supplied with organic matter. As for all brassicas, it must be firm at planting time. If necessary, lime should be added in the winter or spring to ensure that it gets well washed in.

Yield 1 kg (2 lb) per plant.

Purple or white sprouting broccoli picked fresh from the garden in March is the surest sign that spring has arrived. This is followed in early summer by the calabrese. Although closely related to cauliflower, broccoli is easier to grow and, except in really cold weather, the sprouting varieties are perfectly hardy. The only appreciable difference between purple and white sprouting broccoli, besides the colour, is that the purple is hardier.

Sowing and planting

Seed should be sown thinly in nursery rows outdoors, 1.3 cm (½ in) deep and 23 cm (9 in) apart. The best calabrese heads come from direct sown plants that are thinned in the row and not transplanted. Seed can be sown at intervals from early April until early June.

Maximum crop weights of calabrese are produced if the plants are thinned to 15 cm (6 in) apart as soon as they are large enough to handle. Transplanting to this spacing is also recommended, as long as it takes place when the seedlings are still small and there is no check to growth. Do this during showery weather if you can. Allow 30 cm (12 in) between rows. As with cauliflowers, plenty of nitrogen is desirable to grow the plants fast and without a check.

Make a single sowing of sprouting broccoli between mid-April and mid-May and plant out in June/July 60–75 cm (24–30 in) apart.

Cultivation

All broccoli needs regular hoeing to keep down weeds, and plenty of water in dry spells.

Because of their height, sprouting broccoli plants will need support during most winters.

Pests and diseases

As for Brussels sprouts; particularly in respect of pigeons.

Harvesting

Calabrese is ready for cutting when the spears are fully developed but before there is a hint of them 'blowing'. Sprouting broccoli may be picked once the flower buds are visible and can continue until the heads are too thin and weak to bother about. In a mild year, it may start in January but, normally, March is more realistic. It will continue into May.

Nine Star Perennial

Late Corona

CULTIVATION

1. Keep the plants well watered in dry weather; use a fine rose on your watering can.

2. Mulch with garden compost to aid weed control, to prevent the soil drying out and to feed the plants.

3. When top dressing, sprinkle the fertiliser evenly around the plant in a circle the size of top growth.

4. In autumn, earth up the varieties that have to withstand winter to a height of 10 cm (4 in) round the stem.

HARVESTING

1. When harvesting Calabrese, cut the main head first, to encourage the growth of smaller green heads.

2. The side shoots are removed next, to stimulate further growth. Always pick while flower buds are closed.

3. Harvest flowering shoots of other varieties from the top downwards; snap off the first 15 cm (6 in) of each.

AFTERCARE AND STORING

1. After harvesting a crop of heads from perennial broccoli, mulch with garden compost or farmyard manure.

2. To store sprouting broccoli for up to 3 weeks, dig up the plant and hang upside down in a cool place.

SPINACH

Sowing to harvest time 6–10 weeks.

Soil Must be deep, moist and rich in organic matter to encourage the plants to grow quickly.

Yield 230 gm (8 oz) per plant.

Spinach is one of those vegetables you either love or loathe. If you love it, then growing something that has so much vitamin A and iron in it is worthwhile.

It is by no means the easiest vegetable to grow well. It has a natural tendency to bolt, especially if it is sown too early in the spring, but there are certain things we can do to overcome this.

Sowing

The soil for spinach must be deeply dug beforehand and abundant bulky organic matter should be incorporated. Lime should also be added after digging, if required. Spinach is a greedy crop so, just before sowing, give a substantial dressing of high nitrogen fertilizer.

Ideally, summer spinach should be sown in the shade of taller crops so it makes a good inter-crop for use between peas and/or beans. If you sow it every 2–3 weeks from March to July in rows 30 cm (1 ft) apart and 2.5 cm (1 in) deep, this will give a supply of leaves from May to October.

Cultivation

Thin the seedlings to 7.5 cm (3 in) apart as soon as they are large enough to handle. When it looks as though they need more space, thin further to 15 cm (6 in) apart. Use the thinned plants in the kitchen and allow the remainder to mature.

Thinning is an important factor in reducing the incidence of bolting. It is also vital to water freely, especially during dry periods. This is all part of encouraging the plants to grow quickly so that there is less tendency to bolt. Hoe the soil around the plants regularly to keep the weeds down and to prevent the formation of a surface crust.

SUMMER SPINACH

1. Water often in hot weather; use a fine spray or rose on your watering can so soil is not washed away.

2. Spinach is good for intercropping and will grow well in the shade of runner beans or peas.

3. When harvesting, take only a few leaves from each plant at one time; overpicking can kill the plant.

Pests and diseases

The seedlings may suffer from damping off and are also liable to get mildew if they are left crowded for too long.

Aphids are often troublesome.

Harvesting

Pick off and use the outer leaves of the plants as soon as they reach an acceptable size. Regular and continued picking will encourage re-growth.

Spinach may be deep frozen but it is normally more satisfactory to grow a winter variety instead.

4. After the final harvest, chop up the plants and dig them into the soil to act as green manure.

WINTER SPINACH

1. Sow from mid-summer through to mid-autumn. For heavy soils, make small ridges on which to sow seeds.

2. Protect open grown spinach from winter weather with a layer of bracken or clean straw.

3. Cloches are an alternative way to protect winter spinach; cloches also help keep the leaves free of mud.

NEW ZEALAND SPINACH

Sowing to harvest time From seven weeks.

Soil As for summer spinach.

Yield 1 kg (2 lb) per plant but more if you pick frequently and grow them well.

New Zealand or broad leaved prickly spinach is not related to summer spinach at all but it makes a very good substitute and is particularly valuable in the winter as it is perfectly hardy. It forms a low growing, rather creeping plant that does not bolt like summer spinach. The leaves are thick, fleshy and arrowhead shaped. Besides being winter hardy, New Zealand spinach is resistant to drought.

Sowing

Seed should be sown at intervals from mid-May to early September to give a succession. The winter crops come from the August/September sowings. To hasten germination, soak the seeds in water overnight before sowing, then sow in clusters of three seeds per station 1.3 cm (½ in) deep – allowing 60 cm (2 ft) between clusters and the same between rows.

Cultivation

As soon as the seedlings are large enough to handle, single them to one plant per station, that is, 60 cm (2 ft) apart.

Hoe to keep down weeds and water plentifully during dry periods. When the plants are 30 cm (1 ft) across, nip out the growing points to encourage more shoots, and therefore more leaves, to form.

In colder districts, it often pays to cover the plants with cloches or polythene tunnels in October to protect them from the worst of the weather.

Pests and diseases

Remarkably few, apart from the usual greenfly and caterpillar. Nothing difficult to deal with.

Harvesting

Cut a few leaves from towards the base of each plant regularly to encourage it to continue growing and producing. The shoot tips should also be picked frequently to encourage the plant to spread. The leaves and stems are cooked.

If you want to continue picking through the winter, cloche protection is very useful – and it will also protect the leaves from mud.

SPINACH BEET

Sowing to harvest time From 7 weeks, but usually left much longer if required for winter/spring use.

Soil Deep and moist, with plenty of organic matter. Unlike summer spinach, it will tolerate poor and sandy soils.

Yield 0.5 kg (1 lb) per plant but, the more you pick, the more it produces.

Spinach, or Perpetual, Beet is a very valuable winter and early spring vegetable because it comes at a time when there is little else about.

It looks similar to summer spinach and is in the same family, but there the similarity ends. It has no tendency to bolt during the first summer and has a much milder flavour than summer spinach.

Sowing
The soil should be prepared as for summer spinach. The seed may be sown in April, for summer use, or in July for the more important winter/spring crop.

Sow in rows 2.5 cm (1 in) deep and 45 cm (18 in) apart.

Cultivation
Thin the seedlings to 20 cm (8 in) apart as soon as they are large enough to handle. Alternatively, they can be thinned to 10 cm (4 in) and later to the full distance, if you want to use the second thinnings in the kitchen.

Pests and diseases
Virtually none. Occasionally aphids.

Harvesting
The first leaves can be taken from the outside of the plants in the summer but never overdo this if your aim is to use them in the winter and spring.

The plants may be slightly damaged in really bad winter weather but this is rare. Avoid stripping the plants in the winter as they will take a long time to recover.

Spinach beet is best scrapped once it starts to run to seed in the spring.

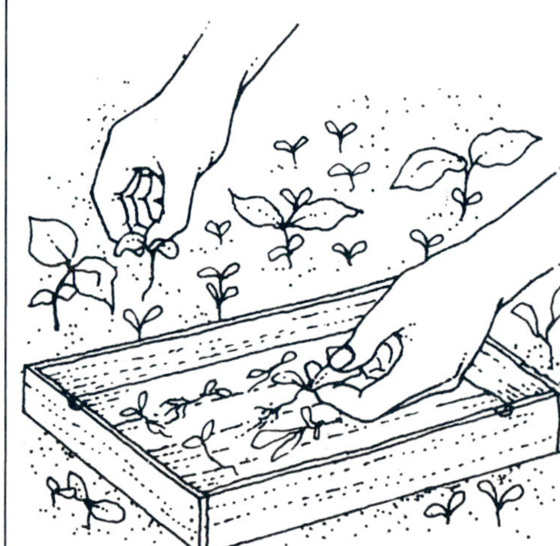

Thinning out seedlings

Picking leaves – take them off close to the ground

SEAKALE BEET, SWISS CHARD

Sowing to harvest time 8–10 weeks.

Soil Should be moist and contain plenty of organic matter but good crops are also harvested from light sandy soils and heavy clay.

Yield 1.5 kg (3 lb) per plant but more if you pick them hard.

Closely related to spinach beet but having a much more prominent midrib. This is the edible part for which the plants are primarily grown.

Swiss chard is also very ornamental with bright red veins. These beet are easily grown and provide a supply of greens throughout the summer and autumn, even during droughts. Those grown for their leaves are cooked like spinach but if they are harvested while young the leaves can also be used chopped in salads. Those grown for their midribs are cooked like asparagus.

Whichever your preference, you are not very likely to find this vegetable available at your local greengrocer – it is one vegetable that commercial growers tend to avoid because it is bulky and wilts very quickly.

Sowing

Prepare the soil as for summer spinach.

In April/May sow three seeds per station, 1.3 cm (½ in) deep with 38 cm (15 in) between clusters and in rows spaced 45 cm (18 in) apart.

If you make several sowings, you can provide yourself with plants for cutting all through the year. Those sown in mid-spring should be ready for harvesting from summer through to early winter. And a late summer sowing will provide you with a winter and spring crop.

Most seedsmen offer two varieties of seakale beet – one green and one red. The red variety has long, crimson stalks with dark green leaves. It is a delicious vegetable and attractive enough to be grown as an ornamental plant.

Cultivation

Single the seedlings to one per station as soon as they are large enough to handle and grow on as for a summer crop of spinach beet.

Your main aim will be to produce a good crop of large leaves, so water the plants liberally, particularly during hot, dry summer spells. If you prepared the ground thoroughly before you started sowing, no additional feeding should really be needed, but if you are growing them on poor soil, you will find it beneficial to apply an occasional feed of dilute, liquid manure.

Keep the ground round the plants free of weeds by hoeing regularly. Alternatively keep the weeds down by placing black plastic sheets between the rows and place stones on top to hold it down. Or, you could mulch with peat or manure – either of which will conserve moisture as well as deterring the weeds.

You can grow a few Swiss chard plants in a trough or large tub provided you can allow a depth of at least 30 cm (12 in) to accommodate the roots. Add well-rotted manure to the potting compost and mix this well in, before sowing the seeds in the same way as directed for outdoor crops. Thin the seedlings to a spacing of one every 30 cm (12 in). Always make sure that the container is kept well watered, and during dry summer spells you may have to increase this to twice a day. Give the container really thorough soakings. Put the container in a cold frame or a greenhouse for the winter months.

Pests and diseases

Swiss chard is virtually trouble-free – disease of any kind rarely troubles it and the only pests you are likely to have to cope with are slugs and aphids.

Harvesting

It is important to remove the coarser outside leaves of the plants to allow the tender inner ones to develop properly.

When large enough, these should be pulled like rhubarb and not cut with a knife because cutting usually makes the plants bleed, as with beetroot. Harvest the leaves regularly, but never strip the whole plant at once.

Harvesting Swiss chard

BROAD BEANS

Sowing to harvest time 9–11 weeks for spring sown varieties; from six months for autumn sowings.

Soil No particular requirements but it must be well drained.

Yield 2.5 kg (5.5 lb) from a row of normal varieties 3 m (10 ft) long. Dwarf varieties, 2 kg (4.5 lb) from a single 3 m (10 ft) row.

There are three main types of broad bean. Longpod varieties, such as Aquadulce Claudia, are recognized by their long, narrow pods. They are the hardiest of all and, therefore, the most suitable for autumn sowing. They give high yields and early crops.

The Windsor group have shorter, wider pods and are best for flavour and later crops, that is, for spring sowing. They are not tough enough to withstand the winter.

The Dwarf varieties are ideal for small gardens, where they can be sown close together. They have short pods and dwarf, bushy growth. For a given area, they do not crop as heavily as taller varieties but are perfect where space is limited. Sow them in spring.

Sowing

The ground should have been well dug and compost added. The nitrogen content of any fertilizer should not be too high, because all legumes manufacture their own.

Longpod varieties can be sown in November, 5 cm (2 in) deep and with 11.5 cm (4.5 in) between the seeds. Rows should be 45 cm (18 in) apart. These spacings give 2 plants per sq. ft and maximum yields. Sow dwarf varieties 23 cm (9 in) each way.

Cultivation

Autumn sown crops benefit greatly from being cloched over the winter.

Keep all varieties well supplied with water once the temperature rises in the spring. This is important from the time they come into flower. And make sure that weeds are kept under control.

Pests and diseases

Aphids, specifically Blackfly, are almost inevitable. Autumn sown crops may be less susceptible than spring sown but are by no means safe.

Chocolate Spot (Botrytis) can look serious but causes little actual damage.

Harvesting

Pick the pods when the scar on the individual bean is still green or white. Black-eyed beans are often mealy and seldom tasty.

Broad beans freeze excellently and make it worth growing plenty, if you like them.

CARE AND CULTIVATION

1. Pick off the growing points to deter bean aphid and to encourage bigger pods.

2. Harvest the beans with a quick downward twist of the hand. The lower pods mature first.

DWARF FRENCH BEANS

Sowing to harvest time 10–14 weeks.

Soil Light and well drained but with ample organic matter.

Yield 3 kg (6.5 lb) from a 3 m (10 ft) row of the normal dwarf varieties; 4.5 kg (10 lb) per 3 m (10 ft) row of climbers.

Unlike broad beans, the whole pod of French beans is eaten so nothing is wasted. They are a valuable source of vitamins and minerals.

Climbing varieties are also available.

Sowing and planting

The earliest sowings can be made in peat pots in the greenhouse during March/April, for planting out in May when the risk of frost is over. Alternatively, seed can be sown outdoors under cloches or polythene tunnels from mid-April.

When grown outside without any protection, sow at fortnightly intervals from late April to late June for a succession. White seeded (fat podded) varieties are slightly tender and should not be sown before late May. Seed is sown 5 cm (2 in) deep, and as the most economical spacing gives three to four plants per square foot, allow 5–10 cm (2–4 in) between seeds. Space the rows 45 cm (18 in) apart. A late sowing may be made in July to give an autumn crop.

Cultivation

Although the closeness of the plants will smother any weeds later on, in the early stages keep weeds down by hoeing. Watering will also be essential during dry spells or cropping will stop and the beans will become stringy. Dwarf varieties will normally need no support but climbers should be treated like runner beans.

Autumn crops benefit enormously from being covered in October, if they are still cropping. This protection speeds up maturity and discourages Botrytis mould by keeping the plants drier.

Pests and diseases

Slugs are often troublesome, attacking the young plants at ground level and cutting them off.

Red spider mite is always bad in a hot, dry summer while, in a wet year, Botrytis often attacks the pods and leaves.

Harvesting

The pods are ready when about 10 cm (4 in) long. Never wait until they become knobbly and stringy; even though there are stringless varieties available now.

If picked over two or three times a week, the plants should continue cropping for 6–8 weeks. French beans freeze well.

CARE AND HARVESTING

1. A mulch of clean straw, moist peat or leaf litter conserves soil moisture and protects plants from early frosts.

2. When harvesting, cut the pods with scissors or secateurs; never pull the pods off, or you may damage the plant.

RUNNER BEANS

Sowing to harvest time 10–12 weeks.

Soil It must be moisture retentive and contain plenty of organic matter. Heavy clays and light sands are seldom satisfactory unless greatly improved.

Yield Climbing varieties can give 18 kg (40 lb) per 3 m (10 ft) row. Dwarfs will yield something under half that.

Runner beans are one of the most, if not *the* most, prolific and cost-effective garden vegetable. For a very small outlay, you can pick beans from July right up until the frosts finish off the plants in October or November. And they enrich the soil with nitrogen compounds for a following crop.

They are also very attractive climbing plants with red, pink or white flowers and beautiful bright green leaves. The most commonly grown are the climbing sort but these can be converted to bush beans by continually nipping out the tips of the shoots. Alternatively, Hammond's Dwarf Scarlet can be grown; this is easily the best non-climbing variety and excellent where space is limited or the site is particularly exposed.

Sowing and planting

The traditional runner bean trench still gives the best results. Prepare it well in advance by digging over an area 60–75 cm (24–30 in) wide, to a full spade's depth or, preferably, double-dig it. Incorporate lashings of garden compost or well rotted manure into the bottom of the trench.

The earliest sowings can be made in heat in April, using peat pots. The exact sowing time should accord with the fact that it will not be safe to plant them out until late May or early June. The earliest outdoor sowing should be in late April under cloches or polythene tunnels.

For growing without any protection, sow (or set out plants raised under cover) during May to give a plant density of one per square foot. A convenient spacing is 15 cm (6 in) between seeds/plants in double rows 45 cm (24 in) apart.

Cultivation

Climbing runner beans will need the support of canes or stout twine. Canes are sturdier but, of course, more expensive. They should be pushed into the ground between each seed/plant and have the top tied to that of the opposite cane with garden twine. The whole row is then made stable with a cane tied along the ridges thus created. An alternative is to drive a strong post into the ground at each end of the row and run a wire between them. From this can be hung either bean netting or strings for the plants to climb up. Tie the plants loosely to their support as soon as possible. Once they start to grow, they will hang on and climb by themselves.

Hoe the ground regularly to keep the plants clear of weeds. Water copiously, especially during dry spells, and encourage the flowers to set by watering gently overhead or spraying in the evening. Mulching the plants from July onwards with a good thick layer of rotted compost or grass mowings will further keep the weeds at bay and help to retain moisture.

CULTIVATION AND CARE

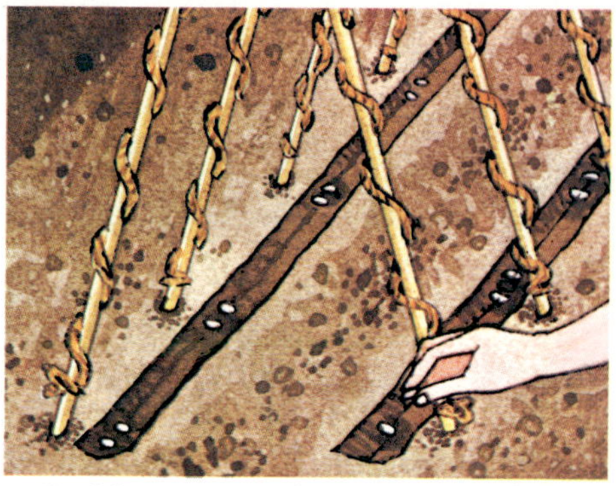

1. Position canes and twine; sow in deep drills, two seeds per cane.

2. As seedlings start to grow, cut or pull out the weaker of the two.

In late July, and again in August, feed the plants with manure or compost water to sustain them during cropping.

Once the plants have reached the top of their support, nip out the growing point.

Pests and diseases
The seeds may be eaten by slugs or millepedes if they are taking a long time to germinate. Mature plants are often attacked by aphids, frequently blackfly. Botrytis fungus may be a problem in wet summers.

Harvesting
Pick the beans when they are young and tender, never wait until they are stringy and lumpy simply for the sake of having a greater weight to pick (this is less likely to happen if you use the modern stringless varieties). By picking the beans regularly when they are quite small, the plants should keep cropping for about three months.

Any that you don't want to use straight away can be stored in a cool larder for a couple of days – or in the refrigerator for slightly longer. Also, runner beans freeze excellently so a surplus is no problem to deal with.

3. Weed around young plants taking care not to damage them.

4. As plants wind themselves up the framework, tie in any stray growth.

HARICOT BEANS

Sowing to harvest time 9–13 weeks.

Soil Light, well drained and with plenty of organic matter.

Yield 1.5 kg (3 lb) from a 3 m (10 ft) row.

These are the white, dried beans that the French love to use in stews and casseroles. The best thing about growing your own is that they have so much more flavour than shop ones, which could be of any age and are usually dried mechanically.

Sowing
Prepare the ground and sow the seed in May in the same way as for dwarf French beans.

Cultivation
This is also the same as for dwarf French beans except that the pods are left on the plants to mature and ripen. If the autumn is wet and cold, the plants should be dug up and the pods ripened indoors.

Pests and diseases
As for dwarf French beans.

Harvesting
In early autumn, when the pods have turned yellow, pull the plants out of the ground and hang them up in a dry and airy shed. When the pods are brittle, shell them and leave the beans to dry on newspaper for a few more days. The dry beans are best stored in cardboard boxes so that they can breathe. If tins or jars are used and the beans are not absolutely dry, they may sweat and spoil.

HARVESTING AND DRYING HARICOTS

1. Harvest in mid-autumn, when pods are pale brown and beginning to split; if it is cold and wet, dig up plants and hang indoors to ripen fully.

2. Spread shelled beans on trays, and dry them in a well ventilated room.

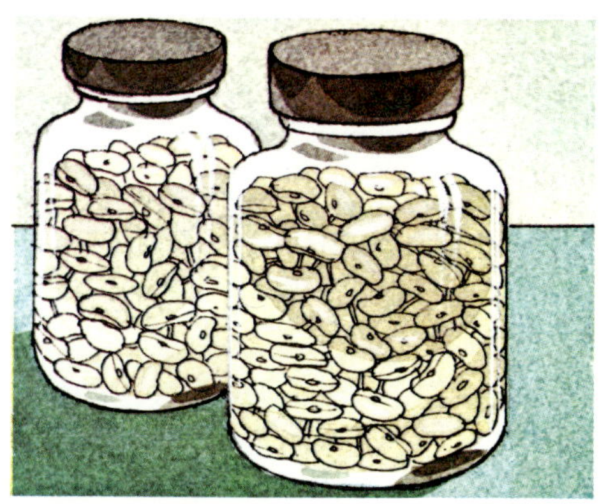

3. If absolutely dry, you can store in glass jars with tight-fitting lids.

GARDEN PEAS

Sowing to harvest time 32 weeks for autumn sown wrinkled varieties, 8–10 weeks for spring and summer sown round varieties.

Soil Well drained and rich in organic matter.

Yield 2–4.5 kg (4–10 lb) from a 3 m (10 ft) row.

These may be either the kind that are removed from the pod or the 'mange tout' and Sugar Snap kinds that are eaten whole. Peas have always been a popular garden vegetable. They are nowhere near as easy to grow well as one might think, but the taste of fresh garden peas makes the effort worthwhile.

From the hardiness point of view, round-seeded varieties are the strongest and quickest to mature but those with wrinkled seeds are sweeter and heavier cropping. The French varieties of wrinkled pea are known as 'petit pois'.

Sowing

The plot should be dug in the autumn or winter and plenty of organic matter incorporated. If the soil is acid, lime should be applied after digging. Any pre-sowing fertilizer must be relatively low in nitrogen as peas are legumes and make their own in nodules on the roots.

The varieties sown will be largely determined by when they are wanted to mature. For peas in May or June, you will have to sow a round-seeded variety in October or November and overwinter them under cloches. For cropping later in June or early July, sow a round or early wrinkled variety in March or April. Once again, they are earlier and safer if cloched. For peas in late July, sow a maincrop wrinkled variety in May. This is also the time to sow the petit pois and sugar snaps. In favourable districts, you can have peas in August and even September by sowing in the first half of June.

All peas are sown the same. First, make a drill 15 cm (6 in) wide and 5 cm (2 in) deep. To give every plant sufficient room to perform at its best, sow the seeds no less than 7.5 cm (3 in) apart, if possible, in two rows (in the 15 cm [6 in] drill) with the peas 7.5 cm (3 in) apart in the rows. Drills should be 60 cm (2 ft) apart.

Cultivation

Newly sown seed, and subsequently the seedlings, should be protected from sparrows with either nylon netting or special pea guards made of wire netting. Hoe the ground regularly to keep the weeds under control and prevent the soil capping.

When the peas are 15 cm (6 in) high, push twiggy sticks into the ground each side of the drill to provide support. Alternatively, stretch suitably sized netting along the centre of each drill between posts at each end.

Peas need plenty of moisture to thrive so a mulch of garden compost or lawn mowings is of great benefit during the summer.

Pests and diseases

Sparrows attacking the seedlings are probably the worst pest but aphids and the caterpillars of the pea moth can be serious if not dealt with. Mildew may be bad in a dry year.

Harvesting

Start picking the pods of normal 'shelling' peas when they appear to be well filled but before the pod begins to get dry and crinkly. Mange tout varieties should be picked before the seeds have swollen in the pod. Sugar snap can be allowed to fill a bit more and may even be treated as shelling peas if the pods become tough. You will find that all peas freeze beautifully.

HANDY HINT

Peas are ready for harvesting when the pods are full. Always use a pair of scissors to harvest the ripe pods as picking by hand can pull the plant right out of the ground. After picking, clear the site. Remove any bits of pea haulm and put them on the compost heap.

SOWING AND CULTIVATION

1. Sow first early varieties in double rows under tall cloches. Put a mousetrap at each end.

2. Maincrop varieties can be sown without protection.

3. Hoe carefully around the seedlings to keep down weeds.

4. If the soil is very poor, apply a low-nitrogen fertilizer when the plants are young.

5. Water the seedlings often, especially in dry spells.

6. Protect young plants from birds by using mesh net pea-guards.

ASPARAGUS PEAS

Sowing to harvest time 14–16 weeks.

Soil Well drained and rich in organic matter.

Yield 1.5–2 kg (3–4.5 lb) from a 3 m (10 ft) row.

The pods of the asparagus pea are smaller than ordinary peas and have a sort of wavy frill along the seams. They have a hint of asparagus flavour about them and are eaten whole. The flowers are delightful; reddish and like the sweet pea.

Sowing

The seed should be sown 1.3 cm (½ in) deep and 10 cm (4 in) apart, with 45 cm (18 in) between rows. Because asparagus peas are not 100 percent hardy, sowing should be delayed until late April in mild districts and late May elsewhere.

Cultivation

Protection of the seedlings against birds is necessary.

As soon as the seedlings are large enough to handle, thin them out to 20 cm (8 in) apart. In exposed areas, the support of canes may be needed but these will have to be twiggy because these rather delicate peas do not have tendrils to cling by. Otherwise, the cultivation is as for garden peas.

Pests and diseases

As for garden peas.

Harvesting

Start picking the pods when they are about 4 cm (1.5 in) long; never wait until they are fully grown (twice that size) as they lose a lot of their flavour. By picking regularly and continually, the plants may go on cropping for a couple of months. Store by freezing.

LEEKS

Sowing to harvest 30–40 weeks.

Soil As long as the soil is well drained, leeks will grow almost anywhere; hence their ease of cultivation.

Yield 5 kg (11 lb) from a 3 m (10 ft) row.

Leeks are another of those vegetables that you either love or hate. If you love them, they make one of the tastiest of winter vegetables. They are also incredibly easy to grow.

Sowing

Leeks fit into a cropping programme very well after early peas or broad beans and, in either case, the ground will probably have been manured for the previous crop. If it has *not*, then this should be done before planting.

The seed can be sown under glass or indoors in February/early March, or outdoors in nursery rows during March. The outdoor sowing should be 1.3 cm (½ in) deep.

Cultivation

Whether raised inside or out, when the young plants are about 20 cm (8 in) tall (usually in June or July) they are planted out 15 cm (6 in) apart, with 30 cm (12 in) between rows.

Transplanting calls for a special procedure. 15 cm (6 in) deep holes are made with a dibber and the leeks are dropped into the holes, which are then filled with water. This causes the soil to fall in and settle around the roots. There is no need to fill the holes with soil.

Many gardeners reduce the height of the young plants to about 15 cm (6 in) to lessen transpiration. This looks tidy but there appears to be no scientific evidence that it does any good.

The plants should be kept free of weeds and watered during the summer whenever demanded by the weather and soil conditions. Soil can be drawn up around the neck of the plants if you want longer blanched stems.

Pests and diseases

Onion fly and white rot of onions can trouble leeks as well.

Harvesting

Although the smallest size at which it is economical to harvest leeks is when they are about pencil thickness, it is normal to leave them in the ground until the winter and then lift them as required. They are normally perfectly hardy but it is a good idea to cover the areas between them with straw to prevent the ground freezing solid and making lifting impossible.

If, at the end of the season, you still have a few remaining, but need the ground for another crop, dig them up and heel them in on their sides in a shallow trench elsewhere.

TRANSPLANTING

1. Transplant leeks in early to mid-summer, when they are about 20 cm (8in) high; do this in showery weather if possible.

2. Cut back the roots until they are 2.5 (1in) long; trim the leaf tips back slightly.

3. Use a thick dibber or trowel to form holes about 5 cm (2in) in diameter.

4. Lower the young leeks into the hole and fill with water; the water will wash soil over the base of the plant, to keep it in position.

BLANCHING

1. To keep stems free of soil, place collars round stems up to the base of the leaves.

2. Then draw up soil from between rows, using a draw hoe; repeat as necessary, fitting another collar above the first one.

3. You can start blanching with paper collars; support paper collars with bamboo canes.

4. As the leeks grow on, replace paper collars with 10 × 30 cm (4 × 12in) clay drainpipes – if you require long blanched stems.

GROWING LEEKS IN TRENCHES

1. Cover compost with 15 cm (6in) of topsoil, and carefully plant leeks 25 cm (10in) apart; water thoroughly.

2. Grow quick catch crops, such as radishes or lettuce, on ridges, before soil is needed for earthing-up.

SHALLOTS

Planting to harvest 18–25 weeks.

Soil Well drained land which is rich in organic matter is the most suitable.

Yield 4.5 kg (10 lb) from a 3 m (10 ft) row.

One of the easiest vegetables to grow and a very good substitute for onions if you prefer something milder.

Also good for pickling.

Unlike onions, which produce a single bulb, shallots form a clump of new bulbs around the parent one.

Planting
Prepare the ground well in advance and allow it to settle to a firm, fine surface (as for onions). In the early spring, push the bulbs into the ground so that the necks are just visible, placing them 15 cm (6 in) apart, with 20–30 cm (10–12 in) between rows.

Cultivation
Hoe regularly to keep the weeds down but take care to avoid damaging the bulb(s).

Water as necessary and, in the summer, scrape the soil away from the base of the clumps to let the sun in to help ripening.

Pests and diseases
As for onions.

Harvesting
As soon as the foliage has yellowed in June/July, dig up the shallots and dry them as you would bulb onions. When

dry, clean off any earth and the outer skin.

Remember to save enough of the smallest bulbs for setting next year. The rest can be stored in a net bag in an airy shed.

ONIONS

Sowing to harvest September planted sets mature in early June. August sown seed in late June. Spring planted sets mature in 18–20 weeks. Spring sown seed in 25–30 weeks. Pickling onions are ready in 11–16 weeks. Salad onions can be gathered in 10–12 weeks from a spring sowing but earliest crops come from August/September sowings.

Soil Well drained, light land, rich in organic matter suits onions best.

Yield 3.5 kg (8 lb) of bulbs from seed or sets, 2 kg (4.5 lb) of pickling onions and 1 kg (2 lb) of salad onions; each from 3 m (10 ft) rows.

Very much a vegetable with its friends and foes – though taste can change with age.

A very useful crop that can be easily stored for out-of-season use. Indeed, they have more uses in the kitchen than most other vegetables. They can be fried, boiled, roasted or pickled, and people with a strong constitution even eat them raw.

Sowing seed

When the soil is in good condition near sowing time, tread it down and rake it to produce a firm and fine seedbed; this is the secret of good onions.

In all but the coldest districts, Japanese varieties of bulb onions may be sown in August to overwinter outside and mature in early summer. The normal sowing time, though, is March/April to produce an August/September crop.

Sow thinly 1.3 cm (½ in) deep in rows 30 cm (12 in) apart for bulb and pickling onions, 10 cm (4 in) for salad onions.

Planting sets

Special sets are available for autumn planting and only these should be used; all others must be planted in the spring.

The ground is prepared as for sowing and the sets are planted 10–15 cm (4–6 in) apart with 30–40 cm (12–16 in) between rows.

Cultivation

If sowings of salad onions were thin enough, it should not be necessary to thin them.

Pickling onions should be singled to 1.3 cm (½ in) apart. Bulb onions should be thinned once or twice, to leave a final spacing of 7.5–10 cm (3–4 in). The thinnings can be used for salads.

Onions must be kept free of weeds but take care not to catch them with the hoe. Water as required but stop once the tops have gone over and started to yellow. The soil can then be drawn away from the bulb to improve ripening. Any flowerheads that appear should be snapped off.

Pests and diseases

The worst pest is the onion fly and the most troublesome disease, white rot.

Birds can also be tiresome as they often pull recently planted sets out of the ground. Combat this by snipping off the dry neck of the plant at the top.

Harvesting

Salad onions are gathered in bunches before they start to swell into bulbs at the base.

When the leaves of bulb onions have toppled over and started to go yellow, the crop can be lifted and allowed to dry on a wire netting frame raised a few inches off the ground. Once dry, they can be stored either by plaiting the tops together with raffia or by keeping them loose in net bags.

Very large onions tend not to store as well as the smaller ones, so bear this in mind when drawing from your stock and use the large ones first.

Solidity, quite bolt-resistant, is good for autumn sowing; it gives solid bulbs.

GROWING ONIONS FROM SETS

1. Before planting onion sets, cut off any old leaves that would attract the birds after planting.

2. By mid-spring, plant sets 15 cm (6in) apart in shallow drills 30 cm (12in) apart, with 'necks' uppermost.

3. Have a look at the sets a week or two after planting; press back into the soil any that have moved.

RIPENING AND STORING ONIONS

1. If the ground is wet at harvesting time, ripen bulbs by placing them on a platform raised from the ground.

2. If it is raining at harvesting time, ripen bulbs in a cold frame, as shown here, or move them into a shed.

3. You can store ripe, thoroughly dry bulbs in trays with slatted bases in an airy, dry, frost-proof place.

STORING ONIONS ON A STRING

Tie a length of string into a loop and hang it onto a nail in the wall or roof of the storage place. Knot the loop end of the string around the neck of the bottom onion bulb.

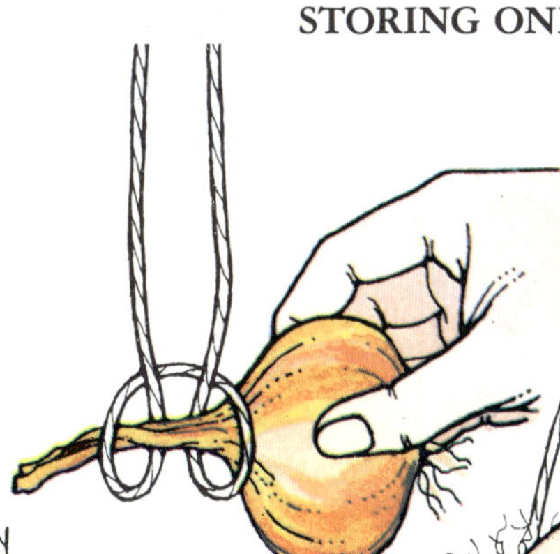

Knot the second onion, twisting the neck through the rope as indicated.

Add the rest of the bulbs one by one, to form a spiral 'rope' of onions.

SWEET CORN

Sowing to harvest 12–16 weeks.

Soil Any soil will do, provided it is rich in organic matter. The site must be sunny.

Yield Normally two ears per plant.

Sweet corn is the refined version of the plant from which corn flakes are made. For years it had to be imported from America, until plant breeders came up with a variety that was successful in the U.K. There are now many. Even so, it is by no means a success every year (lack of sun and warmth), and is really only a viable proposition in the southern half of the country. If you do have a suitably sheltered site, however, sweet corn is well worth a try.

Sowing

The best and earliest crops are had from sowings made under heated glass or indoors in April. There is no point in starting sooner because the plants cannot go outside until the risk of frost is over. Seeds to be raised under cover are sown singly in 7.5 cm (3 in) peat pots.

Alternatively, the seed can be sown outdoors in pairs (two per station) in late May. Sow 2.5 cm (1 in) deep, 45 cm (18 in) apart and in rows 60 cm (24 in) apart. Sweet corn is wind pollinated so it must be planted in near-square blocks; the length of the individual rows is unimportant.

Cultivation

Once the outdoor sown seedlings have developed sufficiently, remove the weaker plant at each station. Those raised under cover can be planted out 45 × 60 cm (18 × 24 in) once the risk of frost is over.

The roots of sweet corn are very close to the surface and, during growth, the plants need plenty of water. Therefore, they benefit greatly from a good thick mulch of well rotted garden compost. Try to avoid hoeing because this can damage the roots.

Pests and diseases

None of any great importance.

Harvesting

The first indication that the ears are beginning to ripen is that the formerly green silks that hang out of the top of the ear go brown. The next step is to expose the seeds and squeeze one or two of them between finger and thumb-nail. If a clear liquid comes out, the cob is not yet ripe. If it is milky and just starting to thicken, the cob should be perfect. Usually, if you leave the cobs too long on the stalks the sugar they contain will begin turning into starch.

Once it has gone doughy, or even mealy, then it is well past its best and really needs to be cooked, scraped off the cob and mixed with other vegetables such as peas or broad beans. The ear should be twisted from the plant or cut off with secateurs.

Store any surplus by freezing.

Break up the stalks with a spade, and put them on the compost heap.

SOWING OUTDOORS

1. Warm soil up by putting cloches on soil two weeks before sowing date.

2. Sow seeds in 2.5 cm (1in) deep drills. Place seeds in pairs 45 cm (18 in) apart.

CARE AND CULTIVATION

1

2

3

1. Start thinning when plants are 20–25 cm (8–10in) high, removing the weaker plants.

2. Water plants well, particularly in dry weather.

3. Mulch with straw in mid-summer to conserve moisture and keep down weeds.

4

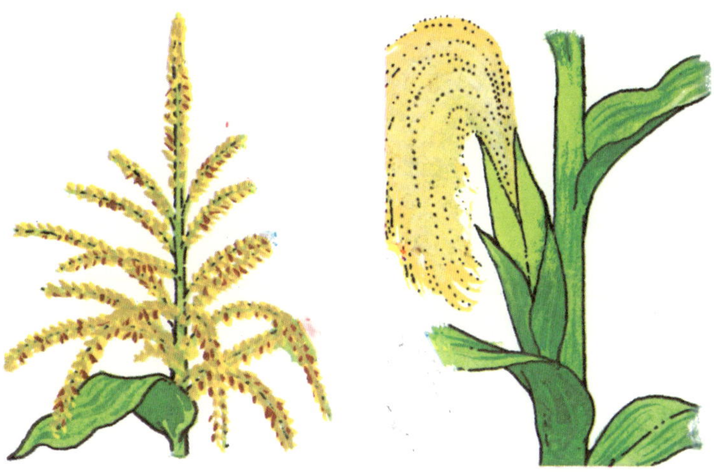

5

4. To assist pollination, gently shake the male tassels to release pollen.

5. Male flowers are the dark brown tassels on the top of the stalk (left). Female flowers are the creamy-white silks lower down the plant (right).

6

7

8

6. Ripe corn has dark brown, damp tassels; those on over-ripe corn are dry and shrivelled

7. Test for ripeness by piercing a kernel; 'milk' will spurt out if corn is ripe.

8. To pick, grasp cob firmly, and pull it downwards from the stalk.

CARROTS

Sowing to harvest time For earlies being grown in frames, about 7 weeks. Maincrop varieties are ready in about 4 months.

Soil Carrots don't only thrive on sandy soils, though they do prefer light land that is not full of stones. Most soil can be made suitable with time and care. What is more important is that the right varieties are grown for the soil; that is, avoid long rooted varieties on heavy or stony land, stick to stump rooted.

Yield Maincrop varieties – 4 kg (9 lb) from a 3 m (10 ft) row. Early varieties will give about half that.

Carrots are one of the most popular vegetables, both in kitchens and gardens. With a little care, they are easy to grow and varieties are available to suit all conditions. The principal virtue of the carrot is its length of season. It can be grown in frames for early crops, when they are used while still young, or left to mature before being lifted for winter use.

Sowing
Like all root crops, carrots do best on soil that was thoroughly prepared for the previous crop. Bulky organic matter should not be used prior to sowing as the difference in soil texture will cause 'fanging' of the roots. Before sowing, rake the soil into a firm and fine tilth.

Sow earlies at fortnightly intervals from March. Maincrop varieties can be sown from April until the end of July. Sow the seed thinly (to reduce the amount of thinning needed later) in 1.3 cm (½ in) deep drills, 20 cm (8 in) apart for earlies and 30 cm (12 in) for maincrop.

Those being grown in frames for very early use can be scattered and raked in. After sowing and covering, firm the drill down with the head of the rake.

Cultivation
Carrots normally need to be thinned out but this can be greatly reduced, or even avoided completely, by using pelleted seed. The advantage of this latter method is that thinning can attract the carrot fly. However, if thinning, do it as soon as the seedlings are large enough to handle and single them to 5 cm (2 in) apart. Thin again, if necessary, to 10 cm (4 in), using the thinnings in the kitchen.

Water the rows straight after thinning to settle the plants back in and to prevent them wilting. If they wilt, a strong scent is given off which attracts the carrot fly. Indeed, carrots should always be kept well watered so that they grow steadily, thus preventing splitting.

Pests and diseases
Carrot fly is certainly the worst pest but aphids can be very damaging if allowed to take hold.

Harvesting
The earliest sowings should be pulled when about pencil thickness but maincrop sowings are lifted when required. Carrots destined for storage are best left until October, to ensure that growth has finished and the roots are mature. They should then be lifted and stored either in bags or dry sand. If the tops are still green when lifting for storage, they should be cut off to leave 2.5 cm (1 in) of stalks.

Carrots grown on stony or freshly manured soils may become forked (left), rather than straight.

CULTIVATION

1. Hoe regularly between the rows of seedlings to remove weeds.

2. When the seedlings are 2.5 cm (1in) high, thin to a spacing of 5 cm (2in) apart. Water the soil before thinning.

3. Firm in the remaining plants and water the ground to deter the carrot fly, which is attracted by the carrot smell.

4. Sprinkle bonemeal between the plants in the rows, and water the ground again.

HARVESTING

1

2

3

4

1. Water the ground the night before harvesting so that the young carrots can be easily pulled by hand.

2. To lift mature carrots in autumn, a fork is necessary.

3. Before storing, use a sharp knife to cut off the tops close to the neck.

4. Autumn crops can be stored for winter use. Pack them evenly between layers of dry sand in a large wooden box, and keep the box in a frostproof shed.

PARSNIPS

Sowing to harvest time From 17 weeks.

Soil As with carrots, the need is for light and rich soils of sufficient depth and freedom from stones to allow the roots to develop properly. Avoid long-rooted varieties in shallow soils.

Deep digging should have been done before the previous crop.

Yield 4 kg (9 lb) from a 3 m (10 ft) row.

An excellent winter vegetable that provides a welcome change from cabbage and Brussels sprouts, and is quite easily grown – given reasonable soil conditions.

Sowing
Seed takes a long time (about 6 weeks) to germinate and should be sown into a fine seedbed, in March or April. Rather than sprinkling the seed, space-sowing three seeds per station is more economical. Sow 1.3 cm (½ in) deep. Broad-rooted varieties should be space-sown 15 cm (6 in) apart with 30 cm (12 in) between rows. Smaller varieties may be 7–8 cm (3 in) apart in rows 19 cm (7.5 in) apart.

Cultivation
Seedlings should be thinned to the above distances if not space-sown, or singled if they have, as soon as they can be handled. (It is not worthwhile to replant these thinnings elsewhere.)

Keep them well watered to encourage steady growth and prevent splitting. Hoe to keep the weeds down but be careful not to catch the shoulders of the parsnip with the hoe; such a wound can be an entry point for canker.

Pests and diseases
Aphids and carrot fly (as for carrots) but, additionally, leaf miner and canker. Avonresister is resistant to canker.

SOWING AND CULTIVATION

1. Work the soil to a fine tilth and prepare drills 30 cm (12in) apart and 1.3 cm (½in) deep.

2. Sow three or four seeds at each station, spacing them 15 cm (6 in) apart from each other.

3. It is a good idea to raise a catch crop of lettuce between the parsnips, to mark your row.

4. Thin the seedlings when they are about 5 cm (2") tall, leaving only the strongest at each station.

5. Water if the weather is dry. This is especially important during the crop's early stages.

6. Hoe as necessary, taking care not to damage the shoulders of developing roots in any way.

Harvesting

The roots are best left until well frosted in the autumn; this seems to bring the flavour out. They can then be lifted and stored damp, to stop them drying out, but are really best left in the ground until wanted. In cold districts, a wise precaution is to cover the rows with straw before the winter to prevent the ground freezing solid and making lifting impossible.

HARVESTING

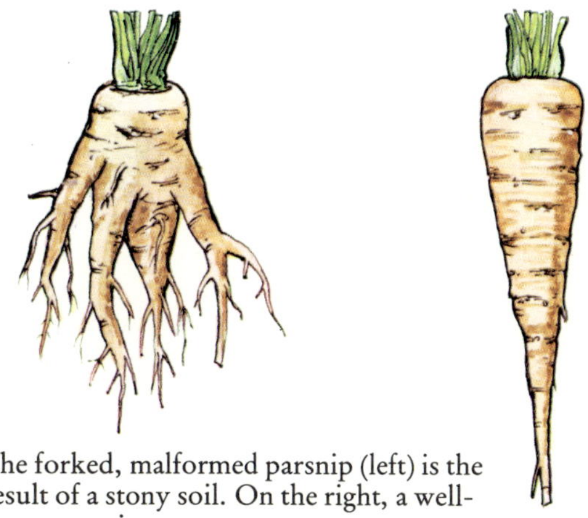

The forked, malformed parsnip (left) is the result of a stony soil. On the right, a well-grown specimen.

Begin at the end of the row and dig a hole close to the first parsnip, making sure it is as deep as the length you expect the parsnip to be. Loosen the soil around the parsnip and you will then be able to lift it easily without damage. Lift the next parsnip by removing the soil next to it into the hole you made for the first one and continue like this down the row.

Although parsnips are best left in the ground, it is a good idea to store some for when frost makes lifting impossible. Store them in boxes, using layers of peat or dry sand.

SWEDES

Sowing to harvest 13 weeks.

Soil Any fertile soil will grow swedes and, unlike carrots and parsnips, they have no limitations as regards stony or heavy land.

Yield 5 kg (11 lb) from a 3 m (10 ft) row.

Along with parsnips, swedes are essentially a winter root vegetable. They are normally served mashed to avoid the fibrous material that is often found in old roots, and taste rather like strong turnips. They are traditionally called 'neeps' in Scotland.

Swedes are hardier and sweeter than turnips, and they rarely become woody.

Sowing

Growing swedes could hardly be simpler, provided that the ground is reasonably fertile.

In cold districts, the seed should be sown by mid-June but, where it is warmer, this can be delayed until the end of the month. Sow thinly 1.3 cm (½ in) deep in rows 38–45 cm (15–18 in) apart.

CARE AND CULTIVATION

1. Three weeks after sowing, or when seedlings are at the rough-leaf stage, thin to 23 cm (9in) apart.

2. Keep down weeds by hoeing between rows and hand weeding between plants.

3. Keep the plants well watered until established; mulch with damp peat in very dry weather.

4. Protect the overwintering swedes from attack by pigeons and rabbits with netting or rabbit fencing.

Cultivation

Thin the seedlings to 23 cm (9 in) apart as soon as they are large enough to handle.

Swede tops make a pleasant change as a spring vegetable and they can be had simply by leaving part of a row unthinned.

Pests and diseases

Being of the same family (*Cruciferae*) as

HARVESTING AND STORING

1. To harvest, gently ease swedes out of ground with a garden fork.

2. Top and tail the swedes before storing for future use.

3. Storing in a clamp: dig drainage trench; place swedes on layer of straw.

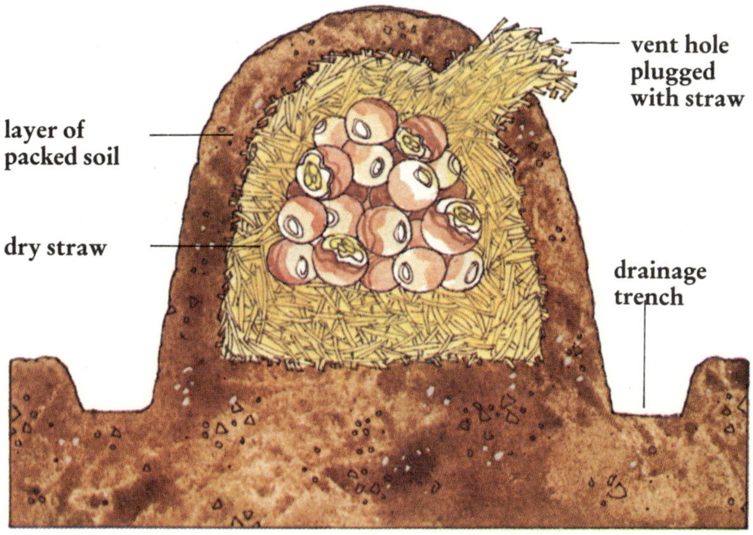

4. Build up heap of swedes. Cover them with another 10 cm (4in) layer of straw. Put a similar depth layer of soil over the straw, leaving a vent for access and air circulation.

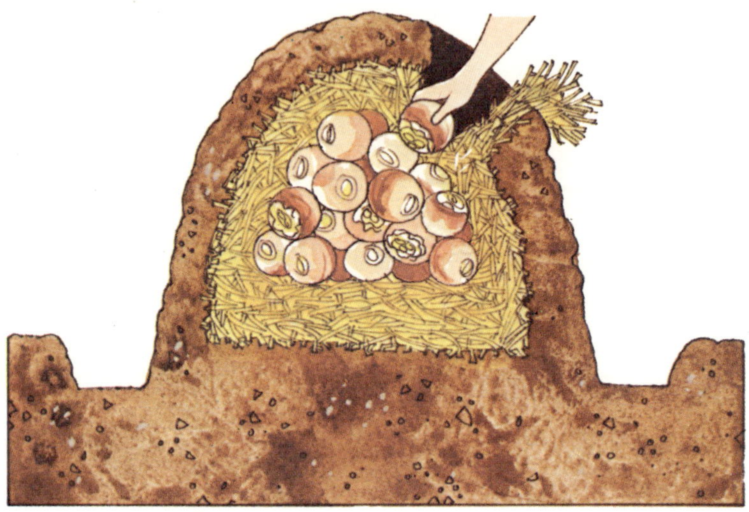

5. Remove swedes as you need them by unplugging the straw in the access vent and lifting the roots out. Replace the straw plug carefully.

PRODUCING BLANCHED STEMS

1. Dig up swedes in late autumn; cut back neck and root, plant in box filled with soil or peat. Water well and store in dark place.

2. Cut blanched shoots when they are 20 cm (8in) long.

brassicas, swedes are subject to much the same problems – flea beetle, cabbage root fly and clubroot disease.

Harvesting

Swedes can be lifted for use, and as required, from October onwards. In mild areas, they can be left in the ground over winter. If being stored, twist off the top growth and keep the swedes in sand or dry peat until needed.

TURNIPS

Sowing to harvest 6–9 weeks for early crops; 10–12 weeks for maincrop.

Soil Any fertile soil well supplied with nutrients and moisture is fine for turnips.

Yield 4 kg (9 lb) from a 3 m (10 ft) row.

Turnips come in all shapes and sizes and in a variety of colours from pure white to yellow; there are also turnips with purple skins and others with greenish gold.

Few people simply tolerate turnips – they are either loved or loathed.

Sowing

The soil for turnips should be dug and limed if necessary and broken down before sowing. Aim for a firm, fine seedbed, and be prepared to tread it down.

For early use, sow in succession from mid-April onwards in drills 1.3 cm (½ in) deep and 38 cm (15 in) apart. Sow maincrop turnips in late July, for lifting in October/November.

For turnip tops, sow in late August in rows 23–30 cm (9–12 in) apart.

Cultivation

Early and maincrop sowings should be thinned to 7.5 cm (3 in) apart once they have their first true leaves. Before crowding occurs, thin again to 15 cm (6 in) apart; use the thinnings in the kitchen.

Turnips should be grown fast to prevent them getting strong flavoured and woody so will need copious watering in dry weather. Hoe frequently to keep the soil open and free of weeds.

Pests and diseases

Flea beetle may seriously damage the seedlings. Cabbage root fly and club root can attack at all stages of growth.

Harvesting

Early sowings can be lifted when they are needed. They are at their best when about the size of a tennis-ball but are usable up to golf-ball size. Lift maincrop in October/November, dry them off, twist off the tops and store the roots in dry sand or peat.

CARE AND CULTIVATION

1. Thin to 15 cm (6in) apart for early crops and those for use as greens; space maincrops 22–30 cm (9–12in) apart.

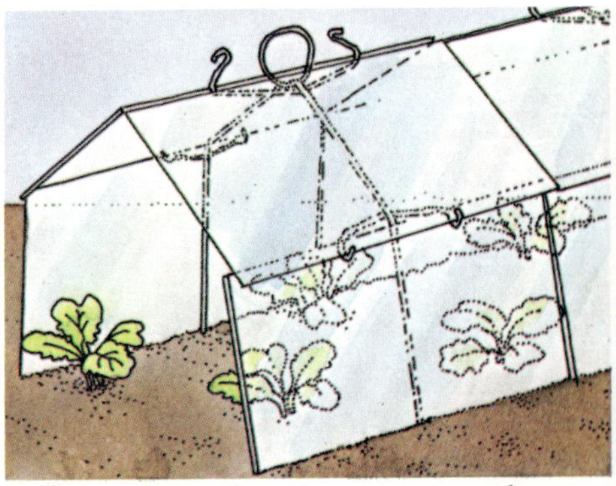

2. For early sowings in open ground, protect the plants with cloches if the weather turns cold or frost threatens.

3. The turnips should receive a steady supply of water while growing, or they will bolt without forming roots.

4. Keep the soil well hoed, being careful not to damage the roots; this controls weeds and keeps soil aerated.

HARVESTING AND STORING

1. Pick early turnips when they are the size of a tennis ball; maincrops can be left in the ground until needed.

2. Pull turnip tops when they are 15 cm (6in) high; do not pull more than two leaves from a plant at one time.

3. In cold areas, lift maincrops in late autumn for storing; place roots in boxes between layers of peat or sand.

Red Globe

SALSIFY AND SCORZONERA

Sowing to harvest 16 weeks.

Soil Any soil, provided it is rich in organic matter and well drained. This usually means that double digging is needed as both have a long tap root. Otherwise, and in stony ground, the roots are likely to divide.

Yield 3 kg (6.5 lb) from a 3 m (10 ft) row.

Salsify, which is white-skinned, has a distinctive and somewhat fishy taste, hence it's common name of 'vegetable oyster'. Scorzonera is black-skinned and less fishy. Both are valuable winter root vegetables.

Sowing
A fine and crumbly seedbed is needed. Sow thinly in March/April in drills 1.3 cm (½ in) deep and 30 cm (12 in) apart.

Cultivation
Thin the seedlings to 23 cm (9 in) apart when they are large enough to handle.

Keep the plants well watered and free from weeds, but hoe with great care as both vegetables are likely to bleed if nicked.

Pests and diseases
Slugs and snails.

Harvesting
Except in the coldest areas, the roots can be left in the ground during the winter until required. Alternatively, in October/November they should be lifted carefully to avoid spearing or breaking them. Then twist off the tops and store the roots for the winter in dry sand or peat in a cool place.

Any dying foliage or discarded roots can be put to very good use on the compost heap.

If you live in an area where it is difficult to obtain seed commercially, it is a simple matter to allow a few plants to run to seed in their second summer. Store the seed in a dry cool place.

The long, tapering roots of salsify make a really delicious vegetable. Scorzonera, known as 'black salsify', has similar, black-skinned roots.

SEAKALE

Season of use March/April.

Soil Well drained and rich in organic matter.

Yield Varies with age but about 1 kg (2 lb) per plant.

This is the cultivated version of the plant that grows wild on the seashore. It is a perennial with a useful productive life of about five years. The curly green leaves are excellent raw in salads but it is the forced and blanched leaf stalks and young shoots, when cooked, that are the real attraction.

Propagation and planting

The easiest way to propagate seakale, and thereby also to maintain a good stock, is from root cuttings, or 'thongs', in early spring. These should be of not less than pencil thickness and 10–15 cm (4–6 in) long. Cut them flat across the top and obliquely at the bottom, to prevent planting them upside-down.

Plant them 30 cm (12 in) apart, with the tips 1.3 cm (½ in) deep. Allow 45 cm (18 in) between rows. You will need about 15 thongs for a useful supply.

Seakale can also be raised from seed but the plants are often variable and not always high quality. However, you can root propagate from selected plants later on.

Cultivation

A number of young shoots will develop from each thong the season after planting. Reduce these to just one per plant and remove any flower stems that appear. Hoe to keep the weeds down and water copiously during dry spells. If possible, give a good mulch of well rotted garden compost to help with both these needs.

Remove the foliage after it has died down in October as it provides an excellent home for slugs.

Twelve months after planting, a few leaves can be taken from the plants but make no attempt to force it. The first two years must be spent in establishing and building up the plants.

The following January, loosen the soil between the rows and ridge it up over the dormant plants; making sure that there is plenty of compost with it. Cover the plants to a depth of about 25 cm (10 in). The blanched stems will be ready in April.

If you have a greenhouse, you can force the plants in boxes under the staging. To do this, lift them in early winter and trim the roots to leave just the thick, central one. Suitable trimmings can be used for propagation. Pack the main roots together in boxes of spent potting compost, place them under the staging and keep them dark. Do this with a few roots at a time to give a succession.

Pests and diseases

None of major importance: slugs and snails are easily dealt with.

Harvesting

The shoots from forced plants are ready for cutting when they are 15–23 cm (6–9 in) long. After harvesting, allow outdoor plants to grow normally. With those forced under the staging, cut the complete crown from the plant when it is ready and throw away the forced root.

PLANTING

1. Dig the soil in autumn. Then add seaweed or manure.

2. Rub off all pointed buds to avoid unwanted flowering shoots.

3. Plant in early spring using a dibber to make holes 23 cm (9in) deep and spaced 30 cm (12in) apart. Cover crowns with crumbled soil, making small mound.

OUTDOOR BLANCHING

1. Remove any weeds and flowering stems as soon as they are seen.

2. Seakale does not like dry soil. During hot, dry weather, water soil frequently, keeping it moist. In spring, a mulch of moist peat will deter weeds.

3. In autumn, remove all the old leaves; fork lightly round roots.

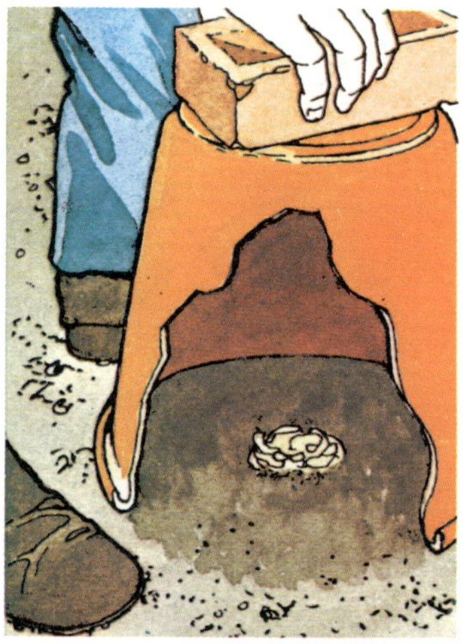

4. Cover crowns with bucket; weight down with a brick.

5. Surround bucket with wire netting, leaving 7.5 cm (3in) space between bucket and netting. Fill space with leafmould to protect from cold.

6. In spring cut the blanched shoots cleanly with a sharp knife.

ASPARAGUS

Season of use From April when the shoots are 15–20 cm (6–8 in) long.

Soil For best results, the soil must be light, sandy if possible, neutral in reaction and have good drainage. Heavy soil can be made quite suitable, if plenty of bulky organic matter is added during preparation of the bed and as an annual mulch afterwards.

Yield 2 kg (4.5 lb) from 3 m (10 ft) of row but increasing with the age of the plants.

In many people's minds, asparagus means luxury. This is only true if you do not have a garden of your own because it is a perfectly easy vegetable to grow. It just costs a lot if you have to buy it in the shops.

Where there is room to grow it, it's worth doing so. Those delicious shoots that you cut in the spring are worth any hard work – assuming, of course, that you like it. Asparagus does take a few years to establish a bed but, once there and if looked after, it has about the same length of life as a fruit tree: around twenty years.

Propagation

It is usually far better to buy professionally raised plants but you can grow your own from seed. This should be sown thinly during April and, preferably, soaked overnight to soften the coat. Cover the seed 1.3 cm (½ in) deep in nursery rows 30 cm (12 in) apart. When the seedlings are some 15 cm (6 in) high, thin them to 30 cm (12 in) apart. Transplant them to their permanent bed in the following April.

Planting

The bed should be prepared during the winter before planting by spreading a good 15 cm (6 in) deep layer of well rotted compost or manure over the ground and working it in two spade's deep. If necessary, add lime to make the soil neutral. One-year-old asparagus crowns should be ordered for April delivery. When they arrive, they should be planted as soon as possible in the prepared ground in rows. If they have to be kept for a few days before planting, make sure that the roots never dry out.

The rows should be in trenches 15 cm (6 in) deep and the plants are set 40 cm (16 in) apart. The rows should be 60 cm (2 ft) apart. Cover the crowns with 7.5–10 cm (3–4 in) of soil, leaving the surplus for gradually filling up the trenches during the summer.

Cultivation

Keep the beds free from weeds and well watered. In June or July dress the bed with a general feed. Cut the 'ferns' down to the ground in early November and top dress the bed with well rotted compost or manure. Every February, give the bed a feed containing plenty of nitrogen.

Pests and diseases

Asparagus seems to be as great a delicacy to pests as it does to humans. The larvae of the asparagus beetle feed on the foliage; cutworms eat the roots and slugs delight in the young shoots.

Harvesting

Refrain from cutting any shoots the same year as planting. In the following spring, you may cut one thick shoot from each plant. Use a saw-edged bread knife to make the cut, 5 cm (2 in) below ground when the shoots are about 15 cm (6 in) long. The following spring, cut and use all the shoots which appear over the first five weeks. Thereafter, the season lasts for 6–8 weeks, depending on the strength of the plants. In a bed's final year, cutting may continue as long as it is worthwhile.

Asparagus freezes well.

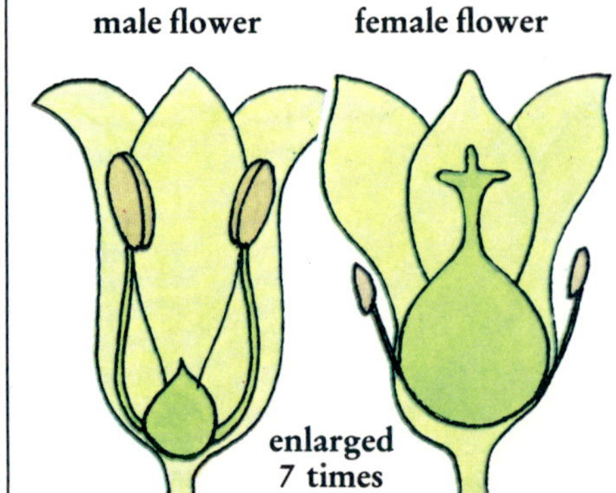

Female asparagus plants are inferior croppers, and plants bearing female flowers should be removed.

CARE AND CULTIVATION

1. Hoe lightly to keep weeds down; do not hoe deeply or you may damage the shallow roots.

2. The first year you harvest, pick only two or three stalks from each plant, early in the season.

3. Cut the shoots with a sharp knife. Try to cut as close to the base of the stalk as possible.

4. After harvesting, keep the beds well watered, particularly in long spells of hot, dry weather.

5. Use bamboo canes or pea-sticks to support summer foliage so it is not blown over by wind.

6. Cut foliage down to ground level in autumn, when it begins to turn yellow, and tidy up the beds.

GROWING ASPARAGUS FROM SEED

1. In spring, just before sowing, rake the soil to a fine tilth.

2. To make seeds germinate quickly, soak them in water before sowing.

3. Sow the seeds thinly in drills 1.3 cm (½in) deep, with 30 cm (12in) space between the drills.

5. Thin seedlings first to 5 cm (2in) apart, and then to 30 cm (12in) apart when they are 15 cm (6in) high.

7. After cutting down foliage, apply a mulch of well-rotted manure, seaweed or garden compost.

8. In late winter apply potash to the bed in the form of wood ash, and rake it in very lightly to avoid damage.

CELERY

Sowing to harvest From about 20 weeks.

Soil Must be well drained but moisture retentive, so plenty of organic matter is called for.

Yield 6.5 kg (14 lb) from 3 m (10 ft) row.

An acquired taste and not loved by everyone, celery produces crisp stalks which are eaten raw with salads from late summer to spring of the following year. It is also splendid as a cooked vegetable or in soups and stews. There are two kinds of celery: the traditional trench-grown varieties that provide stalks from autumn to spring and self-blanching varieties which are ready from late summer. These latter have a milder flavour and have done away with the need for trenches, but they are not as hardy as the trench type.

Sowing

Both sorts are best sown in heat in mid-February and pricked out into seedtrays or individual peat pots when the seedlings are large enough, in order to keep them growing steadily.

Planting

Plant outside in about June when the plants are outgrowing their pots or crowding in the tray. Self-blanching celery is planted 23 cm (9 in) each way so that it is encouraged to blanch naturally by being slightly crowded. The winter

SOWING CELERY

1. Sow the seeds under glass from early to mid-spring. Sow them thinly in seed compost and cover with a fine layer of compost.

2. When you can hold the seedlings between finger and thumb, prick them out 5 cm (2in) apart into boxes.

WINTER CELERY

1. Dig a trench 30 cm (12in) deep and to the appropriate width (see page 78) in late winter. Fork over bottom of trench to loosen soil; work in organic matter. Then cover with 7.5 cm (3in) topsoil. Make finished level of trench 15–20 cm (6–8in) lower than the ground.

2. When plants are about 25 cm (10 in) high begin earthing-up. Remove sideshoots, suckers and tiny leaves; remove and destroy slugs. Wrap plants in newspaper and tie with raffia to keep soil from getting into celery heart. Place 10 cm (4in) soil from adjacent ridge around base of each plant. Earth-up.

3. If your soil is not too dry, plant quick catch crops on the ridge of soil next to the trench. Lettuce, dwarf beans, or radishes can be raised in this way.

4. Earth-up again in late summer and again in early autumn. Each time add another 10 cm (4in) to the soil around the plants. After the final earthing-up, only the leaves should be visible.

5. To harvest, scrape back soil until you see the roots.

6. When the roots are exposed, carefully lever out plant.

1

2

1

2

3

4

5

6

varieties need to be planted in a special trench. This is prepared in advance by digging out the soil 30 cm (12 in) deep and 38 cm (15 in) wide for a single row of plants or 45 cm (18 in) wide for a double row. Dig plenty of bulky organic matter into the bottom of the trench. Then return the soil to raise the bottom of the trench to within 15 cm (6 in) of the top. Use the remaining soil to make ridges 7.5 cm (3 in) high on either side of the trench. Lettuces or radishes can be grown along these.

Set the plants 25 cm (10 in) apart down the middle of the trench if growing a single row. If a double row, space the plants 30 cm (12 in) apart in the row, with 25 cm (10 in) between the rows. Do not stagger the rows as having them opposite each other makes them easier to earth up. Once the trench is planted, flood it with water to settle the soil around the plants' roots.

To improve the blanch of summer celery, plant it in square blocks. Erect a framework of stakes and sacking or plastic around the plants to exclude light. As rows are harvested, move the frame in, to shade remaining celery.

An alternative, but less flexible way is to grow it in a cold frame, as the sides of the frame keep out the light.

Cultivation

When the trench varieties are about 25 cm (10 in) high, blanching can begin. Remove any side shoots, wrap the stems in loosely tied newspaper collars and start to fill in the trench with the soil from the ridges on each side. Finish the earthing up in September so that only the leaves at the top are visible.

Pests and diseases

Celery fly, aphids and leaf spot fungus can all be troublesome but leaf miner is usually the most noticeable.

Harvesting

Lift the self-blanching varieties as you need them. The trench varieties are ready about nine weeks after the start of earthing up. Lift and clean the plants from the end of the row as required but avoid too much disturbance to neighbouring plants.

If a heavy frost is likely, dig out a few plants before the ground can become solid. Dig them out complete with the roots. Remove the outside leaves and any stalks that are damaged. Then pack them upright in a box of moist sand and keep them in a shed or cellar, just above freezing point. Until the celery is used, keep the sand moist.

FENNEL

Sowing to harvest About 20 weeks.

Soil No special requirements, though light and sandy soil is preferred.

Yield 2–3 kg (4.5–6.5 lb) from a 3 m (10 ft) row.

An unusual vegetable and one not grown an awful lot here (though it is very popular in Italy), maybe because of its distinctive taste of aniseed. It is an umbelliferous plant whose swollen stem base is eaten raw in salads, or it can be braised or boiled.

Sowing and planting

The seed is sown in April 1.3 cm (½ in) deep, and may be sown in nursery rows for later planting out or direct into rows 45 cm (18 in) apart. If transplanting, set the seedlings 20 cm (8 in) apart in the row.

Cultivation

Directly sown plants should be progressively thinned to 20 cm (8 in) apart. Start this as soon as they are large enough to handle.

Keep all plants well watered and free from weeds. As the stems start to swell, draw the soil up and around them to blanch them.

Pests and diseases

Almost none.

Harvesting

Lift the plants as required when the swollen stem bases are about 7.5 cm (3 in) in diameter. The surplus crop, including the leaves, can be frozen.

Drawing up earth to blanch the bases.

Fennel plants mulched with black plastic sheeting.

ARTICHOKE (globe)

Green Globe

Season of use Two-year-old plants will crop from June onwards; one-year-olds will crop in the autumn of their first year.

Soil This should be well drained and rich in organic matter.

Yield 4–6 primary heads and 10–12 secondary heads per plant.

Not to be confused with the Jerusalem artichoke (which is a tuber), the globe artichoke is a large and decorative, thistle-like perennial with greyish, deeply cut leaves. It is the fleshy scales around the flower buds that are eaten.

Propagation and planting

It is far better to buy plants from a specialist grower than to raise them from seed, which produces variable plants, most of which will be of poor quality.

To propagate from existing plants, remove rooted side shoots in the spring and pot these up singly in 13 cm (5 in) pots. Once they are growing strongly, they can be planted out into nursery rows or into their final place. When planting out, set the plants into well prepared positions 90 cm (36 in) apart each way. Water in well.

Cultivation

Keep the weeds down and water as necessary during dry spells. Mulching with a good thick layer of well rotted compost or manure is a great help. Apply the mulch annually in the late spring, after the plants have started into growth.

Each autumn, cut the stems down to within 5 cm (2 in) of the ground. Clear away the old leaves and the dead stumps of stems that were cut down twelve months previously. In cold districts, straw should then be placed over the plants to protect them from the worst of the winter.

When a plant has come to the end of its cropping life and you decide to replace it, it can be made to produce a single crop of blanched shoots, called 'chards' in the autumn. Chards are tender shoots which are cooked like seakale beet.

To produce 'chards', cut the stems down to 30 cm (12 in) high after harvesting the flowers; this will encourage new shoots to form. When these are 60 cm (24 in) high, tie them loosely together and blanch them for about 6 weeks with black polythene collars.

Pests and diseases

Largely trouble free.

Harvesting

Cut the flower buds from late June onwards when they are plump and tender but still tightly closed. The primary heads will be ready first; the secondary ones when they are about the size of golfballs.

When grown for chards, the plants should be discarded after harvesting them.

PLANTING AND CULTIVATION

1. Plant rooted offsets in mid- to late spring; space them 90–120 cm (3–4ft) apart, with 1.2m (4ft) between rows.

2. Make sure the artichokes get plenty of water through spring and summer, particularly when the weather is dry.

3. To support tall-growing varieties, tie main stem to a strong stake inserted deeply into the soil.

HARVESTING

1. If any flower buds form in the first year of planting, remove them as soon as they are seen.

2. From the second year onwards, pick the king heads first, when they are about 10 cm (4in) in diameter.

3. To store surplus artichokes, cut them with 30 cm (12in) of stalk, and push the stems into damp sand.

BLANCHED CHARDS

1. In autumn, when leaves are 60 cm (2ft) high, tie them firmly together with soft twine or raffia.

2. Wrap brown corrugated paper around them, or, alternatively, cover them with plenty of clean, dry straw.

3. Lastly, earth up the whole lot with sifted soil or fine ashes, so that all light is excluded from the shoots.

ARTICHOKES (Jerusalem)

1. If you have no small tubers for planting, save on tubers by cutting large ones into small pieces. Each piece should have three buds.

2. Make holes 7.5 cm (3in) deep and 45–60 cm (18–24in) apart.

3. Plant one small tuber or a piece of a larger tuber in each hole and cover over with soil. Shoots should start to appear above the ground within two to four weeks.

4. Weed between the plants, drawing soil up around the stems in a mound.

5. On exposed sites, tie the plants to wires to protect them from the wind.

6. Cut the tops off the plants when they reach about 1.5 m (5ft) tall if not wanted as a screen.

Season of use November to February.

Soil Happy with anything but, preferably, not too heavy or the tubers become even more strangely shaped.

Belonging to the same family as the globe artichoke, this plant is also perennial and very decorative as it produces tall stems carrying large yellow daisy flowers. It requires quite a lot of space but is ideal where it can be used as a screen. The potato-like but rough and knobbly roots are the edible part.

The name 'Jerusalem' is a corruption of the Italian 'girasole' meaning 'turning to the sun', referring to the flowers' habit.

Planting
Plant the tubers in February/March, 7.5 cm (3 in) deep and 45–60 cm (18–24 in) apart, in rows spaced 1 m (3 ft) apart.

Cultivation
All that is really necessary is to keep the weeds down.

Pests and diseases
None worth bothering about.

Harvesting
Once the tops show signs of dying down for the winter (October/November), the tubers can be lifted for use as required. This is normally better than lifting the whole lot together because they shrivel very readily. Be sure to remove all you can find as they become a menace if harvested carelessly so that many small tubers are left in the ground which will produce weedy plants the following year.

PLANTING AND CULTIVATION

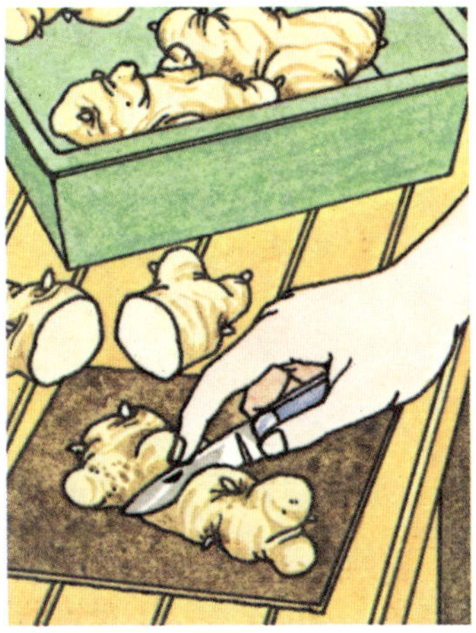

1

2

3

4

5

6

HARVESTING AND STORING

1. Fork the tubers up, being careful not to spear any or to leave any in the ground. If tubers are left, they will grow up next year like weeds.

2. Store a few tubers, sandwich fashion, in containers of dry peat or sand for winter periods when fresh tubers cannot be lifted from frozen ground.

POTATOES

Planting to harvest Earlies: about 14 weeks. Maincrop: about 20 weeks.

Soil Most soils are suitable but they should be well broken up so that the tubers can form properly and not have to fight for their existence among clods.

Yield 6–10 kg (13–22 lb) from a 3 m (10 ft) row.

The potato is a nutritious vegetable and nowhere near as fattening as it is commonly supposed. Some varieties are white, floury and ideal for mashing or baking. Others are waxy in texture and ideal for salads. New potatoes, fresh from the ground, are rich in vitamin C and have a flavour that few shop-bought potatoes can compete with.

Planting

Potatoes are often the most suitable vegetable to grow in what is called 'virgin' land – ground that has not been cultivated as a garden before. In spite of that, they still need good conditions to thrive.

Dig the ground in the autumn and incorporate plenty of bulky organic matter. But avoid adding lime then because it can encourage the fungus disease Scab.

Buy seed tubers of first early varieties as soon as they appear in the shops in the spring and stand them, rose end upwards, in seedtrays or empty egg trays. Place these in a cool but airy and not dark place so that shoots begin to grow from the 'eyes'.

Work on the basis that earlies should be planted about four weeks before the last frost is expected and that maincrop are planted from mid-April to mid-May.

A 9 m (30 ft) of row will take about 4 kg (9 lb) of seed tubers. At the appropriate planting time, take out V-shaped drills about 15 cm (6 in) deep. Those for earlies should be 60 cm (24 in) apart and those for maincrop 75 cm (30 in). The tubers of earlies are planted 30 cm (12 in) apart and those of maincrop varieties 38 cm (15 in).

The tubers should be set rose-end up in the drills, then shallowly covered with good crumbly soil or, if that is not possible, garden compost. This is to ensure that the young roots have a good start in life. Carry on filling in the drill and finish with the row showing as a slight ridge.

Cultivation

If there is still a risk of frost when the first shoots appear, draw a little soil over them for protection and be ready to cover the rows with old sheets or polythene if a severe frost threatens.

When the shoots are about 22 cm (9 in) tall, start earthing up by forking the soil loose between the rows and drawing it up over the tops with a broad swan-neck hoe to produce a ridge some 15 cm (6 in) high. This will also keep the weeds at bay. Earth up again if a lot of top growth forms.

When the young tubers are some 2.5 cm (1 in) across, give the bed a thorough soaking, unless the soil is already very moist.

Pests and diseases

Wireworm can be a real menace by drilling holes into the tubers (old and new), particularly on land that was previously meadow.

Potato Blight is a killer in a wet summer. Not only does the fungus destroy the foliage but it also spreads to the new tubers and completely destroys them. It is recognized by brown spreading marks on the leaves and possibly the collapse of the haulm (top growth). On the tubers, it is seen first as sunken areas on the surface – with a reddish discolouration in the flesh beneath. The best answer to blight in wet areas is to grow only earlies as these are harvested before the disease has built up. Greenfly can also be troublesome.

Harvesting

The only sure indication as to when to lift earlies is to scrape away some soil and look at the progress of the young tubers. When you consider them to be large enough for lifting, dig up only the plants you need; the rest will continue to grow.

Maincrop varieties should be lifted by the middle of October. Make sure that they are reasonably dry and free from mud before bagging up and storing them until needed. Store them in a frost-free place, making sure that it really *is* safe from the sharpest frost.

HANDY HINT

Tubers will turn green if exposed to light – and once that happens, they contain a poisonous substance that makes them dangerous to eat. So, several times during the growing period loosen up the soil between rows and push some up on both sides of the haulms, leaving only the top 15 cm (6in) of leaves uncovered.

GROWING SEED POTATOES

1. Put the tubers in egg boxes, top upwards, to encourage sprouting.

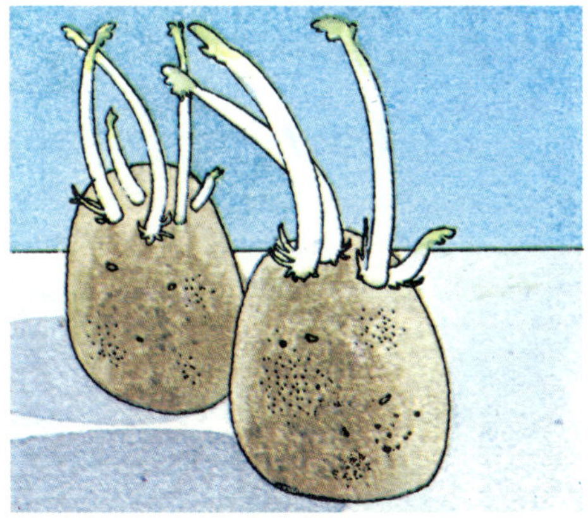

2. Too much warmth or darkness produces shoots unfit for planting.

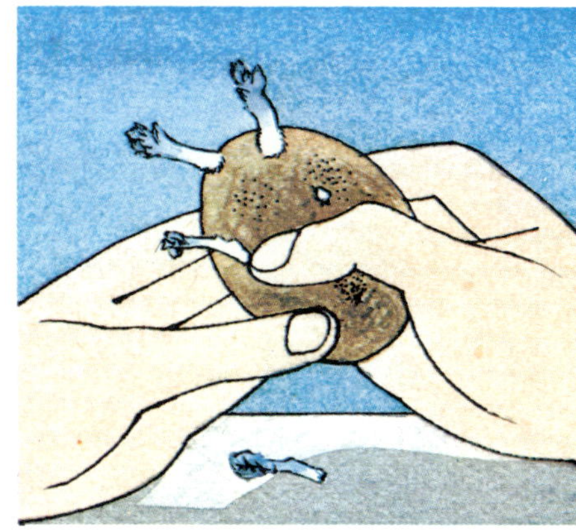

3. Rub off the sprout at the extreme top and all but the two most sturdy.

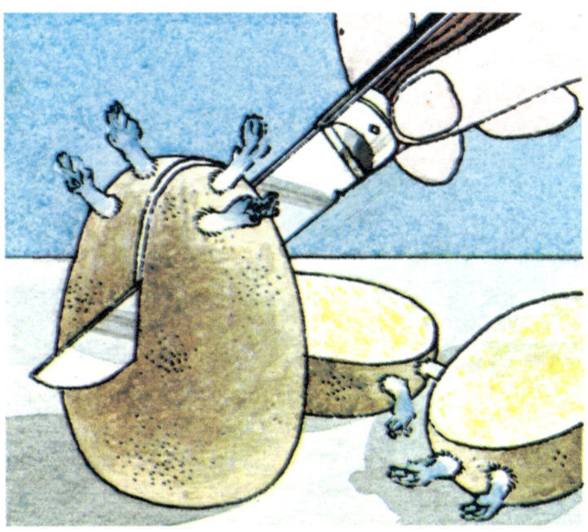

4. Cut large tubers into two. Protect cut surfaces with flowers of sulphur.

5. Prepare ground by digging over and then manuring before sowing.

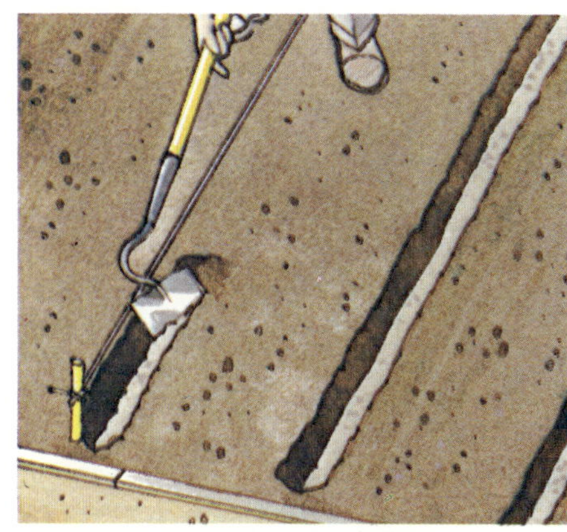

6. Dig v-shaped furrows 8–15 cm (3¼–6in) deep for planting sets.

7. When haulms are 7.5 cm (3in) high, cover them with straw to give protection against damage by frost.

8. Begin earthing-up when the haulms reach 20 cm (8in) to aid production and protect from light.

9. Yellowish leaves indicate the crop is ready. Lift carefully to avoid damaging the tubers.

LETTUCE

Sowing to harvest 9–12 weeks for summer varieties.

Soil Must be well drained and full of organic matter to encourage rapid growth.

Yield 10–30 lettuces from a 3 m (10 ft) row.

There are three main types of lettuce: butterhead, crisp and cos. Butterheads have for years been the standard lettuce grown in gardens but these are being overtaken by the crisp Webb's Wonderful type. Although the large cos lettuce is normally too big for most families, the much smaller Little Gem is very popular as it produces really hard lettuces with plenty of leaf from very little space. Loose 'cut and come again' varieties are also being grown a lot more now.

Lettuces for maturing in winter and early spring are grown throughout under cover.

Sowing

First sowings can be made in January/February in a heated greenhouse, ready for planting outside later. At the same time, make a sowing in a cold frame; this can be followed by an outdoor sowing in

CULTIVATION

1. For early spring sowings outdoors, prepare shallow drills and sow the seed very thinly.

2. Thin when two leaves have formed. If thinnings are to be transplanted, handle gently by one leaf only.

3. Prepare the holes before transplanting, put the seedlings in and water the ground well.

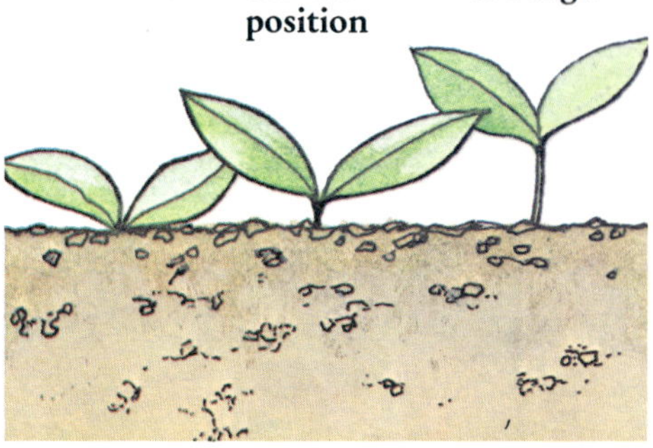

4. Take care to transplant the seedlings with the neck exactly level with the soil.

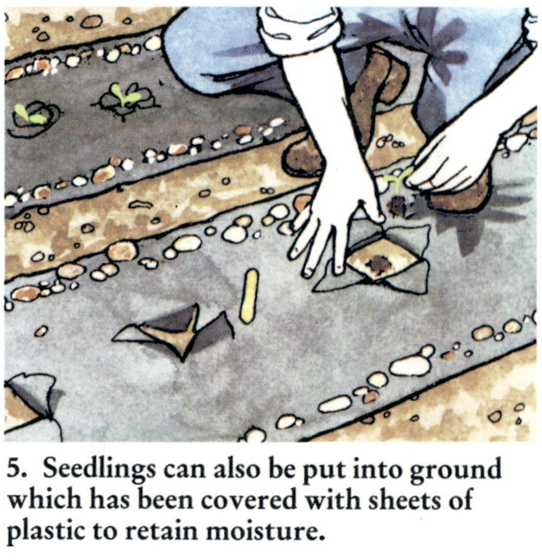

5. Seedlings can also be put into ground which has been covered with sheets of plastic to retain moisture.

6. Weed between the young plants with a draw hoe. This will help to discourage egg-laying insects, too.

7. Lettuces need a great deal of water to grow well. Keep the soil very moist; a trickle hose is ideal.

8. Mulch the young lettuces with well-rotted garden compost, to keep down the weeds and retain moisture.

9. To test for firmness, apply gentle pressure to the heart with the back of your hand.

10. To harvest cabbage or cos lettuces, use a sharp knife to cut just below the lowest leaves.

11. If a variety is not self-blanching, place a tie around the middle, and another around the top a week later.

12. Loose-leaf lettuces are picked by pulling the outer leaves gently. Take them straight into the kitchen.

13. To store, pull up the whole plant and tie a plastic bag around the roots. Keep in refrigerator.

a warm site in March. Follow this with successional sowings every three weeks or so until the end of June.

The seed should be sown thinly, 1.3 cm (½ in) deep, in short rows so that not too many mature at once. The most economical use of seed is to sow a pinch at the recommended spacing for the variety and to single these when large enough. Pelleted seed can be used instead but it is not always as successful as one would like and, at one per station, failures are not welcome. Lettuces are quick maturing so they make an excellent short-term intercrop for growing between recently planted brassicas etc.

Planting

Seedling lettuces grown under cover should be pricked out as soon as they are large enough to handle. If sown thinly enough, though, they can be planted straight out in the open when they have 3–4 true leaves.

Lettuces that are to mature in the current year should not be transplanted after May as the check frequently induces bolting. Planting distances will vary and can be found on the seed packet but 23–30 cm (9–12 in) each way is normal. A good system with those sown direct in the open is to thin at first to half the recommended distance and, later, thin to the full distance and eat the thinnings.

Cultivation

The main thing about lettuces is that summer varieties must be grown as fast as possible. If they grow slowly, they are apt to taste bitter and are more likely to bolt prematurely. This means that good soil conditions and plenty of water are needed.

Keep weeds down by regular hoeing.

Pests and diseases

Sparrows can devastate seedlings. Various root pests may also be troublesome but the worst of all are slugs, especially in a wet summer. These are often accompanied by the fungus Botrytis.

Harvesting

As there is no way at all of storing lettuces, sowings should be made with this in mind and they must be harvested as soon as they are ready, if they are not to spoil. During the summer, they are best cut in the morning so that they are crisp and fresh.

Always use the back of your hand when testing for firmness, as if you use your fingers you can easily bruise the plant. Disease-free roots can be added to the compost heap.

ENDIVE

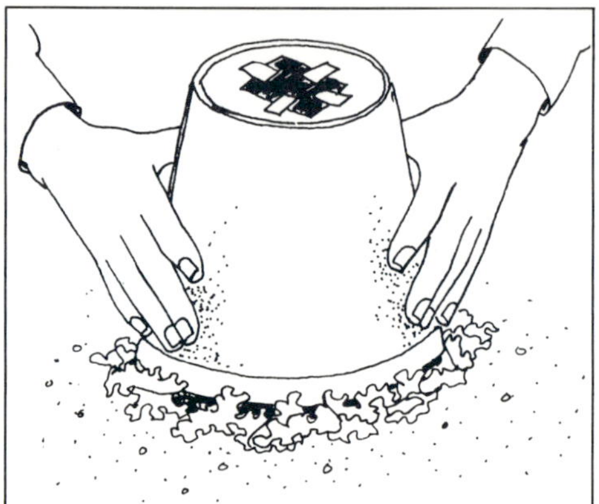

Blanching by covering with a pot

Sowing to harvest 11–13 weeks.

Soil This must be well drained and rich in organic matter.

Yield Usually 12 heads from a 3 m (10 ft) row.

Endive looks just like curly-headed lettuce but it has a rather more forceful taste. It is in season from late August to early winter and, being somewhat hardier than the average outdoor lettuce, it provides a very useful salad vegetable for that time of year.

Sowing

For the earliest crops, sow in drills 1.3 cm (½ in) deep and 30 cm (12 in) apart, in June. The main sowing should be in July.

The Batavian type may be sown in drills 38 cm (15 in) apart in August and early September to provide a salad vegetable for the winter.

Cultivation

As soon as the seedlings are large enough to handle, the standard varieties should be thinned to 30 cm (12 in) apart and the Batavian to 38 cm (15 in).

Endive thinnings do not transplant well. Some people prefer to blanch endive as this removes a lot of the bitterness – simply cover the heads with large flower pots for a fortnight to exclude the light.

Always keep the crop well watered and free of weeds.

Pests and diseases

Nothing out of the ordinary but slugs can be troublesome.

Harvesting

Cut as required.

Pot-grown curly green endive. It is well worth trying this salad crop in containers as well as outdoors.

Blanching by covering cloche with black plastic sheeting

Batavian, broad-leaved endive; this type is slightly hardier than the curly varieties and can be harvested later.

CHICORY

Season of use December to March.

Soil Should be well drained and rich in organic matter. Add lime to acid land.

Yield 12 plants from a 3 m (10 ft) row.

Chicory is an odd vegetable. You cannot eat the roots and, when grown in the open, the leaves are not worth bothering about either. However, when forced in warmth in the dark, the resulting 'chicons' – which look rather like blanched cos lettuce – make an excellent winter salad.

Sowing

Chicory is not a greedy crop so it can be sown on land that was manured for the previous one. Sow the seed thinly in late April or early May 1.3 cm (½ in) deep in drills 38 cm (15 in) apart.

If you try to sow the seed earlier than this, the plants will form very big roots and are likely to bolt or go to seed without producing chicons.

CULTIVATION AND CARE

1. Birds find seedlings of the Sugar Loaf type attractive; protect seed rows with netting if necessary.

2. Chicory is deep-rooted, so water the growing plants only if there is a severe drought.

3. Mulch with clean dry straw in mid-summer to keep weeds down and also conserve soil moisture.

CULTIVATION AND CARE

4. Occasionally, plants will attempt to flower; if this happens, cut out flowering stems at ground level.

5. In summer, pick a few leaves from several plants for use cooked as a spinach substitute or fresh in salad.

Cultivation
When the seedlings are well through, but before there is any hint of overcrowding, thin them to 23 cm (9 in) apart. Keep them weed free and well watered. If ground was well prepared before sowing, no additional feeding is required.

Pests and diseases
Only slugs are likely to be serious but Botrytis can be a nuisance during forcing.

Forcing and harvesting
Once the leaves have died down in the early autumn, lift the roots carefully. Those that are wanted for forcing should be 5–7.5 cm (2–3 in) across the top and about 25 cm (10 in) long. Smaller ones can be thrown out. Trim the parsnip-like roots to 20 cm (8 in) long and tidy up the crown by removing any bits of leaf. Store them in a frost-free place until required for forcing.

Only a few should be forced at a time to avoid over-production. Pack five roots in a 23 cm (9 in) pot of peat/sand or spent seed or potting compost. Cover this with a similar sized inverted pot and put it all somewhere dark and warm. A temperature of 10–13°C (50–55°F) suits well. Check up on progress occasionally and rub off any side shoots that are developing. Cut the chicons when they are 12.5–15 cm (5–6 in) long. Always cut as close to the crown as you can. The roots can be discarded.

FORCING

1. Lift the roots from early autumn onwards; only keep those with a crown diameter of 5–7.5 cm (2–3in).

2. For storing in soft sand in boxes, trim back foliage to within 2.5 cm (1in) of crown and remove all side roots.

3. A month before the chicons are needed, fill pots with damp sand, moist peat, potting compost or soil.

4. Put the prepared roots in vertically, 5–7.5 cm (2–3in) apart so that crowns are 2.5 cm (1in) below soil surface.

5. Invert another pot over the roots to keep the light out; remember to plug the drainage hole with a cork.

6. Begin inspecting pots a month later; the chicons are ready for harvesting when 12.5 cm (5in) tall.

7. Pull up the root and cut off the chicon afterwards; cut as close to the crown as possible.

ALTERNATIVE FORCING METHODS

1. Chicons can be forced in boxes under greenhouse staging; keep out light with black polythene sheeting.

2. You can expose the crown and cut the chicon off in situ; the root will then produce a second, smaller crop.

MUSTARD AND CRESS

Sowing to harvest 15 days for mustard, 18 for cress.

Soil Not really applicable as mustard and cress is invariably grown indoors in trays of peat or peat-based seed compost.

Mustard (more commonly rape) and cress are often grown together; the etiolated seedlings being used for salads and sandwiches. They are probably the first things that most children grow.

Sowing

Cover the base of small plastic trays, or other similar containers, with about 2.5 cm (1 in) of suitable rooting medium and sow the seed thickly on the surface. For a mixture of the two, sow the cress first and the mustard three days later. Place the containers in a warm and dark place to germinate. Alternatively, you can cover the tray with black polythene and place it outdoors under a cloche or in a cold frame.

Cultivation

Once the seedlings have grown to about 5 cm (2 in) high, bring them into full light for a few days to induce them to turn green.

Land cress thrives in the open. Make successional sowings every few weeks from mid spring. Keep well watered and harvest by picking the leaves.

Harvesting

Cut the mustard and cress with scissors once it is sufficiently green. The rooting medium is then discarded. Clean out the tray thoroughly and sow another crop.

Cress should be eaten straight after cutting because it loses its flavour along with its freshness.

Sowing mustard in with cress seedlings

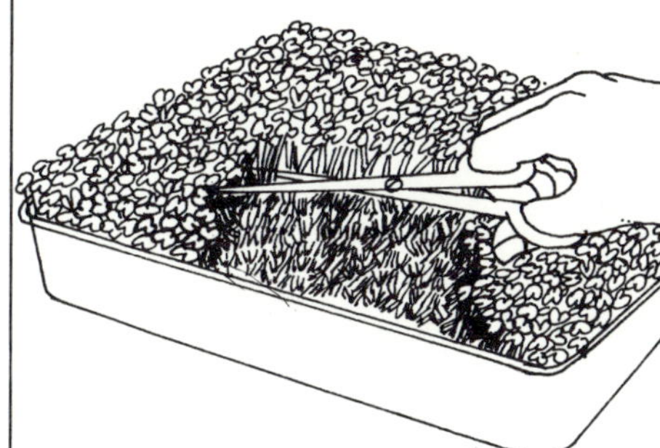

Cutting common cress

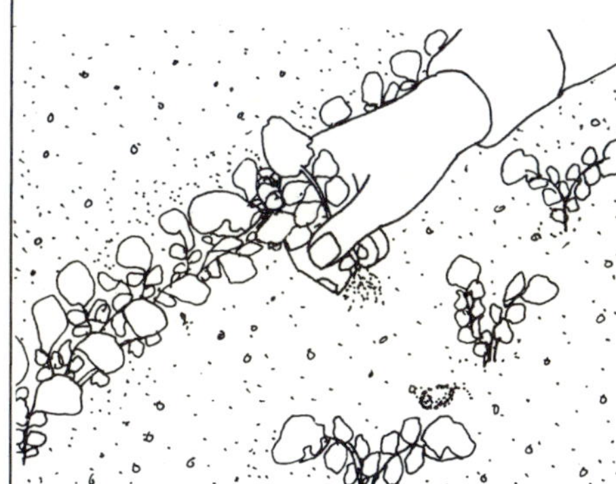

Thinning land cress seedlings

Removing flowering stems from land cress

BEETROOT

Sowing to harvest 12–16 weeks, according to how large they are wanted. If growing them for use as a cooked vegetable rather than for salads, they are normally left in the ground until the autumn.

Soil Preferably light and fertile. Heavy soils can be made quite suitable by the addition of heavy dressings of organic matter.

Yield Crops pulled early: 3 kg (6.5 lb) from a 3 m (10 ft) row. Maincrop: 4 kg (9 lb) from 3 m (10 ft) row.

A very easy root crop to grow but beetroot is not to everyone's taste. Those that do like it, often have it cooked and sliced in salads. It can be either boiled before slicing or boiled and then pickled in vinegar. As well as the normal dark red beet, orange varieties are available.

Sowing

Sow the seeds in succession from April to midsummer, very thinly and 1.3 cm (½in) deep. Those to be pulled early should be in rows 18 cm (7 in) apart; those for maincrop use, 30 cm (12 in) apart.

Cultivation

As soon as the seedlings are large enough to handle, earlies should be thinned and singled to 10 cm (4 in) apart. For the maximum crop of medium-sized maincrop beet, they can be thinned to as close as 2.5 cm (1 in) apart and, later, to 5 cm (2 in). The thinnings can be used for salads.

SOIL PREPARATION

1. Prepare heavy soils in autumn, and leave rough over winter; light sandy soils can be prepared in the spring.

2. Test the soil; if it is acid, apply lime at a rate to give a neutral or slightly alkaline reaction.

3. In spring, work the soil to a fine tilth; prepare drills 30 cm (12in) apart and 1.3 cm (½in) deep.

Pests and diseases

Flea beetle may be a problem.

Harvesting

Lift the early and small beet as required. Maincrop can be left in the ground until about Christmas, when the colder weather makes it wise to lift and store them. The soil should be brushed off them and the foliage twisted off. Store in peat in a reasonably frost-free shed.

SOWING AND THINNING

1. Sow seed clusters 5 cm (2in) apart, in small batches, from mid-spring to mid-summer.

2. After sowing fill in the drills with fine soil, and rake the bed lightly to give an even surface.

3. Thin the seedlings as soon as they are large enough to handle; leave one at each station.

CULTIVATION AND CARE

1. Beetroot needs a steady supply of water while it is growing, during the mid and late summer particularly.

2. Hoe as necessary between rows, being very careful not to damage the roots with the blade of the hoe.

3. For early beet crops, give cloche protection; remove cloches during warm days and replace at night.

4. When harvesting, lift the roots with a fork to avoid damaging the long tap root.

STORING

To store in boxes, line the bottom with sand; place a layer of beetroot on sand, and cover with sand or peat; continue the layers until the box is filled.

RADISHES

Sowing to harvest 4–6 weeks in spring and summer; 10–12 for the winter varieties.

Soil Should be free-draining and rich in organic matter.

Yield 2 kg (4.5 lb) from a 3 m (10 ft) row of summer radishes; double that for the winter varieties.

Radishes are an almost indispensible salad crop and they are as easy to grow outdoors as mustard and cress is indoors. There are both summer and winter varieties but the summer ones are by far the more common.

You should find that an average packet of seed is sufficient for three 3 m (10 ft) rows. And that should yield something in the region of 300 or more radishes, so you get very good value for money.

Sowing and cultivation

Summer varieties should be sown in succession from March to mid-June 1.3 cm (½ in) deep, in rows spaced 15 cm (6 in) apart. Sow thinly to avoid the need for later thinning. Winter varieties can be sown from late July to mid-August in drills 23 cm (9 in) apart. Once there is crowding, thin and single to 15 cm (6 in) apart, using the thinnings.

Hoe to keep down the weeds and water well in dry spells as radishes have to be grown quickly to be good.

Pests and diseases

Flea beetle is the first to be troublesome; this can start straight after germination.

Cabbage root fly very often proves a menace as well.

PREPARATION AND SOWING

1. Well before sowing, dig the soil deeply; add moist peat to very dry or very heavy soils.

2. Work in sifted leafmould or ripe garden compost; avoid digging in heavy manures.

3. Just before sowing, rake the soil surface to a fine tilth and break up any lumps of soil.

4. Make the drills 1.3 cm (½in) deep, and 15 cm (6in) apart; be sure they are absolutely level.

5. Sow the seeds thinly, overcrowding leads to foliage rather than root growth.

1. After sowing, tamp down the soil with the head of a rake, so the seeds are in contact with the soil.

2. Thin the seedlings as soon as they are large enough to handle, to 2.5–5 cm (1–2in) apart.

3. Protect the seeds and seedlings from birds with small mesh wire netting, bird scarers, or cotton webs.

4. Harvest radishes as soon as they are ready; do not leave them in the ground to get hard and stringy.

5. Large winter radishes can be pulled in autumn and then stored in a box filled with damp sand.

Harvesting

Pull the summer varieties as required while they are still young and tender. Once they become woody or start to bolt, scrap the whole sowing.

Winter varieties may be left in the ground until needed or lifted in October/November and stored under cover like carrots.

By giving cloche protection during winter months, you can harvest radishes all year round.

TOMATOES (outdoors)

Sowing to harvest 16–20 weeks.

Soil The best crops are obtained from plants in growing-bags or other containers of prepared potting compost. However, quite satisfactory results are possible in the open ground as long as it has been suitably improved with plenty of bulky organic matter.

Yield 2 kg (4.5 lb) per plant, if grown well.

Unlike indoor tomatoes that need the warmth and protection of a greenhouse, outdoor varieties are capable of producing a perfectly good crop in the open garden. However, do not be misled into thinking that outdoor varieties will do even better if they are grown in a greenhouse. They will not – it is far too warm for them and they will simply grow like weeds.

Both bush and trained varieties are available; the difference being that the bush ones do not need to have the side shoots removed whereas the others do.

Sowing

Even outdoor varieties need to be sown under cover but a warm window sill is just as good as an expensive greenhouse. Sow in mid-April to produce plants of a suitable size to go out after the risk of frosts.

The most successful system is to sow two seeds in a peat pot of seed compost and remove the weaker one when the seed leaves are fully expanded. The size of peat pot depends on what future action you are prepared to take. One of 9 cm (3½ in) diameter will be sufficient until planting out, whereas a tomato in a smaller one will need to be potted on into a 10–12.5 cm (4–5 in) pot. However, it will produce a bigger plant.

Aim for a temperature of about 17°C (63°F) for germination.

Planting

About a week before you plant outside, harden off the plants by gradually giving them cooler conditions. This is normally done by moving them into a cold frame and giving them more ventilation every day.

The best time to plant out is when the flowers on the bottom truss are starting to show colour. Allow three or four plants to each standard sized growing-bag or plant them in the open ground 45 cm (18 in) apart with 60 cm (24 in) between rows. Water the plants well in.

Cultivation

Even bush varieties will need support so a stout cane should be pushed into the ground near each plant. Tie the plant loosely to the cane and keep the new growth tied in as it progresses through the summer. Remember too, that tomatoes are gross feeders and unless they are grown on very rich soil will need regular feeding.

GROWING OUTDOOR TOMATOES

1. Sow tomato seeds in a propagator from late winter onward. Space the seeds about 1.3 cm) (½in) apart.

2. When the seedlings are large enough to handle, prick them off into 7.5 cm (3in) pots filled with compost.

3. When the plants are 12.5–15 cm (5–6 in) high, transplant them to permanent beds and tie to stakes.

4. If growing single-stem varieties, remove side-shoots with a clean knife to control the plant's growth.

5. Give liquid fertilizer as soon as the fruit begins to swell, and repeat every week until harvesting.

7. When four or five trusses have set, stop the stem one leaf above top truss.

8. Harvest tomatoes as they ripen, leaving the calyx on the fruit.

6. If growing bush varieties, put dry straw on the ground under the plants to protect them from soil and slugs.

ALTERNATIVE GROWING METHODS

Single-stem plants growing in a peat bag. Support plants with strings tied to a horizontal wire above.

Plants grown on stakes in a trench and cloched.

A steady supply of water is important, so during dry weather heavy daily watering is necessary.

Bush varieties will need little attention beyond watering, feeding and tying up but trained varieties should have side shoots removed as soon as they appear. Nip the tops out of trained plants at two leaves above the fourth truss, to encourage all the fruits to fill out and ripen. Before the fruit touch the ground, spread a layer of straw beneath them to prevent slug and mud damage. Towards the end of the summer it is a good idea to untie all plants and lay them on straw before covering them with cloches or a plastic tunnel. This helps to ripen the latest fruits.

Pests and diseases

Anyone who has grown tomatoes will know that whitefly is the Number One pest but aphids can also be a nuisance.

Oddly enough potato blight can be bad in a wet year; so can Botrytis.

Harvesting

Gather the fruit when it is well coloured and aim to clear the crop during September (unless you cloche it). Gather any fruits that are clearly not going to ripen outside and place them on a sunny window sill to ripen to a finish. Any very small ones can be used for making chutney. (Ripe tomatoes freeze well but they cannot be eaten raw when thawed.)

CUCUMBER (outdoors)

Sowing to harvest 12–14 weeks.

Soil Even more so than tomatoes, outdoor cucumbers do much better in a well prepared place, or a growing-bag, than when simply grown in garden soil. Along with marrows and courgettes, they thrive on bulky organic matter and being planted in such a bed is just what they like.

Yield 18–20 cucumbers per plant.

Although the cucumber is often regarded as a greenhouse crop, and it certainly does best under cover, excellent modern varieties are now available that grow and crop perfectly well outdoors.

It is a fairly easy crop to grow and the very generous yield makes it well worth the space in any vegetable plot – or greenhouse.

Sowing

Cucumbers are only half-hardy so the plants have to be raised under cover in late March or April.

Peat pots are the best containers for sowing into; allow two seeds per pot. For the quickest germination, stand these in a warm, dark place (such as an airing cupboard) and you should see results in about a week if you selected only plump, clean seeds and discarded the rest.

Planting and cultivation

Once the seedlings have developed their first true leaves, remove the weaker of the two in each pot. By mid-May the plants should be ready for planting outside but they will first have to be hardened off to the cooler conditions.

When planting, allow 60 cm (24 in) between plants and leave the top of the rootball slightly out of the ground to ensure that it will dry out readily and thus avoid neck-rot. It is important to make sure that the cucumbers develop properly without rotting off by resting on the ground. This can be done by covering the ground with a layer of straw.

When a plant has produced seven leaves, nip out the top to encourage side shoots to form. These will produce the cucumbers and should themselves be stopped at two leaves beyond the small fruit.

Keep the ground moist at all times but avoid getting water on the top growth late in the day as this will mean they stay wet overnight, possibly leading to fungus diseases. Feed the plants regularly and discourage slugs by keeping the cucumbers off the ground with slates or small boards.

CULTIVATION

1. Dig compost or manure into trench and cover with soil ridge.

2. For light dry soil, dig in manure and plant cucumbers on flat.

3. Put plant into preformed hole and water in with tepid water.

4. Keep plants well watered if the weather is dry.

5. Nip off the ends of side shoots one leaf beyond the young fruit.

6. Protect cucumbers from soil by placing a pane of glass under them.

Pests and diseases

Apart from slugs, outdoor cucumbers are remarkably trouble-free – unlike their indoor relations.

Harvesting

Gather as required but before the cucumbers start to go yellow. Support ripening fruits on a pane of glass or a tile to protect them from the soil.

COURGETTES

Sowing to harvest 10–12 weeks.

Soil Courgettes are members of the cucumber family and, as such, like much the same organic soil conditions. Growing them on a mature compost heap is perhaps the ultimate in luxury.

Yield Varies enormously but up to about 6 kg (13 lb) from a 3 m (10 ft) row.

These are really just mini-marrows but they taste completely different and are eaten when they are 10–15 cm (4–6 in) long. Modern varieties will carry on cropping all summer and, unlike in the past, most will continue to produce even if some fruits are allowed to grow to marrow size.

Sowing

If you have a greenhouse or enough room on a warm and sunny window sill, the plants can be raised in the same way as cucumbers. Courgettes can also be sown direct outside but it takes longer for them to crop. When the risk of frost has passed, usually in late May, sow three seeds per station 2.5 cm (1 in) deep. As soon as the seedlings have two true leaves, single to one per station.

A good system is to sow the seeds closely and put a large jam-jar over each cluster to act as a small greenhouse. But it must be removed the moment anything appears through the surface.

Planting and cultivation

Late May is also the time to plant outside those raised under cover. Allow 60 cm (2 ft) between bush varieties (the most convenient) and 1.2 m (4 ft) between trailing types.

Keep the plants generously watered at all times, and take out the tops of the shoots of trailing varieties when they reach 1 m (3 ft) long. Once the fruits start to swell, feed the plants regularly to ensure continued cropping.

Weeds are best kept down by mulching rather than hoeing.

Pests and diseases

As with cucumbers, slugs and Botrytis are likely to be the most troublesome, especially in wet years.

Harvesting

Cut the courgettes when 10–15 cm (4–6 in) long. It is much better to keep cutting than to allow them to get larger. Even modern varieties respond best when continually cut.

The cultivation process for marrows is exactly the same as courgettes in every respect except that the 'fruits' are allowed to remain on the plants until they have reached 30–40 cm (12–16 in) long. As with courgettes, they should be picked continually to prevent them becoming woody and to encourage them to continue cropping. They will be ready for cutting approximately two weeks after courgette size.

Marrows can be stored by hanging them up in a frost-free shed but they have to be well past their best for eating before they are mature enough to keep like this for any length of time.

Zucchini

Golden Zucchini

AUBERGINES (outdoors)

Sowing to harvest About 20 weeks.

Soil Aubergines should be grown in specially prepared ground containing plenty of organic matter and, if necessary, grit to lighten it.

Growing-bags are ideal but results are also good in containers filled with proprietary potting compost.

Yield Usually about four fruits per plant.

Although aubergines (egg plants) have increased in popularity as a vegetable over the past 10 to 15 years, they are not the success outdoors in the garden that some people would have us believe. Certainly some of the newer varieties produce far better crops than were hitherto grown but the egg plant remains, primarily, a greenhouse crop in all but a very few really favoured districts. Outdoors, in a wet, sunless summer it will fail to crop.

AUBERGINES IN A GROWING BAG
Aubergines can be grown against the base of a south or west facing wall in sheltered areas. Start the young plants under glass and plant out when danger of frosts is past.

Sowing and planting

Sow the seeds in March in a greenhouse or on a warm window sill at an optimum temperature of 21°C (70°F). Either one or two seeds should be sown in each 7.5 cm (3 in) pot of seed compost. As soon as the seedlings are large enough to handle, single those that were sown at two per pot. Once the roots are seen to be filling the pot, the plants can either go out into their final positions or, if there is still a risk of frosts, they should be potted on into 12.5 cm (5 in) pots.

Cultivation

The plants should be grown outside in as warm and sheltered a position as you can find. A sunny patio makes a good site. They will need to be supported by a cane or stake but, in most cases, the plants will form bushes quite naturally without the need for any stopping to encourage side shoots. Indeed, it is often wise to restrict the number of main branches to 3–4 per plant.

Spray overhead regularly to encourage fruit to set and feed as necessary – certainly not less than weekly once the fruit has formed.

Pests and diseases

Normally trouble-free.

Harvesting

Pick the fruits when they have reached maximum size but while they are still shiny. Once the gloss begins to fade, so does the flavour. Surplus can be stored by freezing.

SOWING AND POTTING ON

1. Sow seeds in early spring in a greenhouse or propagator 2.5 cm (1in) apart; use good quality seed compost.

2. As soon as three leaves have formed, prick out seedlings into 7.5 cm (3in) pots; plant deeply.

3. Keep the soil well-watered; at this stage the temperature can be lowered to 10° (50°F).

4. When pots are out-grown, pot on into 12.5 cm (5in) pots; pinch out growing point when 15 cm (6in) high.

TRANSPLANTING

1. A month before setting out plants, dig soil over and enrich it with well rotted manure or garden compost.

2. Harden plants off in a cold frame; open frame light during the day and shut it at night or in cold weather.

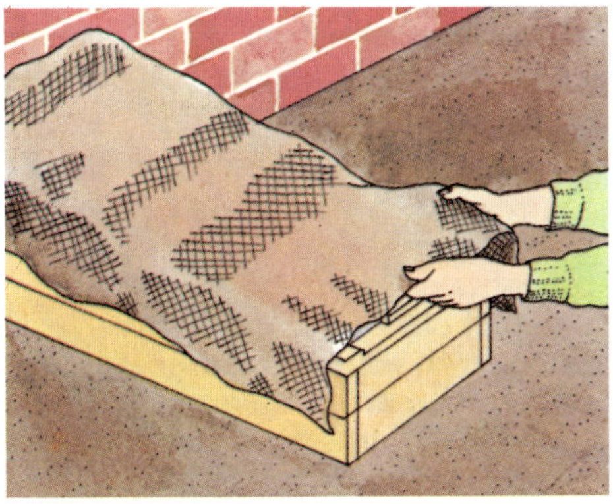

3. If frost threatens, give plants additional protection by placing sacking over closed frame light.

4. Transplant aubergines 60 cm (2ft) apart in all directions; avoid damaging the fragile roots.

CARE AND CULTIVATION

1. While fruits are forming, give plants liquid feed, diluted according to manufacturer's instructions.

2. In hot weather, spray foliage daily with tepid water to discourage attack by red spider mites.

3. Do not allow more than four fruitlets to form; pinch out any extra ones as soon as you see them.

4. Harvest when fruit is about 15 cm (6in) long, and skin is bright and shiny; cut with secateurs.

CAPSICUMS (outdoors)

Sowing to harvest About 20 weeks.

Soil Peppers need better growing conditions than are normally found in ordinary garden soil. This means that it has to be improved by adding plenty of organic matter and, if necessary, grit to ensure good drainage.

Yield Varies with the type and variety but not often more than 1 kg (2.2 lb) per plant.

Capsicums (Peppers) are hardier and therefore easier to grow outdoors than aubergines but they are not as easy as tomatoes. They do have the virtue of having a very long cropping season and many varieties are available. Red ones are possibly the most popular but these are simply green ones that have been left on the plant longer. Orange and yellow varieties are appearing more now; they tend to be sweeter than the red/green.

Sowing and planting

Sow the seeds in March or April, either singly or two per 7.5 cm (3 in) peat pot of good seed compost. Keep in a temperature of about 18°C (65°F) and single those that were sown at two per pot as soon as they are large enough to handle. Once the roots are seen to be filling the pot, the plants can either go out into their final positions or, if there is still a risk of frosts, they should be potted on into 12.5 cm (5 in) pots.

Cultivation

As with aubergines, the plants should be grown outside in as warm and sheltered a place as you can find. A sunny patio makes a good site.

They will need to be supported by a cane or stake and sprayed overhead regularly to encourage fruit to set. Feed as necessary but certainly not less than weekly once the fruit has formed.

Pests and diseases

Normally, only aphids are troublesome.

Harvesting

Red peppers can be picked before they colour up and when they are still green. However, orange and yellow varieties are best left to attain their final colour. Red peppers will keep under cool room conditions until Christmas without any trouble.

If wanted for all year round, peppers can be frozen but are only fit for cooking when thawed.

HANDY HINT

An alternative method of growing peppers is to plunge the pots containing the plants up to their rims in a sunny border, in early summer. Lift pots in the autumn and finish ripening peppers in the greenhouse.

SOWING, CULTIVATION AND CARE

1. If using peat pots, sow two seeds per pot; remove the weakest seedling after germination.

2. If cold weather delays planting out, top-dress the plants with feed and water this in thoroughly.

3. Plant out in early summer when the weather warms up; the plants should be about 20 cm (8in) tall.

4. Give plants cloche protection at night or if weather turns cold; take cloches off during the day.

5. Peppers need plenty of water, particularly at mid-day in hot weather; their thin leaves dry out quickly.

6. Mulch with clean dry straw once the plants are established, to keep weeds down and conserve moisture.

PEPPERS IN GROWING-BAG

In mild sheltered areas, peppers can be grown outside, at the base of a south-facing wall. In early summer, transplant peppers started under glass to a growing-bag outside.

SOWING IN TRAYS

1. Begin sowing seeds from late winter onwards. Space seeds 2.5 cm (1in) apart in all directions in the tray.

2. At the three-leaf stage, prick the seedlings out in 7.5 cm (3in) pots and lower the temperature slightly.

3. Do not allow plants to become root bound; repot them into 12.5 cm (5in) pots and richer compost as necessary.

4. Harden plants off in a cold frame prior to planting outdoors.

HERBS

HERBS TO USE WITH CERTAIN FOODS

SOUPS	Basil, bay, chervil, chives, coriander, dill, marjoram, parsley, sage, savory, sorrel, tarragon, thyme.
FISH	Basil, bay, dill, fennel, lemon balm, lovage, marjoram, parsley, rosemary, sage, tarragon, thyme.
EGGS	Basil, bay, chervil, chives, dill, fennel, marjoram, parsley, rosemary, savory, sorrel, tarragon, thyme.
POULTRY	Basil, bay, coriander, dill, lemon balm, lovage, marjoram, parsley, rosemary, sage, tarragon, thyme.
LAMB	Basil, bay, dill, fennel, garlic, lemon balm, mint, rosemary, sage, savory, tarragon, thyme.
BEEF	Basil, bay, chervil, dill, garlic, marjoram, parsley, rosemary, sage, savory, tarragon, thyme.
VEGETABLES	Basil, bay, chervil, coriander, dill, lovage, marjoram, mint, parsley, rosemary, sage, savory, sweet cicely, tarragon, thyme.
CHEESES	Basil, chervil, chives, coriander, dill, mint, sage, tarragon, thyme.

Even with a wide variety of vegetables, there are still some other plants that no self-respecting gardener should be without – herbs. They take up very little room and are invaluable in the kitchen for flavouring food. They can also be used for all sorts of medicinal purposes but that is beyond the scope of this particular book.

There follow just six of the more common and useful culinary herbs, all of which are perfectly easy to grow and which you should be able to squeeze into the odd corner of the garden. Normally, they are handiest if growing near the back door so that they are convenient for the kitchen. But bear in mind also that most herbs are best in positions where the sun can ripen the foliage properly and give it a full flavour.

Always bear in mind that there must be a harmony between the flavour of the herb and the ingredients of a particular dish – don't use them indiscriminately! The above chart gives guidance on this matter and may also inspire you to extend the range of your herb plot in due course.

CHIVES

These are like mini-onions but it is the foliage that is eaten, not the bulbs. They will grow in any soil provided it is well drained. Split up and replant the clumps every 3–4 years to keep them young and strong. They can be split up and re-planted in the winter or seed can be sown thinly in March. The seedlings should be thinned to small clumps 15 cm (6 in) apart.

Remove the leaves by cutting them close to the ground to encourage more to grow. It is better for the plants if you pick off any flowers as they appear, but they are quite decorative and are usually allowed to stay. The leaves may be gathered and frozen or dried for use in winter.

CULTIVATION

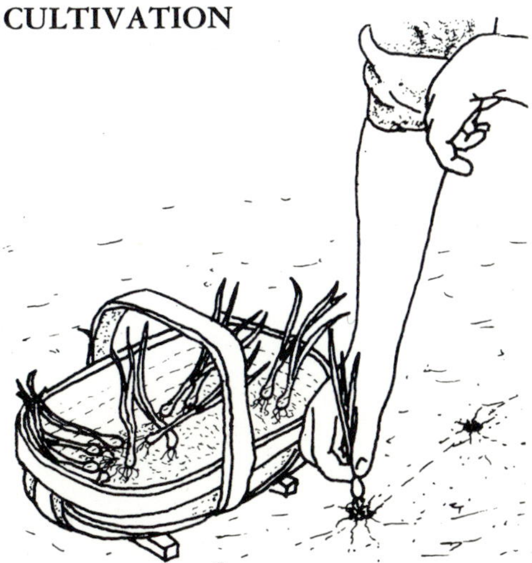

Planting out chive bulbs

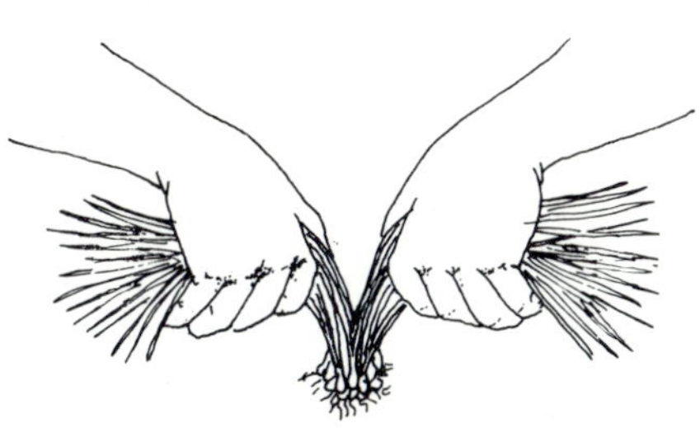

Separating clumps for propagation

Cutting chives for the kitchen

ROSEMARY

Rosemary is an evergreen shrub with charming flower spikes in the summer. It also has a pleasing fragrance, and a distinctive flavour that goes well with roast lamb.

It prefers a sheltered and sunny position on light and well drained land. Propagation is normally by cuttings but it is also quite easy from seed. This should be sown outdoors in April/May and thinned as required to leave a final spacing of 60 cm (2 ft) between plants. Alternatively, plants can be bought from most garden centres.

Cut sprigs of foliage as required. No storage is necessary as it is evergreen but you might like to dry a few sprigs for convenience in the winter.

PARSLEY

This prefers a well drained, rich soil but one that does not dry out readily. It also likes a sunny position. Sow seed in March/April for summer/autumn use or in July for the winter and spring. Sow thinly in drills 6 mm (¼ in) deep. Germination can take up to six weeks. Thin the seedlings to 23 cm (9 in) apart when they start to get crowded. Some of the thinnings can be potted up for growing on a window sill.

Spring-sown parsley will be producing leaves for cutting from mid-summer and onwards until the plant starts to produce flower stems instead of leaves in the following spring.

Use the leaves as required. They can also be stored by drying or freezing.

SAGE

In spite of being a perennial shrub, sage has a useful life of not much over three years so should be propagated with this in mind. It likes a warm and sunny position but has no particular preference as to soil, as long as it is well drained.

Bushes can be bought from most nurseries and should be planted 60 cm (24 in) apart. Pick the leaves as required – bearing in mind that they are very pungent – and dry a few sprigs for winter use. This is the only pruning it should need. Many differently coloured varieties are available, from pale green to deep purple.

MINT

This is an invasive herb that needs restraining. But there are many varieties and it is indispensable for use with peas, new potatoes and roast lamb. It doesn't mind what type of soil it is planted in and will grow anywhere – and everywhere! Keep it in check by growing it in an old tin bucket with drainage holes in the base, sunk in the soil.

It is propagated by digging up the roots in winter, teasing them apart and replanting them. These pieces of root can also be potted up and grown indoors on a window sill. Simply gather the leaves as required during the growing season.

THYME

Like sage, thyme is a short-lived plant that should be propagated regularly to keep a good supply of young and vigorous shoots. Propagation is carried out by division.

It likes full sun but has no particular soil likes or dislikes, except that it should be well drained. Plants can easily be bought from nurseries and should be planted 23 cm (9 in) apart. After the first year they should join up to provide excellent ground-cover.

Pick the leaves as required and for winter use dry some from pickings made before the delightful flowers appear in summer. Many variously coloured and fragrant strains are available.

–FRUITS–

TREE FRUITS

In most good garden centres and nurseries you will see fruit trees in such a wide range of shapes, sizes and varieties that even the most pernickety gardener will be able to find what they want, and to suit all sites and situations. But choosing the right tree to suit your own particular needs is often easier said than done.

'Bush' trees

These are the ones probably most commonly found in gardens, but they are not always the most suitable because even these will reach a height of some 3–4.5 m (10–15 ft), with a similar spread. Also, the trunk is usually too short – about 60 cm (2 ft) tall – for the ground underneath to be of any real use for other crops.

Fruits usually grown as bush trees include apples, pears, plums, cherries and, occasionally, peaches. They should be planted 3.5–4.5 m (12–15 ft) apart.

TREE SHAPES

dwarf bush
1.75 m (6ft)

semi-dwarfing bush
2.9 m (9ft)

bush tree
3.5 cm (12ft)

Cordon trees

Cordons could quite easily have been developed with small gardens in mind, as no other tree form allows so much fruit to be grown in so small an area in so short a time. A cordon is a single stem with no side branches but, instead, a succession of fruiting spurs from top to bottom.

They can be grown either in the open garden or against a wall or fence, and are planted and trained at an angle of 45° to discourage growth and encourage fruiting. The normal method of training is to tie them to canes which, in turn, are fastened to horizontal wires.

Cordons can be grown to more or less any convenient height but not usually more than about 3 m (10 ft). Plant them 60–90 cm (2–3 ft) apart.

Apples and pears are the only tree fruits normally grown as cordons, simply because only they can be sufficiently controlled as regards growth and vigour. However, gooseberries and red currants can also be grown in this way, with a little more effort.

Espaliers

These are trees that have a central stem with pairs of horizontal branches trained from it about every 23 cm (9 in). They, also, are grown on a wall or in the open and are trained to horizontal wires.

Again, apples and pears are normally the only fruits grown as espaliers. They should be planted 3.5–5.5 m (12–18 ft) apart, according to vigour. The height is governed simply by how much room you have and the number of tiers of branches that you can fit in.

Fan-trained trees

These have short trunks with branches radiating out in roughly the shape of a fan. They have to be trained to a wall or fence, or to a frame if grown in the open.

This type of tree is normally most suitable for figs and stone fruits (plums, cherries, peaches, nectarines and apricots), where constant replacing of worn out branches is needed once the trees have reached middle age.

They are really the stone fruits' equivalent of espaliers and, as with these, the height will depend on the room available: 3 m (10 ft) is normal, with a spread of 3–4.5 m (10–15 ft). If more than one tree is grown, allow 3.5 m (12 ft) between them.

Cordons, espaliers and fans all need to be pruned in the summer as well as in the winter so that their vigour is controlled and more energy is channelled into the production of fruit and fruit bud.

Dwarf pyramid

This is another form of 'concentrated' fruit tree. These trees need not be tied down or trained and can be kept to about 2 m (7 ft) high, with a width of 1.2–1.5 m (4–5 ft). They crop early in their life and perform best when kept in

A fan-trained plum in blossom. A fan is a very attractive and manageable tree shape.

check by summer and winter pruning.

Although plums are sometimes grown as dwarf pyramids, this form is best suited to apples and pears because of their more controllable vigour.

The standard

Going from the smallest to the largest type of free-standing tree, we find the standard. This can be anything up to about 15 m (50 ft) tall and is quite unsuitable for all but the largest gardens.

Half-standards

On the other hand, while still being about 6 m (20 ft) tall, half-standards are not nearly so unmanageable and can make attractive specimen trees in a lawn or mixed border.

Apples, pears, plums and sweet cherries can all be grown as standards or half-standards but a lot of thought should be given before committing yourself because it is of little use complaining about their size ten years after planting. They will still be only half grown! One large tree is generally enough for most gardens; any problems with pollination can be overcome by planting one of the dwarfer tree forms nearby.

Pollination

Pollination is vital if good fruit crops are to be had and it is normally carried out by insects, especially bees. Some trees are described as 'self-fertile' because they will set a perfectly reasonable crop, but not an outstanding one, with their own pollen. Apricots, peaches, nectarines, cooking cherries, some plums and all soft fruits are self-fertile. In other words, they do not need the pollen of another variety to set a full crop. Even these, though, do best when they are cross-pollinated and, with other tree fruits, it is virtually essential.

In most cases, there will be a tree in a neighbouring garden that will adequately pollinate your's but, if not, ask a local nurseryman for a suitable pollinator when you are buying the trees. In fact, this may be necessary in years to come if, for no apparent reason, a tree flowers but fails to carry a crop.

A piece of cotton wool tied to a cane may be used instead of a paint-brush for hand pollination, as with this early peach blossom.

CROSS POLLINATION BY INSECTS

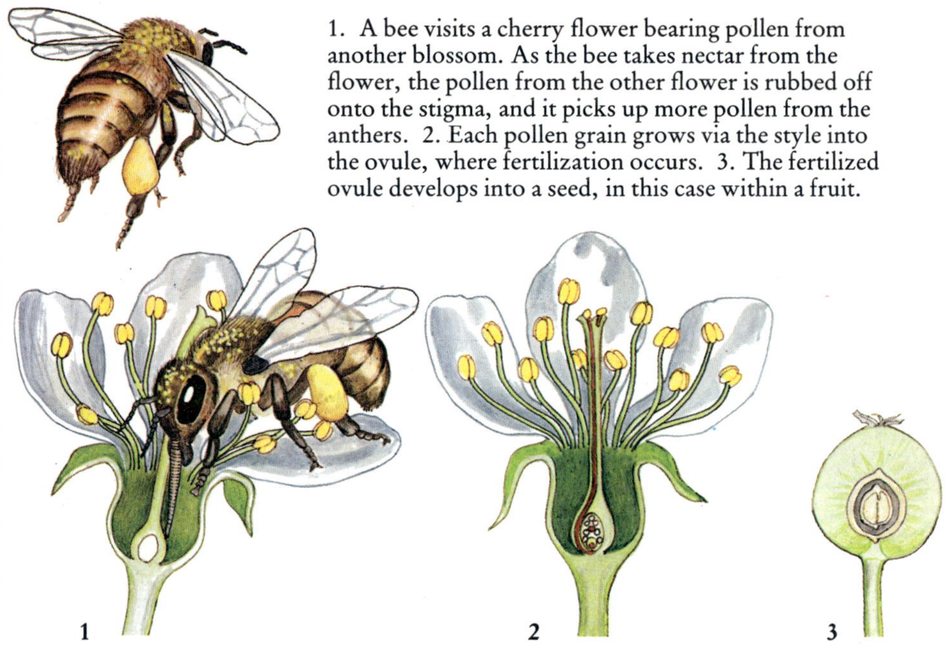

1. A bee visits a cherry flower bearing pollen from another blossom. As the bee takes nectar from the flower, the pollen from the other flower is rubbed off onto the stigma, and it picks up more pollen from the anthers. 2. Each pollen grain grows via the style into the ovule, where fertilization occurs. 3. The fertilized ovule develops into a seed, in this case within a fruit.

Planting

The best time to plant a tree will depend on whether it is bare-rooted or growing in a container when you buy it.

The normal time for planting bare-rooted trees is during the period October to April, though November to March is better. Avoid midwinter if you can as the roots will be completely inactive for some time afterwards and could suffer. November and March are the best months with March slightly ahead.

Trees growing in containers can be planted at more or less any time because the root system is not going to be disturbed. But when planting in the summer, remember to keep them well watered and staked.

The soil for fruit trees should be thoroughly broken up to a good 45 cm (18 in) deep and sufficient soil taken out to create a hole large enough to take the spread-out root system of bare-rooted trees.

Bush trees, half-standards and standards should have a stout stake driven into the bottom of the planting hole before you put in the tree. This avoids possible root damage as a consequence of putting the stake in afterwards. Position the stake on the windward side of the tree, and trim off any damaged roots before planting. Incidentally, any trees that are going to need post and wire supports, or just wire on walls or fences, should have these put in place before planting. Trying to do it afterwards is not only nearly impossible, it can damage the trees. For a row of cordons, horizontal wires should be stretched 30 cm (1 ft), 90 cm (3 ft), 150 cm (5 ft) and 210 cm (7 ft) from the ground. For espaliers, they should be 20–30 cm (8–12 in) apart.

Plant the tree so that the original soil mark at the base of the trunk will be at the same level when all is finished and the surrounding soil has been firmed down. Fill in the hole with good garden soil suitably enriched with well-rotted garden compost or manure. Bone meal can also be mixed in for autumn and early winter planting but, when doing it in the late winter or spring, substitute a more general feed so that the tops, and not just the roots, are encouraged to grow. While planting, joggle the tree about to make sure that the soil falls well down between the roots and carefully firm it with your heel as you go to exclude air pockets.

When the tree has been planted, tie it firmly to the stake with a proper tie made for the job. If the tree is growing in grass, make sure that a circle about 1 m (3 ft) across is cleared around the tree while it is trying to establish itself.

STAKING AND TYING FRUIT TREES

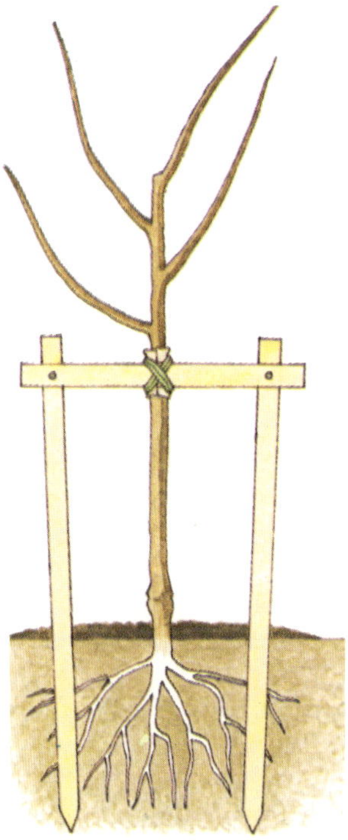

For standards and half-standards, use this double stake.

This is the usual method of supporting smaller trees.

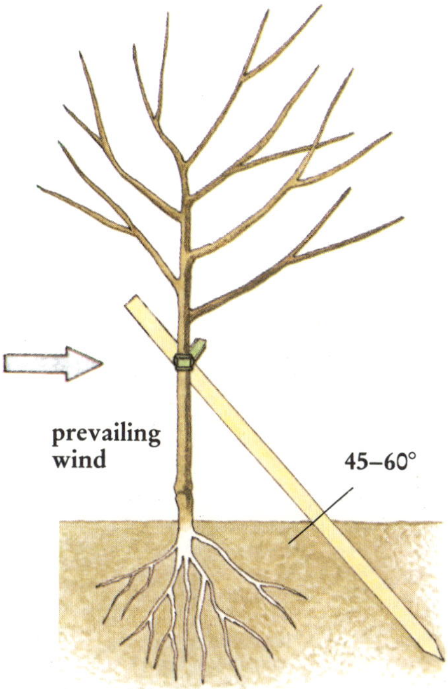

If you did not insert a stake before planting, then put it in at an angle to avoid the roots.

Wrap the tree with hessian and use a strip of old tyre as a buffer.

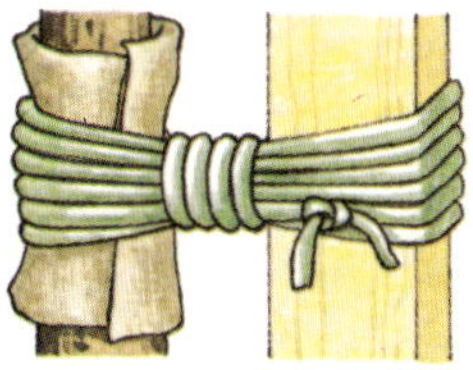

Alternatively, tie the cord at right angles between tree and stake.

The buckle of a plastic tree tie can be adjusted as the tree grows.

A modern dwarf bush apple tree – convenient to look after and ideal for the small garden. Little pruning is necessary as trees of this size fruit better and earlier in their life when allowed to develop more or less naturally. Although this tree is growing in grass, it could just as well be growing in cultivated land, but its vigour would increase.

APPLES

Tree forms Standard, half-standard, bush, dwarf pyramid, cordon, espalier.

Pollination At least two varieties are necessary for effective cross-pollination and fertilization.

Position in garden Dessert varieties, especially red ones, will need a sunny position to bring out the flavour and give them good colour.

Soil The soil should be deep and well drained and yet moisture retentive in the summer. Chalky soils should be acidified if the tree's foliage is excessively yellow.

Yield Ten cordons will produce roughly 20 kg (44 lb) of fruit. Large standards and half-standards might crop four times that amount and bush trees about double.

Planting and cultivation

The soil for apples should be made suitable by the addition of plenty of garden compost. For the first few years put down a moisture retaining mulch around the base of the trees in the spring. Make sure that they never run short of water in these formative years.

Suitable fertilizers should be applied each year, in the early spring. Treat all of the ground beneath the spread of the branches. In June or July, most apple trees shed a fair proportion of their fruitlets. This is perfectly normal but, should it be excessive, it means that the tree is short of food and/or water.

If the crop is particularly heavy, thin the fruits and single them to one per blossom cluster as soon as possible after the natural fruit fall (June drop). This will ensure that the fruits reach an acceptable size.

Pests and diseases

Aphids of many sorts, capsid bugs, sawfly, codling moth, mildew, scab, canker. You name it, most apples get it.

Any fruits that are going to be stored must be free from all signs of pests and diseases (or bruising) or they are likely to rot during storage.

Harvesting

An apple is ready for picking if, when twisted gently, it comes away from the tree quite easily. If you have to tug at it, you are too early. If, however, half the crop is on the ground, then clearly you have left it too late. Store any surplus fruits of mid-season and late varieties by wrapping them individually in newspaper before putting them in boxes.

Pruning

There are so many different methods of pruning that it is quite impossible to cover them all here. However, for those gardeners who are more concerned with keeping the trees tidy and reasonably productive rather than maintaining them in immaculate condition, the following system is normally adequate.

On standard, half-standard and bush trees, diseased, damaged, crossing and crowded shoots and branches should be cut back or removed completely in the early winter. The idea is to produce a tree which allows plenty of light and fresh air to get right into it.

On dwarf pyramids, cordons and espaliers, all new shoots growing directly from the main stem or main branches should be cut back to about 8 cm (3 in) long in late July, and further reduced to 2.5 cm (1 in) in early winter. Shoots growing from existing spurs are shortened to 2.5 cm (1 in) in July/August and are normally left in the winter.

PLANTING AND SUMMER PRUNING OF CORDONS

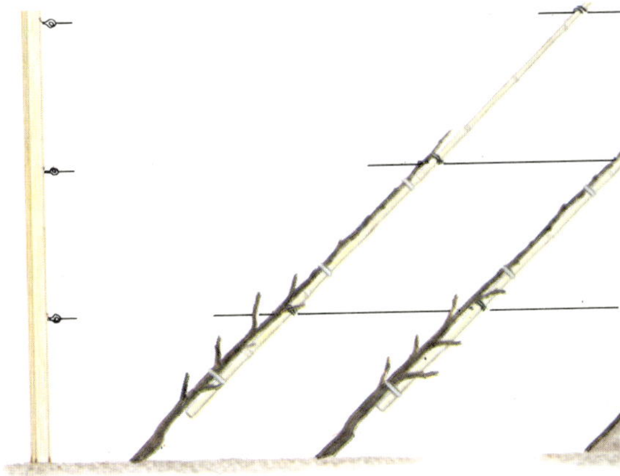

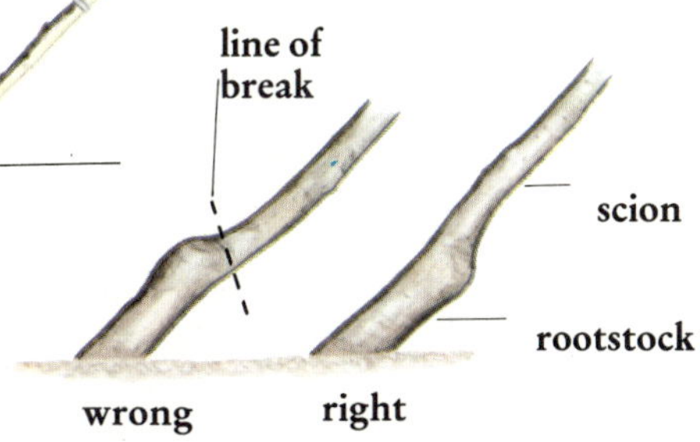

The cordon should be tied to a cane and the cane is tied to wires. Hold the tree at an angle of 45° while you plant.

Plant with the scion leaning above the rootstock, or the tree could break.

Prune the short spurs of the cordon at the points indicated to encourage fruit buds.

WINTER PRUNING PROGRAMME

1. If the nursery has not done so, prune a one-year-old to half its height, leaving three or four good buds.

2. In second year, prune back strong growth halfway and weak growth by two-thirds. Cut to an outward pointing bud.

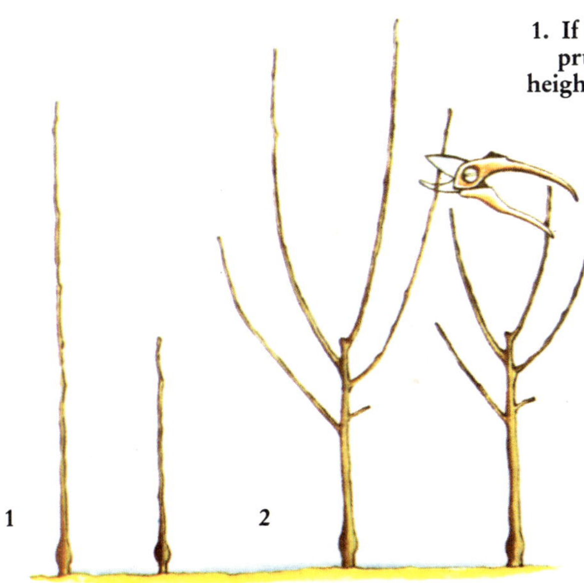

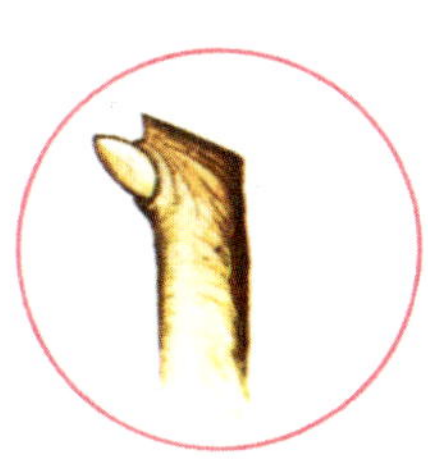

FURTHER WINTER PRUNING

1. By third winter, primary branches will have developed three or more secondaries. New growths from the tip are called leaders. Other secondary branches are called laterals. Both will grow fruiting spurs.

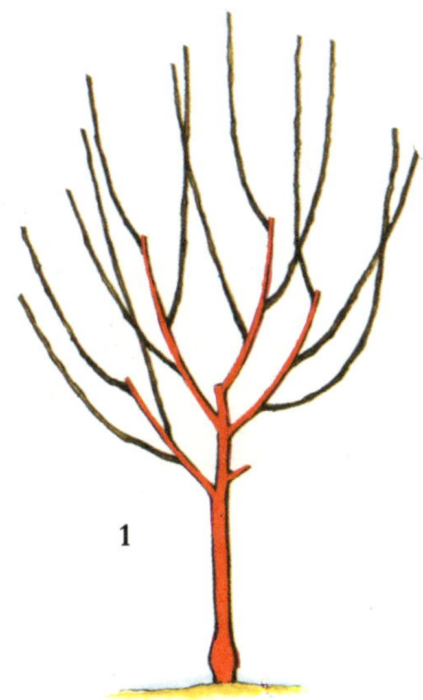

2. Cut back the previous summer's growth by a third if strong or by a half if weak. By the fourth year the tree is fully formed and shaped. Any further pruning will be to encourage fruiting.

PEARS

Tree forms Standard, half-standard, bush, dwarf pyramid, cordon, espalier.

Pollination At least two varieties are needed if maximum crops are to be produced.

Position in garden Pears are easily damaged by strong winds so they must be sheltered. The choicer dessert varieties need the protection of a warm south- or west-facing wall.

Soil Pears are slightly more tolerant of poor soils than are apples but, nonetheless, they should have a good depth of free draining and fertile soil that remains moist in the summer.

Yield About the same as for apples but it should be remembered that pears blossom before apples so they are more likely to be damaged by spring frosts.

Planting and cultivation

Pears are just as easy to grow as apples if you choose the right varieties for your district. For a single tree anywhere, the best variety would be Conference. This is the main commercial variety and has the ability to carry reasonable crops even in the absence of pollination.

The soil should be improved, if necessary, by the addition of plenty of garden compost. In early spring, feed the ground under the spread of the branches with general fertilizer and mulch the ground around the base of the trees with well rotted garden compost or manure. Although pears can tolerate poorer soil than apples, they are less tolerant of dry conditions. If these do occur and nothing is done to correct the dryness, there is a real risk that too many fruitlets will be shed. Trees planted close to walls are particularly vulnerable to this.

Pests and diseases

Aphids of several types, pear sucker, scab and, frequently, birds in the autumn just as the fruit is ripening.

Harvesting

Pears should not be allowed to ripen to a finish on the tree if they are to be at their best; they tend to become dry and mealy.

Earlies should be picked when they are still hard; mid-season varieties when they can be twisted off the tree without bringing half the branch away with them. Late varieties for keeping can also be picked at that stage but, instead of wrapping them up like apples, they should be laid in a single layer on shelves in a cool shed, cellar or garage. Properly stored, they should keep for several months. Bring them into a warm room three or four days before they will be required.

TRAINING AN ESPALIER

1. Espaliers need wire supports, whether in the open or against walls, 30 cm (12in) from the ground, and at 30 cm (12in) intervals. Immediately after planting, cut the leader back to a strong bud 5 cm (2in) higher than the lowest wire. Select two opposite buds to form laterals, notch the lower one, and rub out the rest.

2. The first summer, tie middle shoot to a cane with soft string; when they grow long enough, tie the lateral shoots to canes as well. The middle cane should be vertical, and the two lateral canes at an angle of 45° from the ground. If the side shoots grow unequally, lower the cane of the stronger shoot to slow it down; raise the cane of the other slightly.

3. In autumn, undo the two side canes and bring the branches down to the horizontal wires; secure the branches to the bottom wire. In the second autumn, the same procedure is followed to produce a second tier, and again until the top tier has filled the top wire.

Pruning

Pears are winter and summer pruned and trained in exactly the same way as apples, but there the similarity ends. They will stand being cut harder back than apples, should this be necessary with trees that are getting too big for their position (or boots). However, the best crops are produced on trees which, as one specialist grower described it years ago, 'have been left judiciously alone'. By this he meant that, the less pears are pruned within reason, the better they crop. Remember that; it can be comforting.

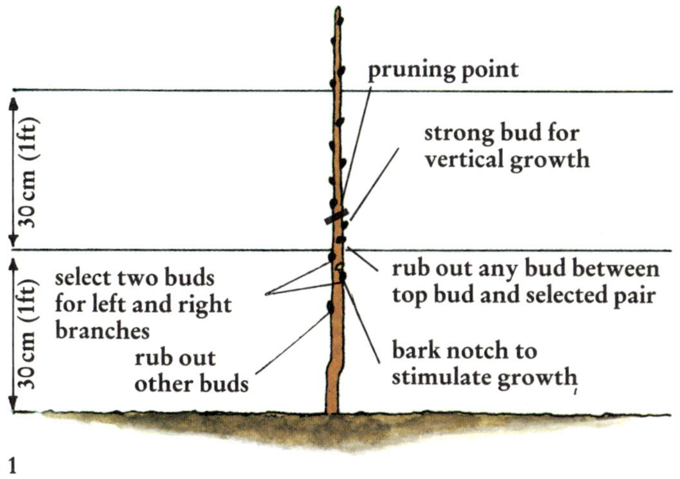

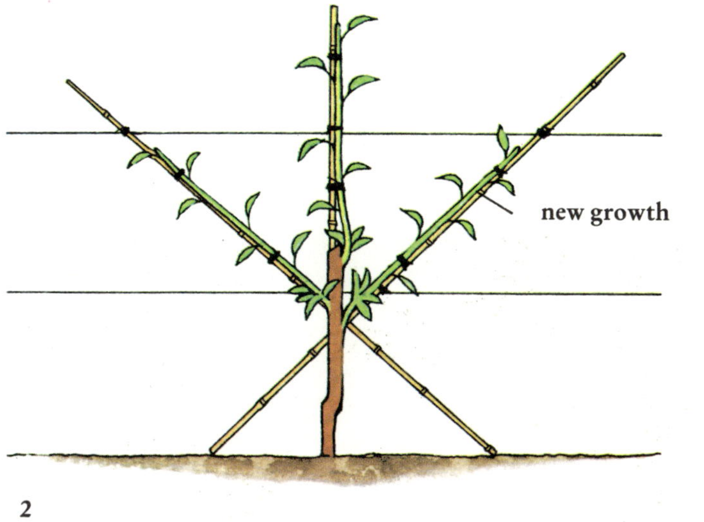

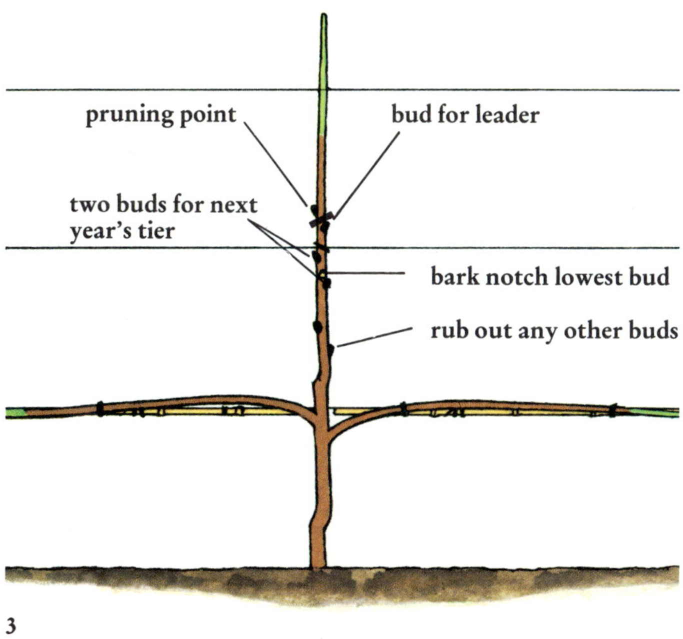

PRUNING ESPALIER LATERALS

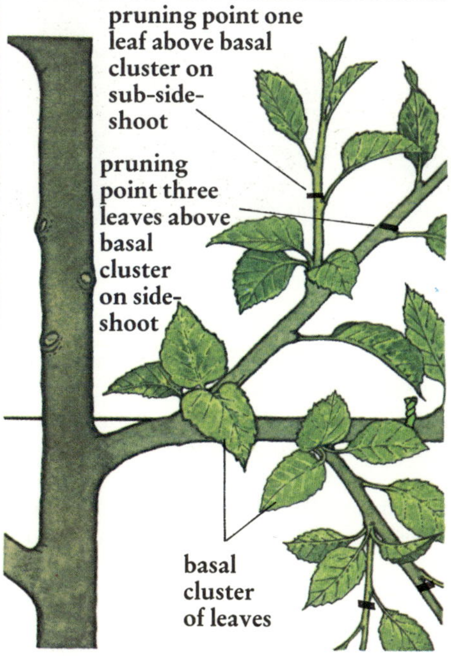

Prune espaliers in mid-summer. Cut mature laterals growing from horizontal branches to three leaves above basal cluster; cut sideshoots back to one leaf above.

THINNING AND HARVESTING

1. To get healthy, good sized pears, thin fruit in late spring and mid-summer; remove mis-shapen fruit.

2. Ripening pears are vulnerable to attacks by birds; protect the fruit by fixing cardboard squares onto stalks.

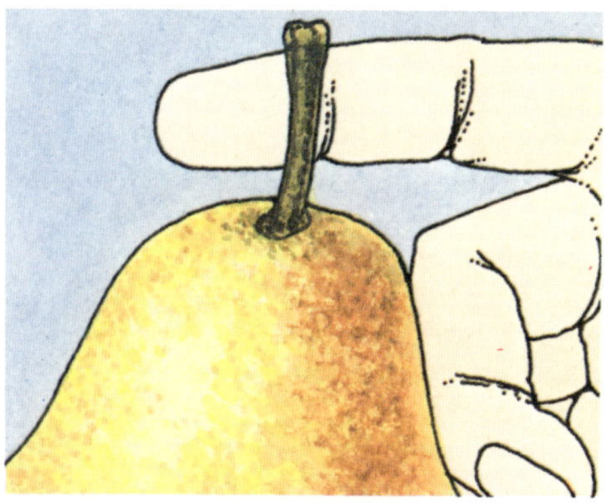

3. If picking pears for storing, pick fruit with the stalk intact, otherwise the pears are liable to rot.

PLUMS AND GAGES

Tree forms Standard, half-standard, bush, fan-trained and, with care, dwarf pyramids.

Pollination The best known plum, Victoria, is also the only one that could be said to be fully self-fertile. Several others are to a lesser extent but the remainder need cross-pollination. To be on the safe side, therefore, always arrange for at least two varieties to be present; even when growing Victoria.

Position in garden As with the choicer pears, high quality gages need a warm and sunny position to give of their best. They will benefit enormously from being fan-trained against a sunny wall.

Soil Soil must be well drained but moisture retentive, that is, the heavier types are more suitable. A certain amount of lime is required but soils with a pH of about 8 and above usually cause severe yellowing of the foliage. Oddly enough, this does not always lead to a serious reduction in crop.

Trees growing on a new and less vigorous rootstock called Pixy are not widely available but are the obvious choice for gardens.

Yield Very difficult to predict because, except in a few very favoured areas, plums frequently fall victim to spring frosts that kill the blossom. However, a mature half-standard or bush tree will normally supply a family's needs.

Planting and cultivation

The trees should be planted in well prepared soil, preferably in March so that the roots soon become active.

Once the trees are established, fertilizer should be given every spring followed by a mulch of garden compost or well rotted FYM. This will not only help the soil to retain moisture but it will also serve to keep the weeds down. Plums need a lot of moisture in the soil – but also good drainage at subsoil level.

When plums and gages carry heavy crops, they do so with a vengeance. So much so that fruit thinning is needed if the fruits are to be anywhere near a respectable size. This should be done in late June or early July, as soon as it is seen that the crop is going to stay put and not thin itself naturally. The normal system is to single the fruitlets to about 5 cm (2 in) apart.

TRAINING AND PRUNING OF

Pruning young pyramid trees should be done in the winter; because the wounds are tiny, the trees are unlikely to get silver leaf.

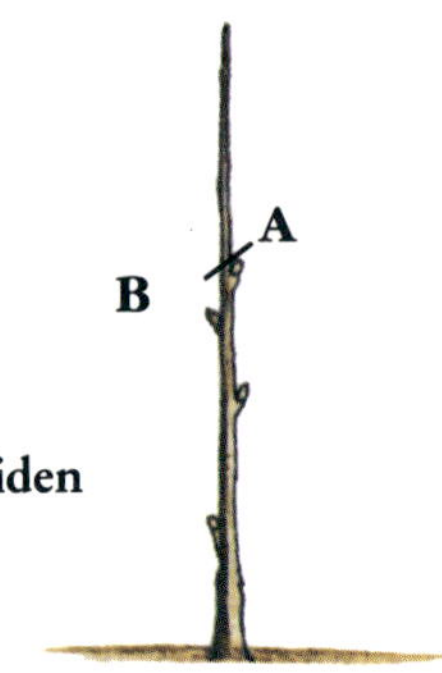

1. Maiden

2. Second winter

1. Cut the maiden back to 50 cm (20in) the first winter the tree is in your garden. Cut back to a suitably placed bud (A). Rub out bud immediately below leader bud (B). Make sure there are 3 or 4 buds left spaced evenly around the stem.

2. The next winter, prune the leader to about 45 cm (18in) to a bud pointing in the opposite direction from the previous year's pruning; this helps keep the growth straight (A). Make sure there are 3 well-placed buds on the remaining part of the leader to make a second whorl of branches. Prune all branches back to 22 cm (9in) (B); this encourages the formation of fruit spurs.

3, 4. Train the leader vertically (A); the second whorl of branches will grow out (B). Cut back the sideshoots formed on the lower set of branches to 4 good leaves during early summer. In the third winter cut back the leader to 45 cm (18in) (C) and the new whorl of branches back to 22 cm (9in) (D).

5. Established pyramid tree.

Pests and diseases

Specific plum aphids can be a nuisance in the late summer, along with wasps at picking time, but the worst of the lot is the Red Plum Maggot; you may find him looking at you with beady little eyes when you bite into what should be a delicious plum.

In rural areas, you may have to guard against bullfinches eating the fruit buds during the winter. Fine netting or small polythene bags will do the trick.

PYRAMID PLUM TREE

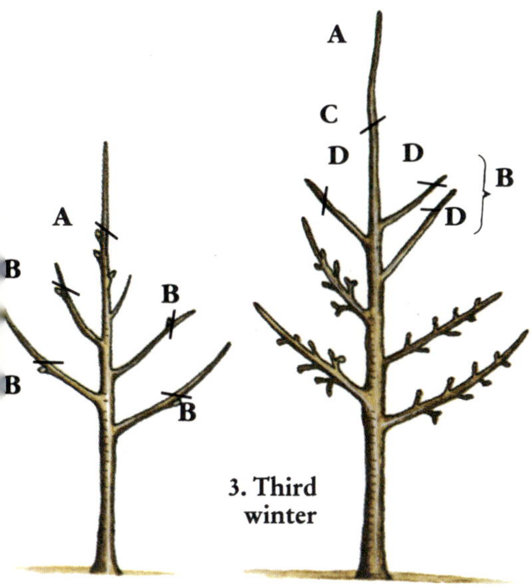

3. Third winter

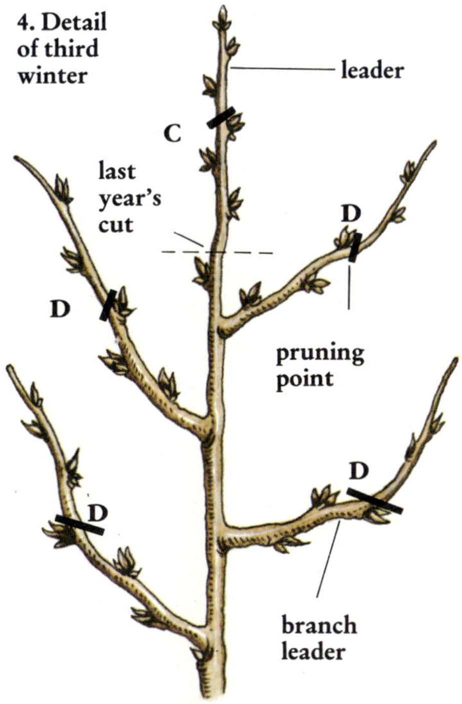

4. Detail of third winter

6. Plums need much less pruning than other fruit trees because they fruit on old and new wood. Generally, pruning should be done in early summer to avoid the risk of dieback and silver leaf. Pinch out vigorous sideshoots to 4 to 6 leaves from the parent stem (A and B). This encourages fruiting spurs to form. Cut out any dead wood back to living wood (C) and if the wound is larger than 2.5 cm (1in) treat it with bitumen paint. When the branch leaders grow longer than 1.2 m (4ft), cut it back by one fourth to one third, depending on the vigour of the tree. Cut back to a suitably spaced spur or sideshoot (D). If the variety has a naturally drooping habit, such as *Victoria*, prune the branch leader back to an upward growing spur or sideshoot. Cutting back the branch leaders encourages the formation of new sideshoots. When the leader grows taller than 2.4 m (8ft), cut it back into the old wood (E). Do this at blossom time, in mid-spring, every three or four years, as necessary.

5. Established pyramid tree

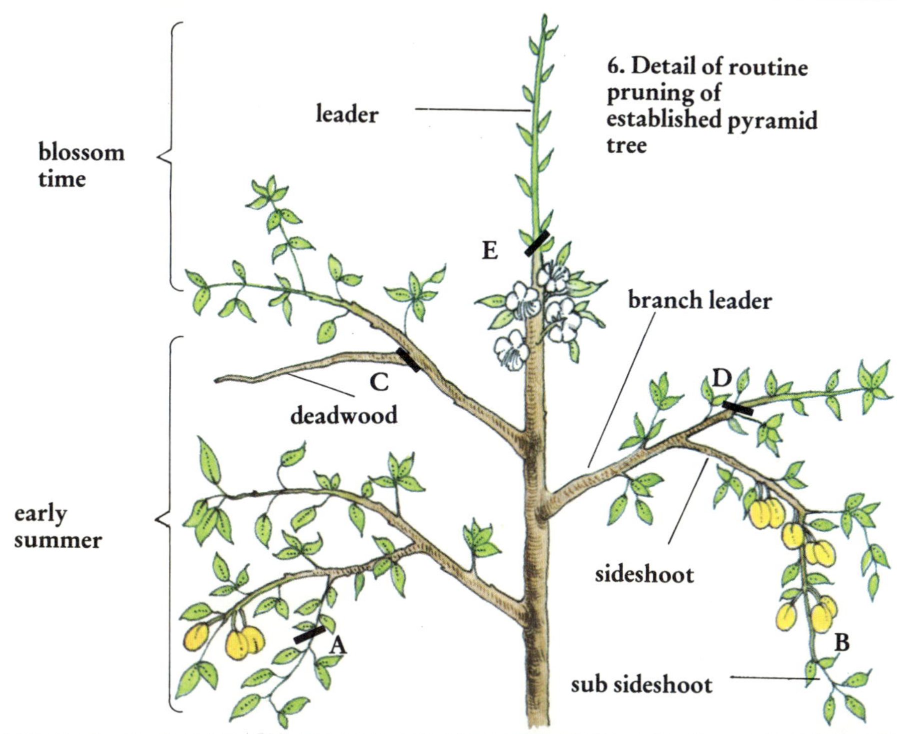

6. Detail of routine pruning of established pyramid tree

Harvesting

The only point to be made about picking plums is that the cooking varieties should be gathered well before they are ripe whereas the dessert gages are much better if left to ripen on the tree.

Pruning

Established bush and half-standards are pruned as little as possible and only then to keep them tidy, open and free from dead shoots and branches.

Pruning should be done in the summer to avoid the risk of infection by the Silver Leaf fungus disease. It can often be done at the same time as fruit thinning.

Fan-trained trees have their shoots tied back to wires until the wall space is filled and then all new shoots that are not wanted for extension growth are stopped at 6–7 leaves during the summer. They are shortened back further to half that length after picking.

Warwickshire Drooper

SWEET CHERRIES

Tree forms Normally only grown as fan-trained on account of their size, but in a large garden you could grow bush trees – using the less vigorous rootstock Colt. However, even when restricted, they make trees that are far too large for almost all gardens.

Pollination Cross-pollination is essential unless the self-fertile variety 'Stella' is grown, which makes this the only one really worth contemplating. Not all varieties are even compatible so check before you buy.

Position in garden When grown against a wall, it should be in a sunny position so that the fruit ripens well.

Soil Sweet cherries prefer a heavy but well drained soil. On lighter land they tend to make smaller trees but these are not nearly so productive as they are normally half-starved.

Sweet cherries are varieties that may be eaten as dessert.

Planting and cultivation

Once cherries are established and have been tamed, they really take very little looking after. However, anything that can be done to even out the water supply will be of benefit, particularly in the summer when a variable soil water level always causes the fruit to split. Plenty of organic matter in the soil and a good mulch every spring will help a lot.

Pests and diseases

The most serious complaint is bacterial canker. This appears in several guises – notably as lesions exuding gum at the junction of branches. Another form is as small brown spots on the leaves in summer which later become holes.

Blackfly are usually a nuisance from June onwards but may also serve the purpose of restricting extension growth. A case of using a pest to one's advantage.

Birds during July – especially starlings – are the other big pest.

A fan-trained morello cherry, in early spring, before the blossom has appeared.

FAN-TRAINING MORELLO CHERRI

1. Cut the main stem of the maiden back to a growth bud 30–45 cm (12–18in) high in early spring. Make sure there are between 2 and 4 growth buds on the stem; two should be opposite each other at least 20 cm (8in) up from the ground (AB).

2. When the two opposite shoots (AB) are 45 cm (18in) long, tie them, and any other shoots, to long bamboo canes; gradually lower the angle of the lower two (CD) so that by mid-summer they are at 45° angles to the ground. If one shoot grows more rapidly than the other, lower the bamboo cane (D) to impede the flow of sap until the slower shoot catches up.

3. The following spring, shorten the side branches to a bud 30–45 cm (1ft–18in) from the main stem (ABCD). Cut out all growth above and below selected branches.

4. During the following season, extension shoots will grow from each of these side branches, and should be tied in (ABCD). Six or eight side shoots will grow along the lengths of these branches. Select two vigorous shoots on the upper side of each branch, and one on the lower side. Rub out any others. These selected shoots form the framework; tie them to the wires.

5. The third spring the tree has been in your garden, cut back these branches to a bud, leaving 75–90 cm (2ft 6in–3ft) of ripened wood (A).

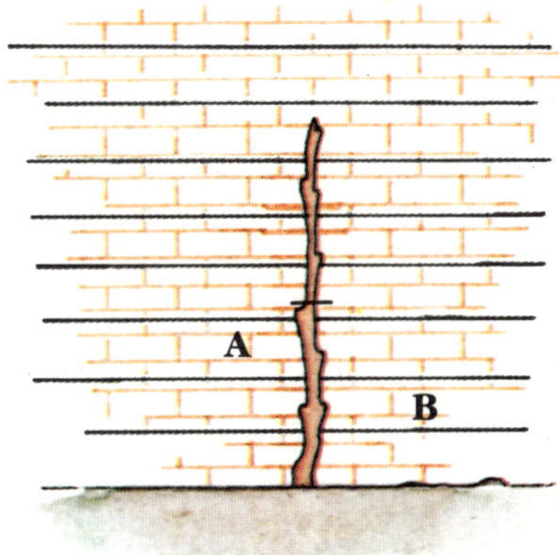

1. Newly planted maiden

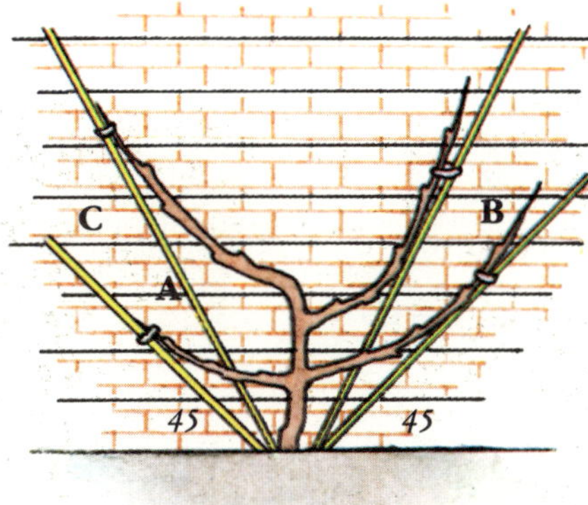

2. Mid-summer

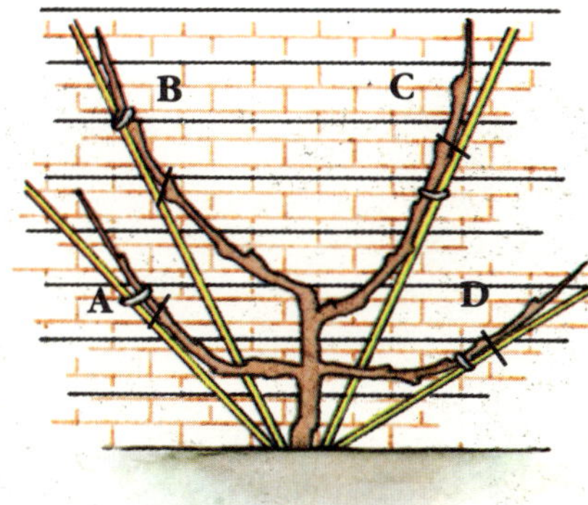

3. Following spring

4. Second mid-summer

5. Third spring

Harvesting
Cherries should be allowed to ripen on the tree.

Pruning
Once a fan is formed, little pruning is required beyond the removal of dead and diseased shoots and branches.

SOUR CHERRIES

Tree forms Bush trees, as well as fans, are quite feasible because of the less vigorous growth they make. The best known variety is 'Morello'.

Pollination Self-fertile.

Position in garden One of the only fruit trees capable of growing well when fan-trained to a north facing wall.

Soil No special requirements.

Sour cherries are the only varieties recommended for any but the largest of gardens.

Planting and cultivation
As Sweet Cherries.

Pests and diseases
As Sweet Cherries.

Harvesting
As Sweet Cherries but should only be used for cooking, jamming, or turning into wines. Far too sour for dessert.

Pruning
As for Sweet Cherries.

PEACHES

FAN-TRAINING

1. In late winter of first year, when buds start to break, cut tree back to 60 cm (2ft) above ground. Leave at least two other buds for left and right branches.

2. The following summer, select two opposite sideshoots for primary left and right branches. Rub out all other growths on main stem; cut back central leaders to just above the higher branch. When they are 45 cm (18in) long, tie sideshoots to canes with soft string. Fix canes at 45° angle to the ground.

3. In the second winter, prune when buds start to break; cut the two side branches to a bud 30–45 cm (12–18in) from the main stem.

4. In the second summer, select two vertical shoots on upper side of each branch and one on underside. Cut back all others to base. Tie them to the wires to form framework of the tree. Leave the leader shoot on end of branch until winter.

5. In late winter of third year, prune back the eight branches to a triple bud (flower and growth buds), leaving 30–45 cm (12–18in) of ripened wood.

6. Unless wall to be covered is very large, after third year pruning should aim to stimulate fruit production; make sure that branches are evenly spaced and not overcrowded.

Tree forms Bush and fan-trained.

Pollination Self-fertile but there is often a need for hand-pollination because peaches flower early in the year.

Position in garden For peaches to be a success, they must have the warmest, sunniest position available. It is sometimes possible to grow them as bush trees in the open garden but the best crops are always from fan trees trained against a warm and sunny wall.

Soil Provided that it is well drained and not too chalky, any soil is acceptable.

Yield A good tree will produce 40–50 fruits.

Planting and cultivation

Peaches should be planted in well prepared soil, preferably in the spring so that they have a complete season in which to become established before their first winter.

As long as local weather and topography suit them, peaches may be grown as far north as southern Scotland. Where there is any doubt about their hardiness or suitability, though, it is much safer to give them the protection of a cold greenhouse. In April put down a mulch of well rotted garden compost or manure to keep in the moisture and control the weeds. This is particularly important with peaches and other stone fruits as they have shallower root systems than apples and pears. For this reason also, any soil cultivation beneath the trees should be kept to a minimum; both as regards frequency and depth.

Plenty of water should be given in the summer so that the soil never dries out and fruit-drop is kept to a minimum. Remember that the base of a wall is probably the driest place in any garden.

If the set is heavy, never be afraid to thin out the fruitlets. This should be done first when they are about 1 cm (⅓ in) across and again, if necessary, when they are the size of walnuts. This final thinning should leave the fruitlets at a density of approximately one for every 20–25 cm (8–10 in) of shoot.

Pests and diseases

Peach leaf curl is certainly the most damaging affliction. It is a fungus disease and will be known to everyone who has grown peaches, nectarines or even flower-

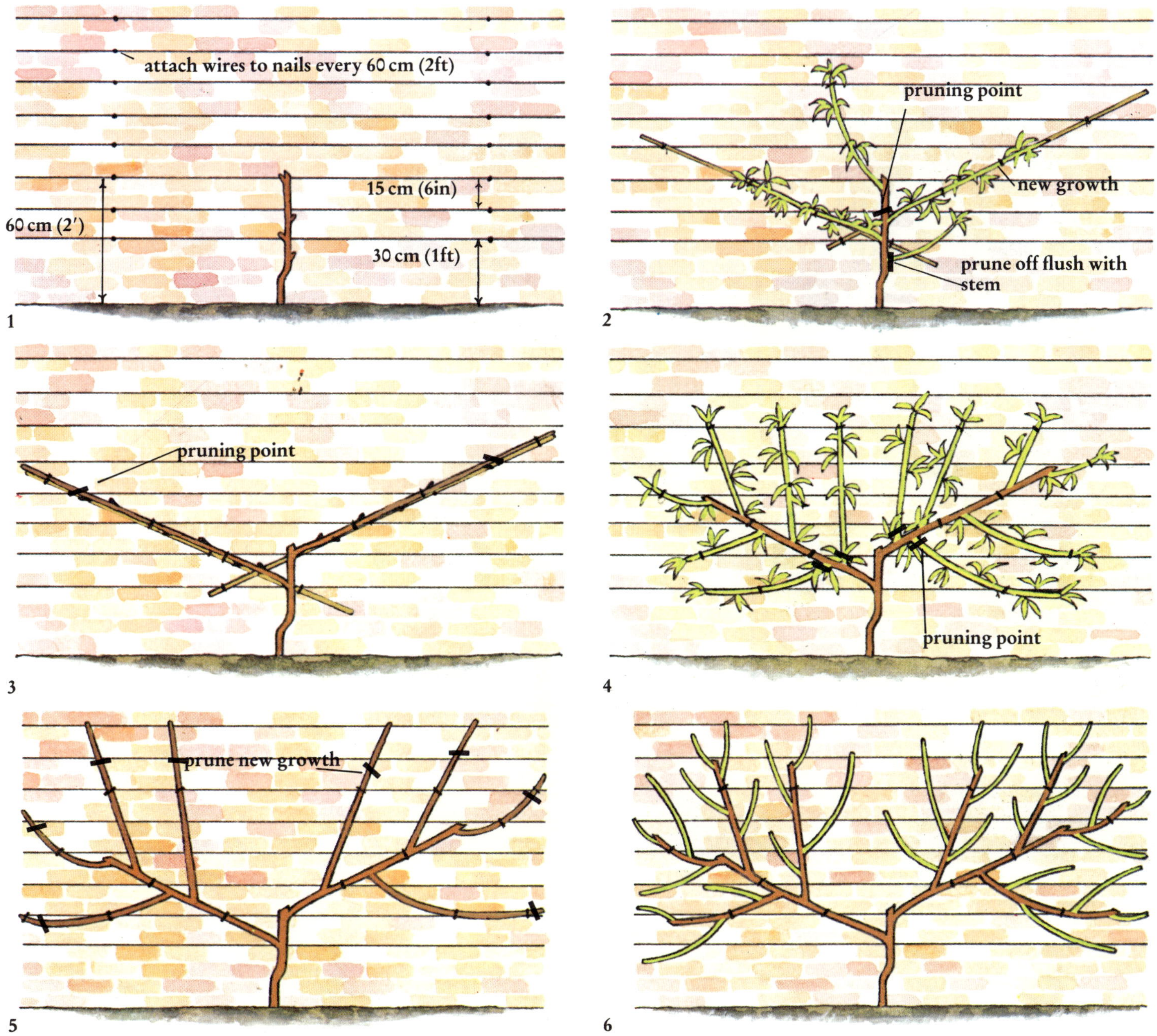

ing almond trees for ornament.

The most effective control is to keep the foliage reasonably dry during the growing season. For fan-trained trees this is achieved simply by putting a small roof on the wall above them. There are details of this in the Pests and Diseases chapter.

Harvesting

Pick the fruits when the flesh around the stalks yields to gentle pressure when squeezed. A ripe fruit should come away from the tree easily. Any that cannot be eaten soon will keep for several weeks in a cool place like a cellar, or even in the bottom of the fridge.

Pruning

Bush trees growing in the open will need very little attention beyond keeping them tidy and making sure that the shape is good. Any dead shoots and branches should be removed. As with plums, this pruning is best done in the summer to help avoid Silver Leaf disease and also so that dead shoots can be seen easily. Once they have lost their leaves in the autumn, they look much the same as any other tree.

The system for fan-trained trees is more detailed. In the spring, new shoots will appear on the branches but only those growing from the top or bottom surfaces of the branches should be kept. Any growing towards or away from the wall should be rubbed off when they are seen.

A little later, further thinning may be needed to leave a shoot every 15 cm (6 in) or so above and below the branches. These are tied in and, once they reach 45 cm (18 in) long, nip the tops out.

Peaches flower and fruit on last year's shoots so, once fruiting has finished, the fruited shoots are cut out, unless they are wanted for extension growth.

The cultivation of nectarines is exactly the same. However, it must be borne in mind that they are even less hardy than peaches so are best confined to greenhouses, though they may succeed outdoors in the extreme south.

APRICOTS

Tree forms Fan-trained.

Pollination Self-fertile but, as with peaches, hand pollination is always advisable because pollinating insects are scarce in the early spring when the trees are in flower.

Position in garden Apricots need a warm and sunny spot even more than peaches as their tenderness is similar to that of nectarines.

Soil Any soil is suitable as long as it is free draining and fertile.

Planting and cultivation

Planting should take place in the spring so that growth starts soon and the trees establish quickly. Fertilizer is usually not needed at planting time as it can cause excessive shoot growth.

As with peaches, fan-trained trees are far more successful than bush. Those trained to the wall in a cold lean-to greenhouse are the best of all.

Annually, in early spring, apply a fertilizer rather richer in potash than in nitrogen. This will encourage the formation of fruit buds and make the tree

PLANTING

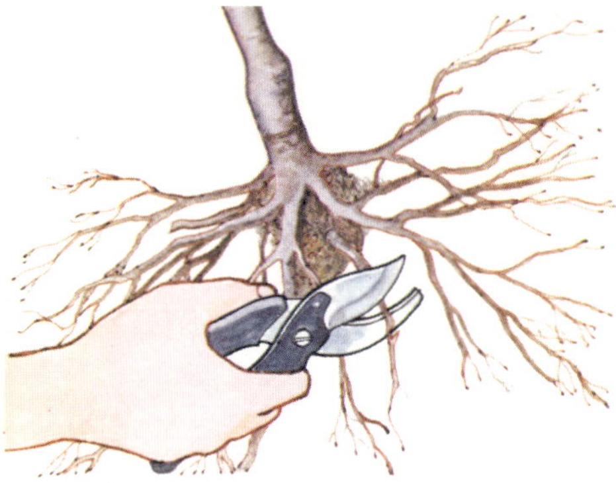

1. Cut back damaged or broken roots with secateurs.

2. If the roots are dry, soak them in a bucket of tepid water.

3. Erect training wires 15 cm (6in) apart using vine eyes.

4. Plant the tree with the soil mark just at the soil level. Leave the soil in a slight mound and rake the surface to make it porous. Then tie the tree to the wires.

5. Use a child's paintbrush to transfer pollen from one flower to another to obtain a good fruit set.

generally stronger and more robust. Follow this with a good mulch of garden compost or manure. Thinning of the fruitlets is seldom necessary but if it is felt that there are too many to make good sized fruits, they should be singled to about 10 cm (4 in) apart when they are the size of a walnut.

Keep the soil well watered throughout the early summer to ensure good sized fruits. This is especially important when the fruitlets are swelling but, once they have reached maximum size, less water will encourage the flavour to come out.

Pests and diseases

Apart from red spider mite, none are likely to be too troublesome.

Harvesting

Apricots should be picked as soon as they are ripe and part easily from the tree. If they are left too long, they are inclined to dry out rather and, anyway, the wasps and birds will soon find them.

Pruning

Apricots do not carry the fruit on young shoots in the same way as peaches. They bear best on spur systems built up over the years. This means that, after the initial formation of the fan, little pruning is needed beyond the removal of overcrowed, diseased and dead shoots and branches and the shortening back of new shoots into spurs.

FIGS

Pollination They are self-fertile and do not need hand pollination.

Position in the garden Although fig trees ares still often grown in the open, they appreciate the warmth of a sunny wall and, therefore, do better when trained roughly to a fan shape.

Planting and cultivation

Figs succeed best when root growth is restricted and many of the old country houses grew them in specially prepared raised and completely enclosed beds. In bleak districts they are best grown against a south-facing wall or in a cold greenhouse.

The strangest thing about growing figs over here is that, although the flowers appear throughout the growing season, it is only those produced in late August that we want. These overwinter as fruitlets which carry on growing and become mature figs in the early autumn of the following year.

Trees in the open are seldom attended to but it pays to treat those trained against walls with rather more care. The embryonic figs, therefore, are picked off until late August. Those then formed are left to grow and mature in the following year.

Pruning

This is normally restricted to the removal of dead, dying and overcrowded shoots and the tying in of replacements.

Pests and diseases

Coral Spot fungus may attack the wood from time to time. Infected shoots and branches should be cut out and burnt.

DEFRUITING IN AUTUMN

When harvesting outdoor figs, also pick off any fruits which are larger than a pea. They will never mature outdoors. The embryo fruit buds at the tip, however, should be left. They will form next year's crop.

STRAWBERRIES

Pollination Self-fertile. Hand pollination is quite unnecessary, except when the plants are being forced in a greenhouse.

Position in garden Like all fruits, strawberries should have a sunny position so that the fruit is properly ripened. In most gardens, the crop will be grown in the same area as the vegetables. Row spacing is convenient for this and strawberries occupy the ground for no more than three cropping seasons.

Soil In spite of being relatively small plants, strawberries need good soil – it should be deep, fertile and well drained.

Yield 2–3 dozen plants are enough for the average family.

Planting and cultivation

The two main groups of strawberry are the summer (July) fruiting varieties and the perpetual fruiting kind normally induced to fruit only in the autumn. A third group covers the tiny alpine varieties; these can be grown from seed but the other two groups are propagated from runners.

Summer varieties should be planted during August or September if they are to give a good crop in the following summer. Perpetuals are planted from October to March and will give a good crop in their first year, following planting at any time during this period.

The ground should be well prepared with plenty of garden compost or manure incorporated, and it should be firmed down before planting. No pre-planting fertilizers are normally required.

The young plants of summer varieties should be planted firmly 38–45 cm (15–18 in) apart, depending on the standard of the soil and the vigour of the variety, with 75 cm (30 in) between rows. Keep the plants well watered after planting so that they establish quickly. This helps to ensure a good first crop. The same planting rules apply to autumn varieties, except that they are normally less vigorous and need only be 30–40 cm (12–16 in) apart within the row.

In the spring, before the developing fruits of summer varieties touch the ground, straw should be spread beneath the plants to stop the fruits getting mud-splashed. Failing straw, special strawberry mats can be bought or you can lay special slitted polythene between the rows.

After fruiting, it is normally wise to cut off all the foliage, flower stalks and runners (if they are not wanted for propagation). A lot of pests and diseases are removed with these and the plants quickly put out fresh and vigorous leaves to build up strength and fruit buds before the winter. Both the straw and the tops should go on to the compost heap. Once that is out of the way, give the plants a high potash feed to encourage them still further.

Perpetual varieties required to fruit throughout the autumn should have the flower buds nipped out until the end of May. Those developing after that are left to set fruit. Ground covering is also needed for these varieties but it is normal to feed them in the spring rather than after fruiting, and foliage should not be cut off after fruiting.

Pests and diseases

Undoubtedly the worst problem is Botrytis (Grey Mould). This turns the fruits of all varieties into little grey balls of fluff and is particularly bad in a wet season.

Harvesting

Strawberries should always be allowed to ripen on the plant. Autumn varieties are improved if they are protected by cloches or polythene tunnels once the weather starts to deteriorate – usually towards the end of September.

Other methods of cultivation

Strawberries can be forced in a greenhouse perfectly easily by bringing them in under cover at the end of February. Alternatively, first-year plants in the open can be cloched at that time.

For forcing in the greenhouse, the plants should be grown in pots or proprietary Tower Pots.

For growing outside, strawberries are often planted in once-used growing-bags or in special strawberry barrels. Both have the advantage of mobility in case of frosts or simply for showing-off to neighbours in a prominent position.

PREPARATION AND PLANTING

1. Double dig the soil at least a month before planting, digging in plenty of manure or garden compost.

2. If plants are in peat pots, soak pots in water, then plant with rim of pot level with soil surface.

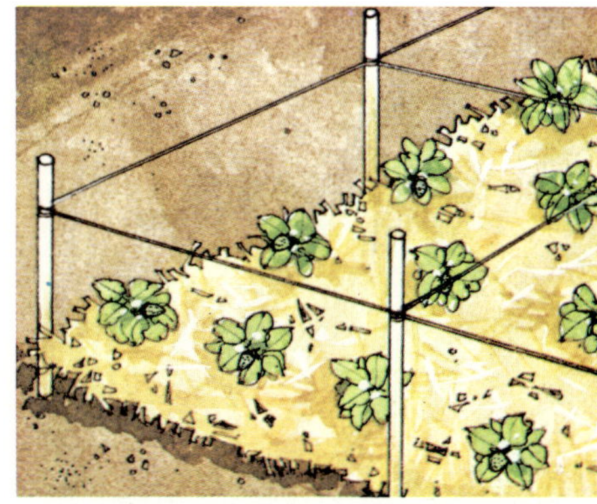

3. To protect crops from birds, make a frame for netting by stretching wires between vertical posts.

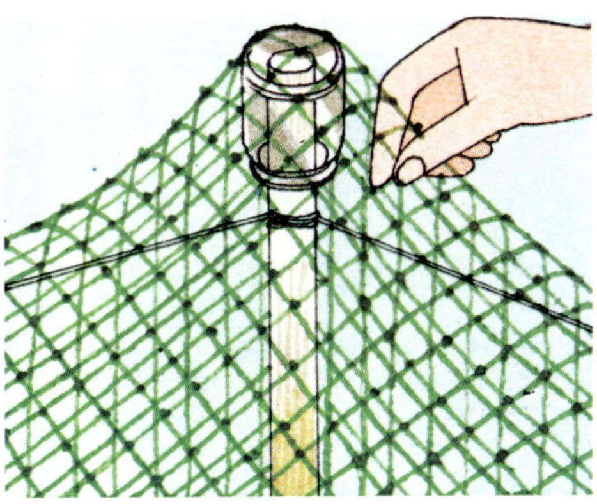

4. Invert jars over posts before putting on netting; this stops the netting from catching on the posts.

5. Water frequently and thoroughly until plants are established, particularly in hot, dry weather.

6. Protect ripening fruit with a layer of barley straw, special strawberry mats, or plastic strips.

CONTAINER GROWING

(right) **Old barrels make excellent containers for strawberries; make sure there is a central core of drainage material running up through the middle, so the compost does not become waterlogged.**

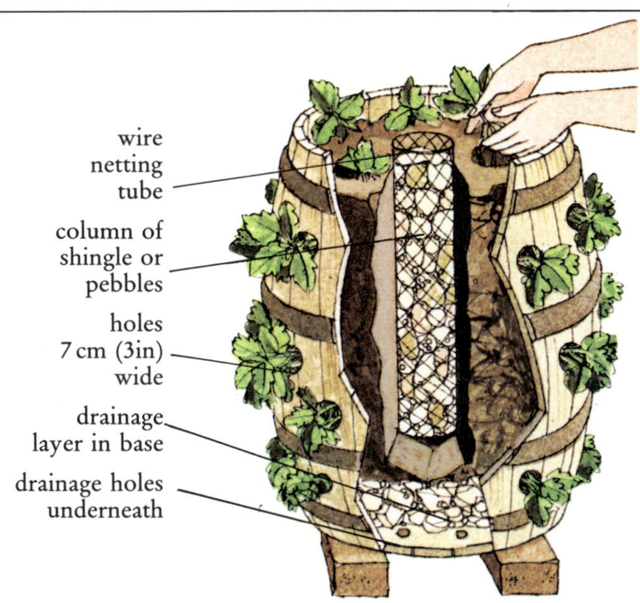

RASPBERRIES

Pollination Self-fertile and late flowering, so protection from frosts is unnecessary.

Position in garden Raspberries take up much more room than strawberries but are still best grown in rows in the vegetable section. Autumn fruiting varieties in particular need a sunny position or they tend to be tasteless.

Soil The canes are very shallow rooted so a great depth of soil is not needed, but it must be free draining and fertile. Raspberries seldom grow successfully on chalk because they are particularly susceptible to lime-induced trace element deficiencies.

Yield 24 canes should be enough for the average family.

Planting and cultivation

Summer and autumn fruiting varieties should both be planted in the spring, to ensure established plants by their first winter. The ground must have been well prepared beforehand with the addition of plenty of garden compost or manure. Both types should be planted in rows 1.5–1.8 m (5–6 ft) apart, according to their vigour, with 40 cm (16 in) between canes. Use the greater row spacing for autumn varieties. At this spacing they should be allowed to form a hedge and not be restricted to single clumps of canes (stools). Either before or after planting, cut the canes back to 30 cm (12 in) high.

Only summer varieties need a permanent post and wire support. This should be installed before planting. The traditional system is to have either one or two wires stretched 60 cm (24 in) above the ground and another at 1.4 m (54 in). If a pair of wires are used for the lower of the two, the canes can be passed between them for support. If only one is used, the canes are tied to it. All are tied to the top wire. Drive in a post at both ends of each row of the autumn fruiting canes so that a line can be passed down either side when the canes are half-grown, to stop them flopping about. Mulching raspberries is a particularly good idea as it greatly assists the shallow root system.

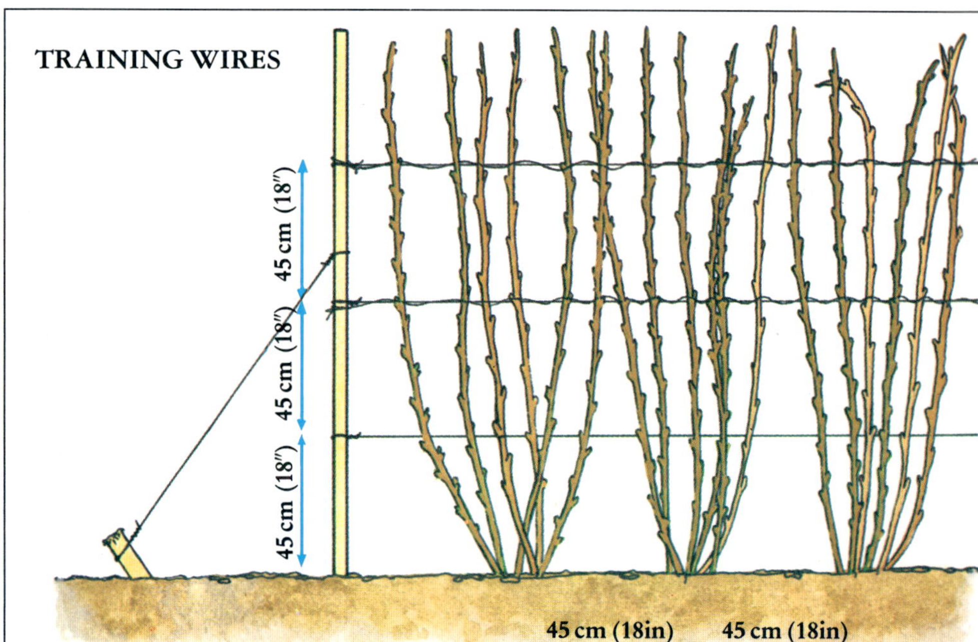

Tie canes individually to parallel horizontal wires as they grow. Erect wires at 45 cm (18in), 90 cm (3ft) and 1.2–1.5 m (4–5ft) from ground.

Pests and diseases

As with strawberries, the worst fungus disease is Botrytis infecting the berries in a wet summer.

Aphids are also troublesome in their own right but their main threat in regard to fruit is in transmitting virus diseases from infected canes to healthy ones.

Harvesting

Pick the fruit as it ripens; the surplus can be frozen.

Pruning

Summer varieties are best pruned soon after picking by cutting the fruited canes right down to the ground. Any pests and diseases will not then be spread to the new canes, which can be tied in to the wires.

Autumn varieties should be cut to the ground in the spring, just as new growth starts.

CARE AND CULTIVATION

1. In the first summer after planting, when the young canes are 25 cm (10in) high, cut out old canes entirely.

2. As the canes grow, tie them to bottom wire with soft twine, and then to middle and upper wires.

3. Mulch in mid-spring with garden compost or well-rotted manure to deter weeds, conserve soil moisture.

4. If bushes are not growing in a fruit cage, give temporary protection when fruit begins to form. Use 2.5 cm (1in) nylon mesh netting over stout wooden posts. Bricks will keep net from blowing away in strong wind.

5. Harvest on dry sunny days. Support laterals with one hand while picking berries with the other.

6. Tip prune in late winter: cut strong-growing canes back to a good bud 15 cm (6in) above top wire.

7. After fruiting, cut old canes back to ground level in autumn; tie in new canes to the wires.

GOOSEBERRIES

Pollination Self-fertile but some protection may be needed against spring frosts.

Position in garden No particular preferences but dessert varieties should be in the sun to sweeten them.

Soil Limy and chalky soils are tolerated, along with most others, but they must be well drained.

Yield Six bushes (not cordons) will provide more than enough for the average family.

Planting and cultivation

Bare-rooted bushes can be planted at any time from November to March. Container-grown bushes are also best planted then but can really go in at any time. They should be planted a little shallower than the soil ring on the stem indicates, to make sure that the bush is on a 'leg' (short trunk). Before planting, be sure to remove any buds or suckers that you find below the main shoots. Also remove any suckers on the roots.

Plant bushes 1.2–1.5 m (4–5 ft) apart; cordons should be spaced to allow the upright arms to be 30 cm (12 in) apart. All respond well to the ground being mulched beneath them annually in the spring.

Take care when hoeing not to damage the fine, surface roots. This is why a mulch is so much better for keeping the weeds down.

Pests and diseases

The worst pest is certainly the caterpillar of the gooseberry sawfly; the worst disease, gooseberry mildew.

Harvesting

In late June, when the berries are still firm, pick the fruit intended for cooking. Leave those for dessert until they are fully ripe; this will be a month or so later. The best time to pick dessert varieties is in the afternoon or early evening, while they are still warm from the sun – this will ensure that you get the best flavour from the fruit. Also, try to pick the fruit on a dry day.

Pruning

In the early winter, as soon as the leaves have fallen, the leading shoot on each branch is cut back by half and the side shoots to two or three buds.

Some thinning out of the centre of the bush may be needed from time to time, as may the replacement of any branches that are old and worn out – a sort of horticultural euthanasia. The same system is adopted for cordons, though the leading shoot must be tied in to a cane as growth progresses during the summer.

It is also an advantage to prune both types of plant towards the end of June, to help the fruit ripen better. In this case, leave the leaders untouched but cut back the side shoots to about five leaves. Any shoots that appear on the leg of either bushes or cordons should be removed as soon as they are seen or they will simply grow up the centre of the bush and dominate it without contributing anything. It is also advisable to remove any basal growths appearing from ground level.

FORMATIVE PRUNING

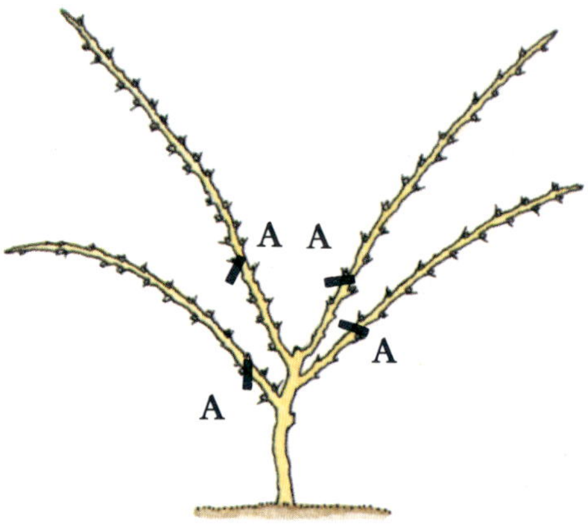

1. First year pruning

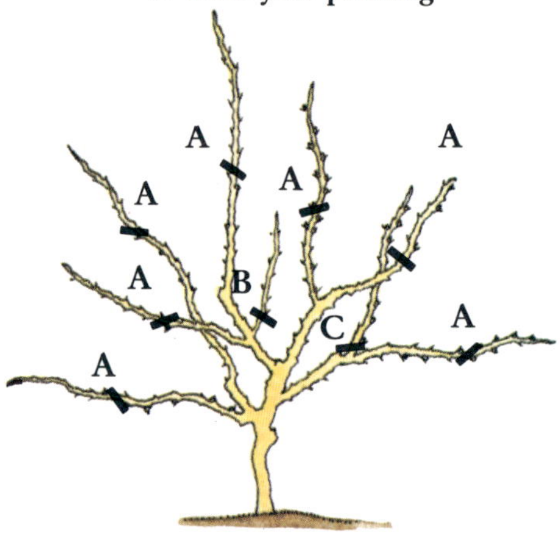

2. Second year pruning

1. The first pruning consists of cutting back three or four strong shoots to an outward pointing bud, three or four buds from the base (A). Remove weak shoots completely.

2. One year later, cut back 5–8 strong shoots to half their length, to an outward pointing bud (A). Shorten smaller sideshoots to one bud from the base (B); remove completely any weak or badly placed shoots (C). When pruning to form the framework of the bush, aim for an open-centred bush.

MAINTENANCE BUSH PRUNING

Established gooseberry bush (unpruned)

There are two methods of pruning an established bush; regulated and spur pruning. The former consists of removing overcrowded, weak and old wood, pruning branch leaders back by a quarter, and pruning one-year-old shoots to 7.5 cm (3in). To spur prune, cut back all sideshoots to one or two buds, to encourage the formation of fruiting spurs. Spur pruning results in larger, but fewer, gooseberries.

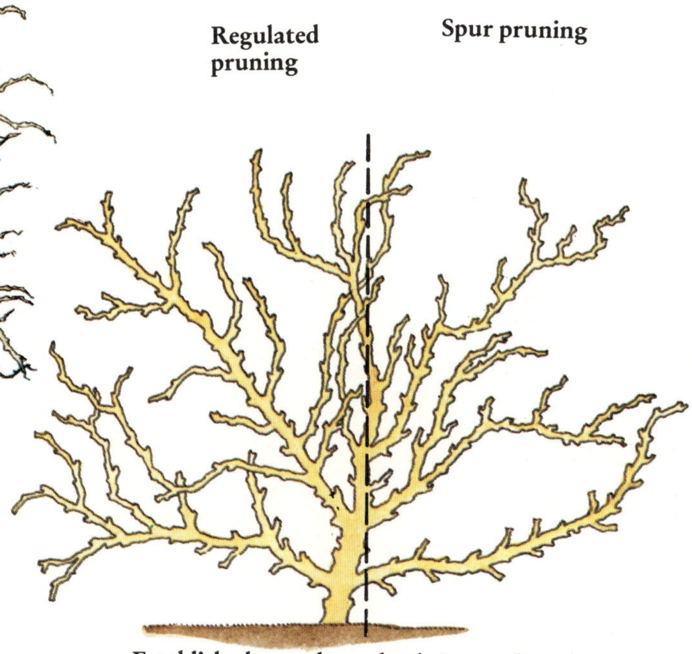

Established gooseberry bush (pruned)

PRUNING ESTABLISHED GOOSEBERRY CORDONS

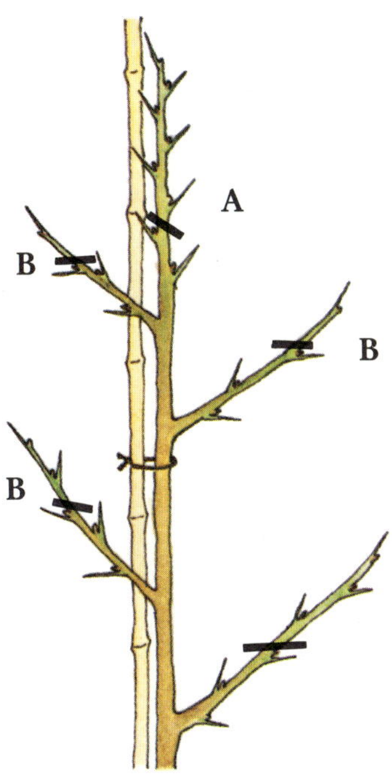

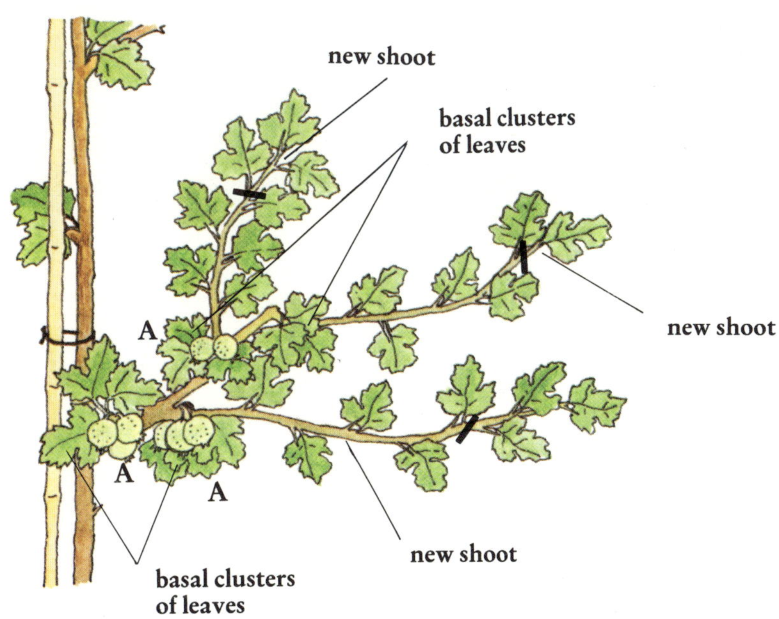

Winter pruning consists of shortening the leading shoot to leave one third of its new growth (A), and pruning laterals back to three buds (B). Pruning laterals encourages the formation of fruiting spurs. In areas where bird damage to gooseberry buds is severe, leave pruning until early spring.

In mid-summer, prune back laterals to 5 or 6 leaves, not counting the basal clusters (A). This pruning encourages the formation of fruit buds. As American gooseberry mildew appears first on the tips, tip pruning at this time helps to control the disease.

If the cordon has reached the desired height, you can cut back the leading shoot during routine summer pruning. Sometimes, sucker-like shoots appear near the base of the cordons; cut these off cleanly as soon as they are seen, as they will drain the cordon of energy needed to produce the fruit.

RED AND WHITE CURRANTS

Pollination As for gooseberries.

Position in the garden Although red currants are used primarily for cooking, they should have a sunny position to ripen both the fruit and the shoots for the development of next year's fruit buds.

Soil Red currants are rather less tolerant of chalky soils than are gooseberries.

Red and white currants may be grown as either bushes in the open ground or as trained cordons, which can be single or double, that is, they can have either one or two vertical arms.

White currants are the same as red currants except for the colour – in fact, they are thought to be simply a colourless variety.

Planting and cultivation

These requirements are the same in every respect as for gooseberries.

Pests and diseases

Even these are similar to the gooseberry's, although attacks are likely to be less severe.

Aphids and blackbirds will also be troublesome.

Harvesting

Pick both red and white varieties in complete clusters, not invidually.

Pruning

As for gooseberries.

PRUNING CORDON-TRAINED CURRANTS

As soon as the fruit shows the first signs of changing colour, cut sideshoots to five leaves.

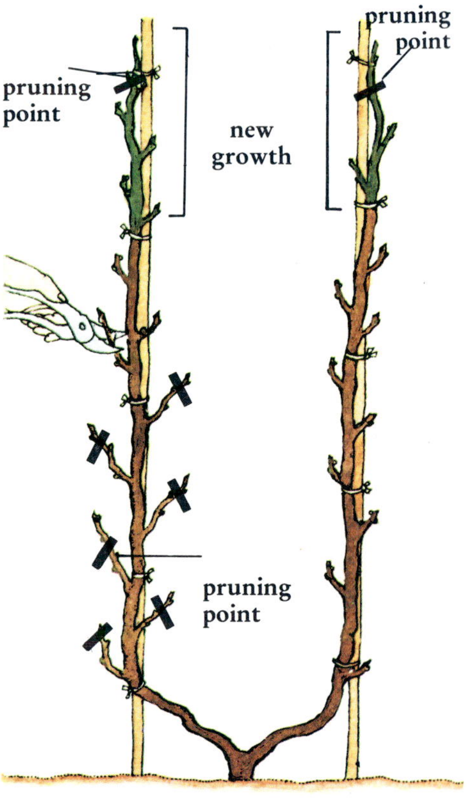

In winter, cut the new extension growth by a third and shorten the sideshoots to just two buds.

BLACK CURRANTS

Pollination Black currants flower early in the year and are therefore very susceptible to frost damage. Where this is particularly likely, a late flowering variety such as Jet is to be recommended.

Position in the garden A sunny place is preferred, to build up the sugar and vitamin C content.

Soil Black currants are heavy feeders and, to do well, need deep rich soils containing a lot of organic matter. The ground should also be moisture retentive but not to the extent that it tends to become waterlogged.

Unlike red currants, black currants can only be grown as bushes, not cordons.

Planting and cultivation

Despite both being currants, the cultivation of reds and blacks is about as different as it could be. Whereas reds produce their best fruit on spur systems built up on semi-permanent branches, black currants fruit best on very young wood so the bushes must be kept growing strongly throughout their life.

Again, while reds are grown on a leg, blacks are grown as a stool– with most of the shoots coming from below ground. Planting should be at a depth slightly deeper than that indicated by the original soil ring. After planting, all shoots must be cut to within about 2.5 cm (1 in) of the ground, to encourage quick establishment and strong new shoots. After placing each bush in its hole, work in soil round the roots, firm well.

Fertilizers will be needed each spring to maintain growth and this treatment should be coupled with an annual mulch to help with water retention in the soil.

Pests and diseases

Apart from run-of-the-mill aphids, the only pest likely to make serious trouble is the big bud mite, or gall mite. This not only turns growth buds into galls, which prevents them from opening properly, but the mite is also responsible for carrying the virus disease, Reversion. This slowly weakens the bush to the point at which it is no longer worth keeping.

Harvesting

When wanted for dessert, such as in fruit salads, black currants should be absolutely ripe. Slight unripeness, though, is tolerable when they are being used for cooking. Any surplus can be frozen.

PLANTING A BUSH

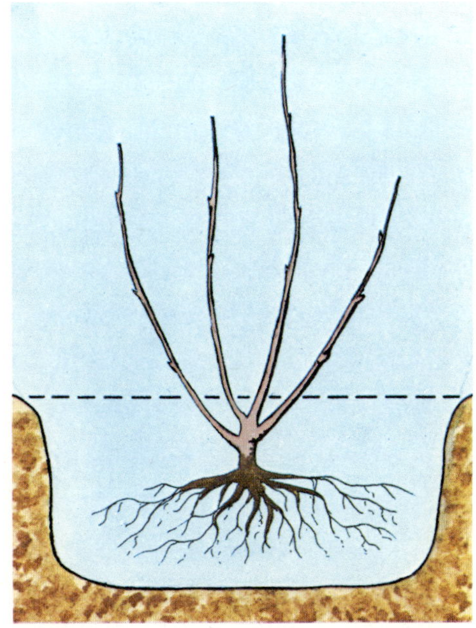

1. Plant the bush with enough room for the roots to spread. Place the soil mark about 5 cm (2in) below ground.

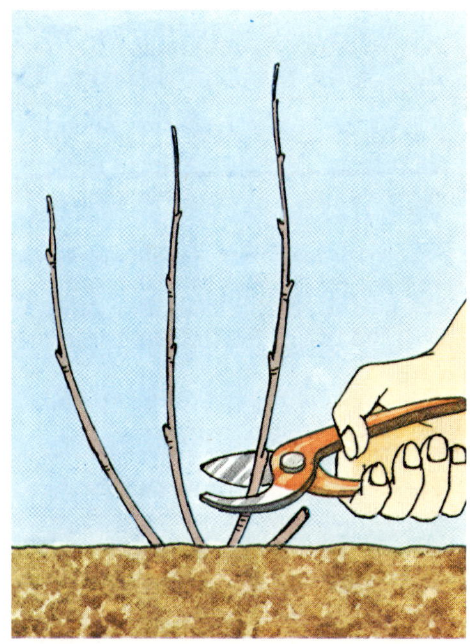

2. Fill in the hole and gently heel in the soil to firm the ground. Immediately after planting, use secateurs to cut back every shoot to 2.5 cm (1in) above the ground.

Pruning

Remembering that the bushes must be kept young, pruning should be aimed at removing older and less fruitful branches. In practical terms, this means cutting out any branch that is more than four years old.

BLACKBERRIES AND HYBRIDS

Pollination As with raspberries, no provision need be made for cross-pollination as all are self-fertile. Also, they flower late enough to avoid the dangers of spring frosts.

Position in garden As blackberries and all the hybrids can be treated as dessert fruits, they need sun to ripen them properly. They can also take up quite a large area as even a single plant of sunberry or Himalaya Giant blackberry will need about 4.5 m (15 ft) of row.

If there is a choice, loganberries should be given the warmest position as, originating in California, they are the least hardy.

Soil No special requirements, but they should be rich in organic matter and free draining.

Slight acidity is preferred to chalk, as blackberries in particular are likely to exhibit mineral deficiency symptoms.

These are all cane fruits and, besides the several varieties of blackberry, we can include the loganberry, tayberry, sunberry, boysenberry and (not yet released) the tummelberry.

All need the support of a permanent post and wire framework. The most versatile arrangement, and the one that will cater for all the different blackberries and hybrids, involves stretching horizontal wires 90, 120, 150 and 180 cm (3, 4, 5 and 6 ft) above the ground.

In the first season there will only be a couple of fruiting canes, but from the second summer there will be eight or more and training should commence.

Several systems of training are possible depending on the vigour of the fruit in question.

WEAVE TRAINING

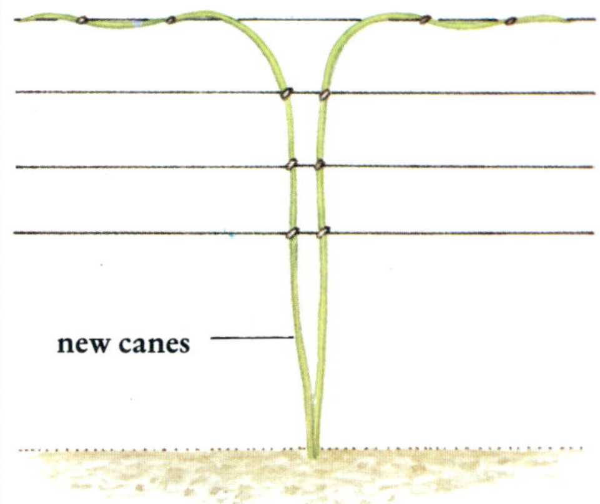

1. The first summer after planting, only one or two canes are produced; tie them up and along top wire.

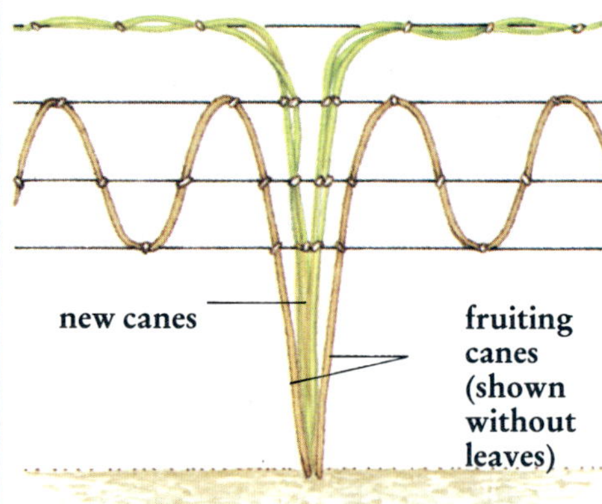

2. Untie and begin training these canes along wires the following summer; tie new shoots as before.

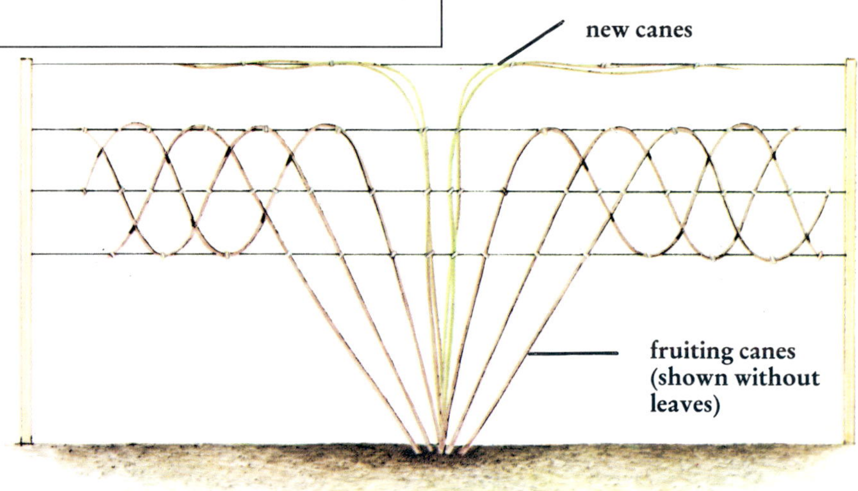

3. Established plants have eight to ten fruiting canes; start with middle pair of canes and weave along wires; leave centre empty for new canes.

Planting and cultivation

Even a single plant of a good variety can carry an enormous crop so it is well worth paying attention to soil preparation.

Although these cane fruits are normally quite hardy, it is safer to plant them in the early spring, rather than in the autumn, so that they do not have to spend their first winter unestablished. And the post and wires support should be in place before planting. The distance to allow between plants will vary with their vigour but should be roughly 3.6 m (12 ft) for most blackberries, 4.5 m (15 ft) for Himalaya Giant and sunberry and 2.4 m (8 ft) for the rest.

When planting, have the top of the rootball at soil level – with the dormant buds at the base of the cane no more than 1.3 cm (½ in) below the surface. After planting, a good mulch of well rotted garden compost or FYM should be put down to protect the shallow root systems of the hybrids. If planting takes place when the canes are dormant, cut them down to 30 cm (12 in) high.

During the first season, the new growth should be tied to the wires at regular intervals to prevent damage. In subsequent years, the new canes are best trained up the centre of the plant so that they do not become entangled with those that are about to fruit.

Fertilizer should be applied in the spring and, in most cases, potash will be more important than nitrogen as growth is usually adequate.

Pests and diseases

Botrytis (Grey Mould) rotting the berries can be a nuisance in wet summers and during the autumn.

The maggots of the raspberry beetle also have a nasty habit of appearing after the fruits have been picked and are about to be eaten. Keep an eye open for aphids, because if they are not dealt with quickly they will spread cane fruit viruses. Birds should not be ignored either, or they will strip the canes of berries when they are still only half ripe.

Harvesting

Most of these cane fruits ripen over a period of several weeks so they should be picked over at least twice a week. They all freeze well. If some form of shelter, such as a sheet of polythene, can be erected over the later maturing ones in September, the fruits will stand a much better chance of ripening.

Bear in mind that overripe berries are more prone to insect or viral attack; remove and destroy any you find.

CULTIVATION AND CARE

1. Top dress plants in early summer with well rotted manure or garden compost 2.5 cm (1in) thick.

2. If the weather is dry while the fruits are forming, water with a perforated hose laid along rows.

3. Check thornless varieties for thorny suckers. Cut them off below ground, where they join the root.

4. In autumn, after fruiting is over, cut old canes down to ground level. Clear them away and burn them.

5. Untie and spread out new canes. Retain 8–10 of the strongest canes and tie them in to the wires for fruiting.

GRAPES

Pollination No special requirements.

Position in garden Outdoor grapes need all the sun and warmth that they can get, so the hottest spot in the garden should be reserved for them. Even so, the young shoots are still liable to be frosted in the spring so be on your guard.

Soil The best crops are produced on light and sandy soils as these tend to dry out soonest and, therefore, induce a higher sugar content in the fruit. However, any reasonably good soil will be adequate as long as it is well drained.

Planting The distance between plants will depend entirely upon the method of training that you intend to adopt. If you are going to grow them trained to a warm wall in much the same way as in a greenhouse, then they will need to be 90–120 cm (3–4 ft) apart for a single rod or 150–180 cm (5–6 ft) for a pair. This is a very similar set-up to that for growing cordon gooseberries. However, the Guyot system only needs 45 cm (18 in) between plants.

Growing grapes outdoors in this country is not as chancey as it used to be because we now have modern and more reliable varieties. However, it still needs care and attention if they are to be a success.

Cultivation and pruning

While creamy white or green grapes are classified as 'white' and dark red or blue-black varieties are classified as 'black', they all have greenish flesh. Red wine gets its darker colour simply because the skin is included, too. Whether you are growing wines for dessert use or for wine making, in both cases, the rods are cut back to two buds from the ground straight after planting. Vines produce their grapes on the current season's shoots and, after fruiting, these shoots are cut hard back.

With the cordon method, either one or two rods are retained from the first season's growth. It or they are cut back by half in the winter. Subsequently, all side shoots are treated as fruiting laterals and are stopped at two leaves beyond the flower truss. At the end of the season these laterals are cut back again to the main rod.

In the Guyot system, only one rod is allowed to develop in the first year. This is cut back to 20–30 cm (8–12 in) in the winter and only the top two shoots are allowed to develop in the following year.

In the winter, one is shortened to six buds and tied to a horizontal wire 15–23 cm (6–8 in) from the ground. This will be next year's fruiting rod. The other is cut back to two buds and in their turn, the resulting shoots are treated in the same way as the previous two.

After fruiting, the whole cane is cut back to its point of origin and the process goes on year after year, with two canes growing and one fruiting.

Both these systems are equally suitable for dessert and wine grapes. Only the varieties will be different.

Pests and diseases

The worst problem is likely to be mildew but birds can also be a nuisance when the grapes are ripening.

Harvesting

Grapes should be picked only when they are fully ripe but dessert varieties can be kept in good condition for several weeks if they are cut from the vine with a short section of lateral. This is then placed in a bottle of water so that the grapes are kept plump and tasty.

WALL TRAINED GUYOT VINES

Guyot trained vines can easily be adapted to grow around windows and doors; south facing walls are best. For bigger crops, grow several small vines rather than one enormous one.

PRUNING FOR A DOUBLE GUYOT

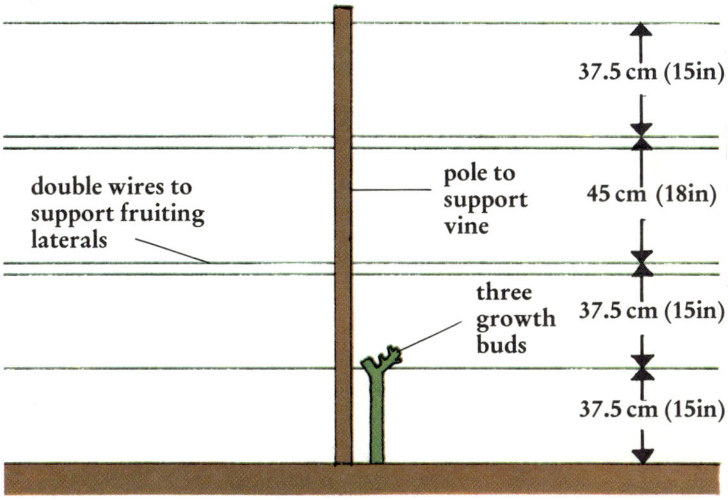

1. For a double Guyot system, cut the vine back to three buds just after planting in autumn or spring. Posts and wires can either be erected before planting or delayed until the following season; each post supports a single vine.

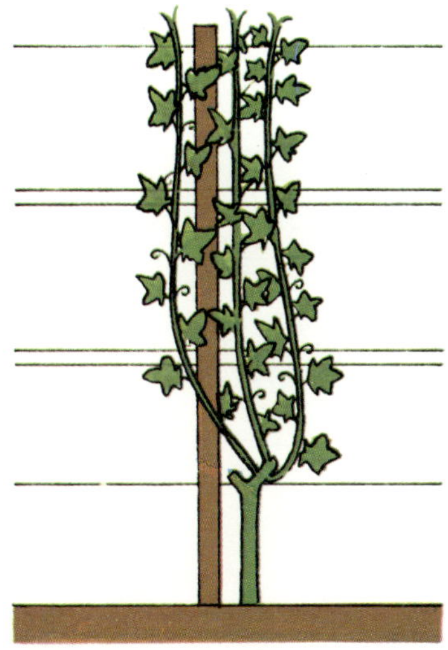

2. Next season these will produce three good shoots; tie them in to the cane for support.

3. Next winter, shorten the two best to 75 cm (2ft 6in). Shorten the third shoot to three good buds.

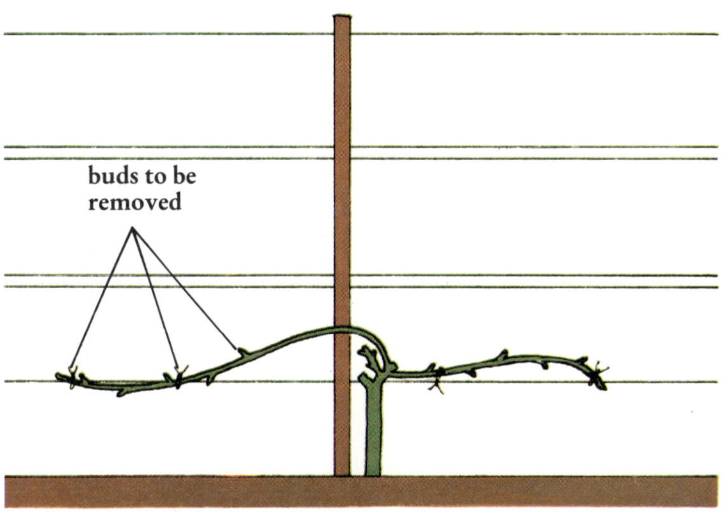

4. In early spring, when the sap rises, tie the two shoots to the bottom wire right and left. The third shoot is left to send out replacement shoots; remove any other shoots which develop.

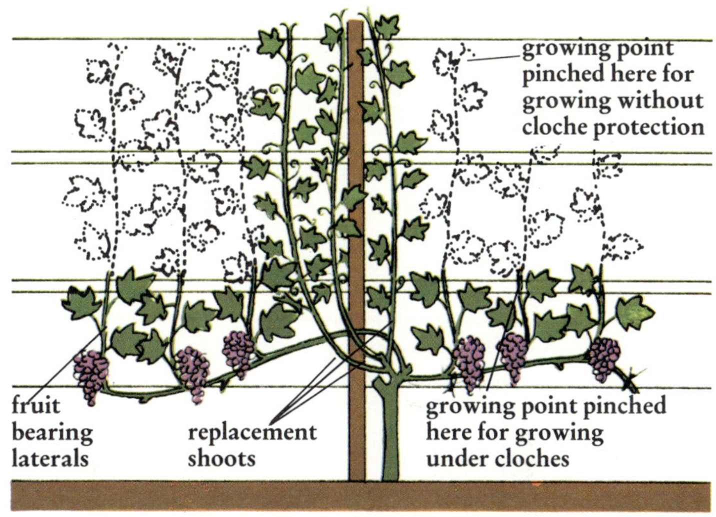

5. Select six to eight laterals per vine; remove the rest by cutting them off close to the horizontal rod. Tie replacement shoots vertically. Pinch out growing points when shoots reach top pair of wires.

CULTIVATION AND CARE

1. In summer, pinch back to one leaf sideshoots which develop in leaf axils; use scissors or thumb and fingers.

2. To get perfect bunches of large, well formed berries, thin the bunches while they are still immature.

3. Harvest grapes on a dry sunny day. Cut the bunches with scissors; do not tear them off the vine.

MELONS

Pollination Hand pollination may be required in cooler districts where the covering is seldom removed.

Position in garden A sunny place is needed if the fruits are to be sweet, well flavoured and juicy.

Soil Any good garden soil is suitable but probably the best crops are grown when the plants are in pots or beds of garden compost or in growing-bags. In any event, the ground should contain a very high proportion of organic matter.

Yield Each plant should be allowed to produce only four or five fruits.

Melons are members of the cucumber and marrow family. As such, they are too tender to be raised and planted outdoors until the risk of spring frosts is over. They therefore need to be grown under cover until being planted outside at the end of May. Even then, they still have to be grown under some form of protection like a cloche or tunnel, or in a cold frame, if they are to be worthwhile.

Planting and cultivation

Sow seed in individual peat pots indoors or in a greenhouse during April. Time this so that the plants are sufficiently advanced (but not pot-bound) for planting out in late May.

When planting, the actual distance to allow between plants will vary with the method of covering but you should reckon on each plant having about 0.5 sq. m (6 sq ft) of space. This, for example, would mean planting them 60 cm (2 ft) apart in a 90 cm (3 ft) wide frame.

Varieties differ in the way in which they produce their fruiting (female) flowers. Some have them on the lateral shoots – those growing from the main stem. Others wait until the sub-laterals (those growing from the laterals) have appeared. Whichever type is involved, all plants are stopped at their second true leaf to encourage side shoots. Female flowers will then normally be produced but, should they not be, then these laterals are stopped at seven leaves to induce sub-laterals.

When you see female flowers appearing (those are the ones with a tiny melon behind the petals), you know that everything is all right. The males have longer flower stalks and no embyronic fruits.

Hand pollination may then be needed. Once a good number of flowers have set, retain no more than four or five of the best fruitlets. They should also be nearly equal in size, to avoid any one dominating the others and prospering at their expense. The fruit should however, differ from plant to plant to ensure a succession.

Never allow the ground to dry out or fruitlets will begin to drop and you will have to start all over again.

Pests and diseases

The worst pest is likely to be red spider mite. You can avoid this by keeping the plants and ground well watered.

Mildew may be troublesome as well.

Harvesting

Although some say that you can smell melons when they are ripe, you can also smell them when they are not(!), so a much more reliable guide is to examine the stalk when you suspect ripening. A crack will appear where it joins the fruit. When this is complete, it is a sure sign that the fruit is ripe enough to be picked and eaten. The flesh at the flower end will also be soft.

SOIL PREPARATION AND SOWING

You can grow melons either under cloches or in frames. In frames dig a hole about 30 cm (1ft) deep at the back of the frame and half fill it with well-rotted manure. Put the soil which you have dug out back into the hole and leave in a mound.

PLANTING OUT

1

2

1. Plant with about 1.3 cm (½in) of the rootball above the soil surface to prevent collar rot.

2. As a further precaution, insert two pots into the soil, one on each side of the plant. Water into the pots so that moisture reaches the roots but cannot collect around the collar, where it could cause rot.

CARE AND CULTIVATION

1

2

1. Pinch out the tops to encourage side shoots.

2. However trained, the melons should be pinned down to the ground with bent pieces of wire.

3

4

3. When the fruits become the size of a walnut, select one on each main branch and pinch out all others. Then cut the fruiting shoots off after the second leaf beyond the fruit.

4. Support the developing fruits on a tile or flower pot. When small cracks develop around the fruit stalk, harvest by cutting away on either side of stalk.

RHUBARB

Position in garden Traditionally, rhubarb is dumped in the most hostile part of the garden that can be found, and there it is left to get on with it. This is no way to treat any plant; especially one that is expected to produce a crop for you. Give it a little care and it will respond dramatically.

Soil Very tolerant with no special likes or dislikes.

This is one of those plants that no one really seems awfully sure about. It is classified by the Royal Horticultural Society as a vegetable and yet many more people eat it with custard than with meat, another vegetable or two and gravy.

Most families find that two plants are more than enough.

Planting and cultivation

Under good soil conditions, rhubarb can make an enormous plant. Luckily, it does not object to overcrowding, so 75–90 cm (30–36 in) is enough between plants. If it can be planted in October or early November, so much the better. If not, leave it until March.

Always plant firmly, with the central bud just visible above the surface. A good mulch of garden compost or FYM is then appreciated, but keep it clear of the actual crown. Thereafter, an annual spring mulch is recommended.

Any flower stems that appear during the growing season should be pulled out completely as soon as they are seen.

If possible, rhubarb plants should be renewed every 3–4 years to prevent a build-up of disease and decline in vigour.

Pests and diseases

The only organism that is likely to make trouble is a bacterial rot that infects most crowns once they have been in place for a few years.

Slugs can be a menace with forced crops and, again, in the autumn if dead leaves are allowed to remain on the ground for any length of time.

Harvesting

No crop should be pulled during the first season after planting. The aim must be to encourage the plants to establish quickly. In the following year, two or three light pullings may be taken but should not continue beyond about mid-May. Thereafter, pulling can start in March and continue until late June. You should be able to take leaves from a well growing plant every 4–6 days.

Always select stems that have fully unfolded leaves, and always take care to leave the plant at least three stems. Also, stop harvesting the stems after three months so that the plant has a good respite in which to recover and renew its strength for next year.

Forcing

Although outdoor rhubarb can be advanced quite easily, the main object of forcing is to produce blanched and much more tender sticks.

This is done by covering the crowns in December or January with either straw or something like an upturned dustbin. The Rolls Royce treatment is an upturned bucket covered with fresh manure; this will heat up and bring growth on splendidly. Once the quality of the sticks begins to decline, uncover the plants and make no attempt to force them again the following year. They have done what was expected of them and must be allowed to recover by being grown naturally for another year.

Index

Page numbers in bold refer to illustrations

Acknowledgements

A-Z Collection: 42, 80(r)
Bernard Alfieri: 35(tr), 51, 56, 95, 106(t)
Pat Brindley: 44, 53, 59, 68, 71(bl), 72, 98, 99(r), 107(b), 108, 109, 114
Nick Carman: 5, 6
Bruce Coleman Ltd: 118(t)
R.J. Corbin: 10/11, 16, 21, 32, 46(1), 49, 58, 70(t), 78, 100(t)
Eric Crichton: 54, 56
C. Donaldson: 106(b)
Derek Fell: 107(t)
Valerie Finnis: 24, 112
Brian Furner Horticultural Pictures: 18, 19, 46(b), 57, 64, 80(1), 84, 87(t,b), 102, 107(c)
Iris Hardwick Library: 76, 82, 134
R. Hatfield: 23
J. Hovell: 28
George Hyde: 39(t,b), 132, 136
ICI: 35(b)
Leslie Johns: 105
Mark Lawrence: 89
David Levin: 91
J. Markham: 38(1,r)
Murphy Chemical: 35(tl)
Clay Perry: 52, 60(t), 62, 100(b), 138
Donald Smith: 110, 120, 126, 130
Harry Smith Horticultural Photographic Collection: 48, 50, 71(br), 74, 86, 92, 94, 96, 99(1),111, 116, 117, 122, 124, 128, 131
Sutton Seeds: 60(b)
Syndication International: 25
Jerry Tubby: 12, 46(t)
Michael Warren: endpapers, 8/9, 40, 41
Michael Wickham: 104